HARMONICS OF THE SPHERES

TOWARDS A UNIFIED UNDERSTANDING OF ASTROLOGY

MIKE EYRE

Harmonics of the Spheres:
Towards a Unified Understanding of Astrology

First edition (2020)

mikeeyre71@gmail.com

Ruby Star Press

ISBN: 978-1-9161708-0-3

To Mum and Dad,

with much love and gratitude.

TABLE OF CONTENTS

TABLE OF FIGURES

ACKNOWLEDGMENTS

My heartfelt thanks to everyone who has offered help and encouragement during the writing of this book, especially my partner, Aileen, whose support and counsel I value enormously.

I am also grateful to the many astrologers whose books have made it possible for me to write this book – in particular Dane Rudhyar and Liz Greene – and to all those who play a part in making Rudhyar's work accessible online.*

A very special thank you to Antony Milner (friend and student of the late Dane Rudhyar), who was asked by Leyla Hill (formerly Leyla Rael) to check the references I have made to her own work and that of Rudhyar. Largely due to a lack of forward planning on my part, this occurred with only a two-week window remaining to make changes to the book. During this period, Antony found time to carefully read the book from cover to cover and make helpful suggestions concerning where greater clarity was needed, where additional references would be useful to the reader, and where additional subject matter could be included to make the work more complete. Antony was also a great help with the proper referencing of Rudhyar's works.

Thank you also to Vic DiCara, for patiently answering my questions on Vedic astrology and checking the references to his work on the nakshatra sutras; to Steven Forrest, for checking the references to his work on the lunation cycle; and to Rok Koritnik, for checking the references to his work on divisional charts.

Thank you to the developers of the excellent, free-to-use Inkscape vector graphics software; and to Esoteric Technologies for allowing me to use planetary and other astrological glyphs from the *ET Symbol 3* font (Solar Fire).†

---

* For written works, go to Khaldea.com/rudhyar/ For recorded talks, go to RudhyarAudioArchives.com.

† Zodiacal sign glyphs are from the Wingdings font and used under license. The charts and aspect grid at the end of the book were generated using Solar Fire.

INTRODUCTION

One of the first things we learn as students of astrology is that the odd-numbered zodiacal signs (beginning with Aries) are traditionally referred to as the *masculine, positive* or *yang signs,* while the even-numbered signs are referred to as the *feminine, negative* or *yin signs.* In *The Pulse of Life,* however, Dane Rudhyar* suggests that a yang emphasis runs through the first half the zodiac (the *individual signs*) and a yin emphasis runs through the second half (the *collective signs*). So if a cycle of changing emphasis between yang and yin unfolds both once and six times during each unfoldment of a zodiacal cycle, does it do so at other frequencies; and does the same apply to other celestial cycles? This book is an initial response to these questions – to be viewed as an exploratory work rather than a source of definitive answers.

At the heart of this book is the notion that each astrologically significant celestial cycle unfolds as a *cycle of being* – an idea conceived by Rudhyar. While the book draws heavily on Rudhyar's work, it also incorporates my own viewpoint. I urge the reader to look also at the relevant works by Rudhyar, some of which are available to read at Khaldea.com/rudhyar/, or to listen to at RudhyarAudioArchives.com.

Some readers will skip some or all of the account of celestial motions given in Chapter 1, perhaps referring back to some sections later on if necessary. The inclusion of the Chapter is important, I feel, because learning about celestial motions, and calculating and drawing a few charts by hand, helps to ensure that we do not lose touch with what we try to interpret when we examine our charts, grids, tables and graphs. Furthermore, the *birth sphere,*†

---

* *The Pulse of Life* (1st ed. 1943). Now out of print, but available to read at Khaldea.com/rudhyar/

† The hardware necessary to create such a sphere has been around for some time, in the form of a multi-directional projector mounted inside a translucent plastic sphere. The ones I have seen have a diameter of approximately 50cm. At present, these spheres are typically used to replicate the appearance of revolving celestial bodies, but could be used together with astrological software to show moving or stationary images of the celestial sphere that include house cusps, etc. Unfortunately, at the time of writing, this hardware is still extremely expensive; the ones I have seen currently cost around £10,000 each. As Antony Milner pointed out

predicted many decades ago by Rudhyar, may become a reality in the near future, and at that time, Chapter 1 will hopefully serve as a useful guide to the large number of circles that it will be possible to view on such a sphere. Some parts of Chapter 1 attempt to clarify points on which many current astrology texts that discuss celestial motions are vague or contradict one another. A possible adaptation of an existing house system (though not a widely used one) is suggested on the final page of Chapter 1.

With regard to references, titles are given in the main text and footnotes, with the date of publication of the edition used to determine page numbers, and (if different) the date of publication of the first edition. In each case, the publisher of the edition used is given in the References section.

For those interested in the astrological timing of the writing of this book, it was June 2013 when the questions mentioned in the first paragraph of this introduction arose and this book began to take shape. At that time, transiting Uranus and Pluto had just begun to square one another and make strong aspects to my natal Sun, Venus and Uranus,[*] with my secondary progressed Sun and Mars following closely behind transiting Uranus and Pluto, respectively. With transiting Uranus and Pluto in (tropical) Aries and Capricorn, respectively, it seems fitting that the book attempts to look more deeply into the time-honoured, segment-based approach to astrology in the light of the "new and liberating generalised conceptual framework"[†] introduced by pioneer of harmonic astrology, John Addey.

Finally, thank you for buying this book; I hope you find it useful. To be notified when subsequent volumes are released, please follow me on Facebook[‡] or send your email address to me.[§]

Mike Eyre

Lancaster, UK

February 2020

---

to me, a virtual birth sphere – viewed through virtual reality goggles (presumably from 'inside' the sphere) – is probably closer to being introduced.

[*] My natal chart and aspect grid are shown on pages 265 to 267.

[†] From Charles Harvey's Introduction to John Addey's *Harmonics in Astrology* (2009)

[‡] facebook.com/MikeEyre1971

[§] MikeEyre71@gmail.com

CHAPTER ONE

CHARTING CELESTIAL MOTIONS

This chapter describes how the positions of celestial factors change over time from the viewpoint of an observer on Earth, and the various frames of reference that astrologers use to chart these changes.

The Celestial Sphere

From the *geocentric* – or *Earth-centred* – viewpoint, Earth's centre is located at the centre of a *celestial sphere*, with all other celestial bodies positioned on the inside of the surface of this sphere (see Figure 1.1).

The points of intersection of a plane and a sphere always form a perfect circle. If the plane passes through the centre of the sphere, the centre of the circle coincides with the centre of the sphere and the circle is referred as a *great circle*. If the plane does not pass through the centre of the sphere, the circle is referred to as a *small circle*.

The *ecliptic plane* is the plane in which Earth orbits the Sun; it passes through the centres of Earth and the Sun and meets the celestial sphere at a great circle called the *ecliptic*. Thus, the ecliptic is the apparent path of the Sun (or more accurately the centre of the solar disc) around the celestial sphere. The straight line that is perpendicular to the ecliptic plane, and that passes through Earth's centre, meets the celestial sphere at the *north ecliptic pole* and the *south ecliptic pole*.

Earth's rotation axis meets Earth's surface at the *geographic poles* – or *terrestrial poles* – and meets the celestial sphere at the *celestial poles*. The *equatorial plane* is perpendicular to Earth's rotation axis; it passes through Earth's centre, meets Earth's surface at the *terrestrial equator* (see the black line around Earth in Figure 1.1), and meets the celestial sphere at the *celestial equator*, which is a great circle. The angle between Earth's rotation axis and a straight line between the ecliptic poles – i.e. the angle by which the equatorial plane is inclined to the ecliptic plane – is approximately 23.4°

(approximately 23°26′). This angle is often referred to as Earth's *axial tilt* or as *the obliquity of the ecliptic.*

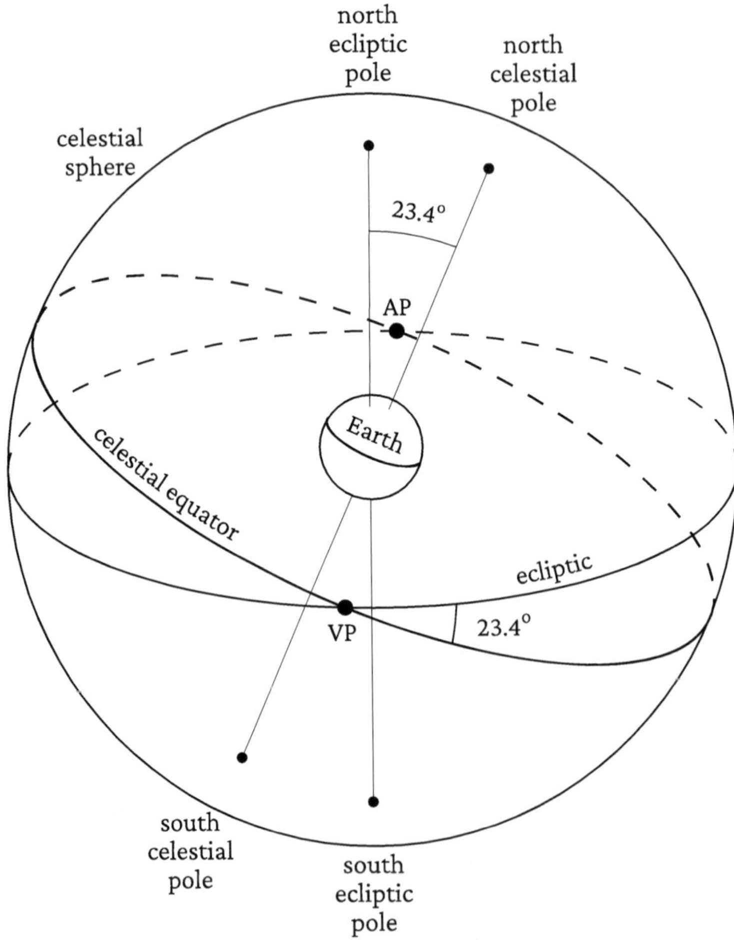

Figure 1.1 The ecliptic and celestial equator

The *nodal axis* – or *nodal line* – of two planes is the straight line at which the planes intersect, and the two points at which a nodal axis meets the celestial sphere are referred to as *nodes*. Thus, the nodes of two planes are the points of intersection of the circles formed where those planes meet the celestial sphere. If two planes pass through Earth's centre, the nodal axis of those planes also passes through Earth's centre, and the nodes are diametrically opposed (positioned at exactly opposite points on the celestial sphere). Thus, the points at which two great circles intersect are always diametrically opposed.

The nodes at the intersection of the ecliptic and the celestial equator are referred to as the *vernal point* and the *anti-vernal point* (marked VP and AP, respectively, in Figure 1.1). Since the ecliptic plane and the equatorial plane pass through Earth's centre, the vernal and anti-vernal points are diametrically opposed. Following the ecliptic eastwards around the celestial sphere (anticlockwise when viewed from the north ecliptic pole), the celestial equator is crossed northwards at the vernal point and southwards at the anti-vernal point.

The orbital planes of the Moon and the planets of our solar system are inclined to the ecliptic by less than 8°, and so as these bodies move around the celestial sphere, they remain within a band that extends approximately 8° north and 8° south of the ecliptic. Ancient Greek astrologers referred to this belt as the *zodiakos kyklos* (meaning *circle of animals* or *figures*), and today we refer to it as the *zodiac belt*. Of the celestial bodies that have been discovered in our solar system since the zodiac belt was defined, many do not remain within the zodiac belt because their orbital planes are more steeply inclined to the ecliptic.

Position on the Celestial Sphere

The position of a celestial body at a given moment in time is recorded as the centre of the area that it occupies on the celestial sphere. The two coordinate systems commonly used by astrologers to label points on the celestial sphere are the *ecliptic coordinate system* and the *equatorial coordinate system*. Each of these systems is based on the same principles as the *geographic coordinate system*, which is used to label points on Earth's surface.

In the geographic coordinate system, a line of *terrestrial longitude* – also called a *meridian* – is a line on Earth's surface that runs perpendicular to the equator from one geographic pole to the other. The line of terrestrial longitude that passes through the Greenwich Observatory in London is defined as 0° and is called the *prime meridian* or *Greenwich meridian*. A line of terrestrial longitude takes its name from the arc-length measured eastwards or westwards along the terrestrial equator from the prime meridian to the line. Thus, terrestrial longitude is measured from 0° to 180° east and west of the prime meridian, with exactly 180° east and exactly 180° west referring to the same line. Positive and negative values may be used to denote easterly and westerly terrestrial longitude, respectively; for example, 70° east and 70° west may be recorded as 70° and -70°, respectively.

Also in the geographic coordinate system, a line of *terrestrial latitude* – also called a *parallel* – is a line on Earth's surface that lies in a plane that is parallel to the equatorial plane. A line of terrestrial latitude takes its name from the arc-length measured northwards or southwards along any line of terrestrial longitude from the terrestrial equator to the line. Thus, terrestrial latitude is measured from 0° to 90° north and south of the terrestrial equator. The terrestrial equator is the line of 0° terrestrial latitude and the north and south geographic poles have terrestrial latitude 90° north and 90° south, respectively. Terrestrial latitudes of, say, 30° north and 30° south may be recorded as 30° and -30°, respectively.

In the ecliptic coordinate system, a line of *celestial longitude* – also called *ecliptic longitude* – is a great semicircle* on the celestial sphere that runs perpendicular to the ecliptic from one ecliptic pole to the other. The lines of celestial longitude that intersect the ecliptic at the vernal point and anti-vernal point are defined as 0° and 180°, respectively. A line of celestial longitude takes its name from the arc-length measured eastwards along the ecliptic from the vernal point to the line. Thus, celestial longitude is measured from 0° to 360°, with exactly 0° and exactly 360° referring to the same line.

As discussed below, astrologers also measure celestial longitude between 0° and 30° of a particular zodiacal sign. To avoid confusion, celestial longitude measured eastwards from the vernal point between 0° and 360° may be referred to as *absolute celestial longitude.*

Also in the ecliptic coordinate system, a line of *celestial latitude* – also called *ecliptic latitude* – is a circle on the celestial sphere that lies in a plane that is parallel to the ecliptic plane. A line of celestial latitude takes its name from the arc-length measured northwards or southwards along any line of celestial longitude from the ecliptic to the line. Thus, celestial latitude is measured from 0° to 90° north and south of the ecliptic. The ecliptic is the line of 0° celestial latitude and the north and south ecliptic poles have celestial latitude 90° north and 90° south, respectively. Celestial latitudes of, say, 30° north and 30° south may be recorded as 30° and -30°, respectively. With the exception of the ecliptic, each line of celestial latitude is a small circle.

Looking at Figure 1.2, we can see that point X has absolute celestial longitude 40° and celestial latitude 50°N.

---

* A *great semicircle* is one-half of a great circle.

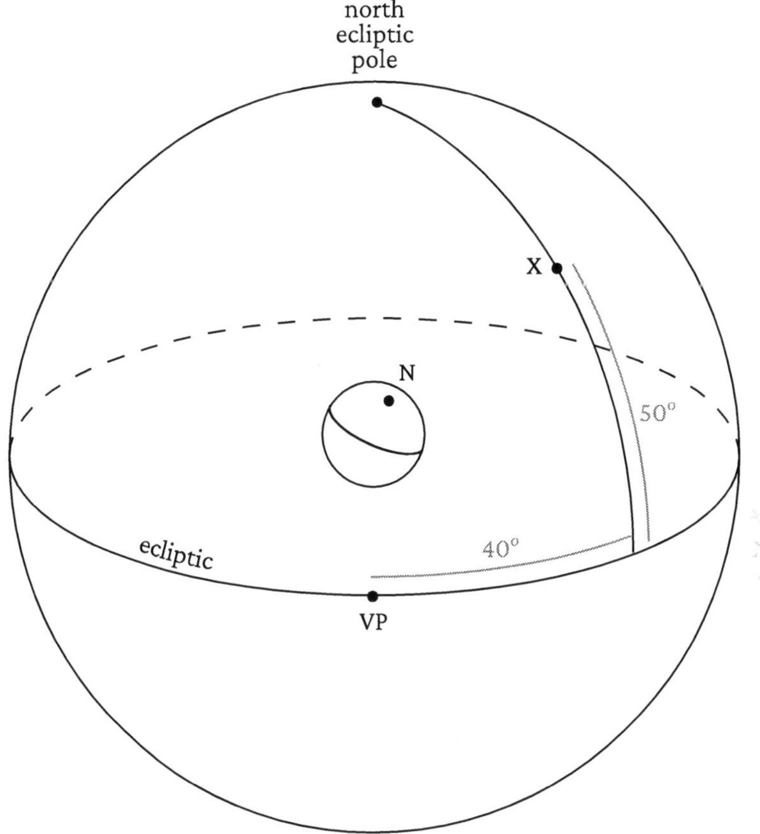

Figure 1.2 The ecliptic coordinate system

In the equatorial coordinate system – also called the *celestial coordinate system* – a line of *right ascension* is a great semicircle on the celestial sphere that runs perpendicular to the celestial equator from one celestial pole to the other. The lines of right ascension that pass through the vernal point and the anti-vernal point are defined as 0 hours and 12 hours, respectively. A line of right ascension takes its name from the arc-length measured eastwards along the celestial equator from the vernal point to the line, with 15° of arc corresponding to 1 hour. Thus, right ascension is measured from 0 hours (or 0°) to 24 hours (or 360°), with exactly 0 hours and exactly 24 hours referring to the same line.

Also in the equatorial coordinate system, a line of *declination* is a circle on the celestial sphere that lies in a plane that is parallel to the equatorial plane. A line of declination takes its name from the arc-length measured northwards or southwards along any line of right ascension from the celestial equator to the line. Thus, declination is measured from 0° to 90° north and south of the celestial equator. The celestial equator is the line of 0° declination and the north and south celestial poles have declination 90° north and 90° south, respectively. Declinations of, say, 50° north and 50° south may be recorded as 50° and -50°, respectively. With the exception of the celestial equator, each line of declination is a small circle.

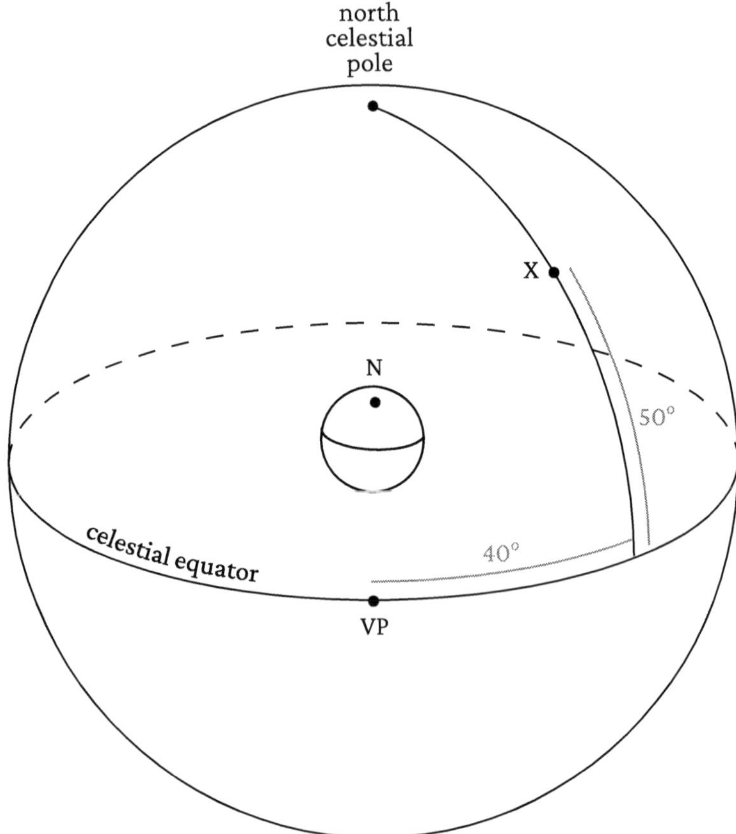

Figure 1.3 The equatorial coordinate system

Looking at Figure 1.3, we can see that point X has right ascension 2h40m and declination 50°N. (40° x 1 hour per 15° of arc = $2^2/_3$ hours.)

When the declination of a celestial body exceeds the maximum northerly or southerly declination of the ecliptic, it is said to be *out of bounds*. In January

2020, Earth's axial tilt was 23°26'12.0" and so at that time, a body was out of bounds if its northerly or southerly declination exceeded this value. Earth's axial tilt is currently decreasing by 0.47" per year (approximately 0.04" per month).

Most techniques used by astrologers do not refer to the celestial latitude, right ascension or declination of factors, but only to celestial longitude. The great significance of celestial longitude in astrological interpretation is reflected in the way the celestial sphere is converted to a two-dimensional chart for the purposes of interpretation: each point on the circumference of a chart wheel is taken to represent all points on a particular a line of celestial longitude.

Zodiacal Cycles

The term *zodiacal* may be used to refer to any cycle or angular relationship that is measured in celestial longitude. However, the term *zodiacal cycle* is usually only used to refer to a cycle of changing celestial longitude measured in relation to an *Aries point* on the ecliptic. There are two types of Aries point. One type is defined in relation to the position(s) of one or more stars, in which case the resulting zodiacal cycle is referred to as *sidereal* (from the Latin for *pertaining to the stars*). The other type is a node, and is referred to as the zodiacal cycle's *Aries node.* A frame of reference based on celestial longitude and measured from an Aries point is referred to as a *zodiacal wheel,* or simply as a *zodiac.*

For the purposes of interpretation, a zodiac may be divided into various numbers of distinct stages (i.e. segments) using lines of celestial longitude, one of which always passes through the zodiac's Aries point. The twelve-fold division is an especially useful frame of reference, because in a given zodiac, particularly significant shifts of meaning occur at twelve lines of celestial longitude, including the line that passes through the Aries point. Where the twelve-fold division is used, the segment to the east of the Aries point is referred to as *Aries*; the segment to the east of Aries is referred to as *Taurus*, and so on, using the names shown in Figure 1.4.

When a zodiac is divided into twelve equal segments, each segment is referred to as a *zodiacal sign.* A minority of those astrologers who use a sidereal zodiac divide it into twelve unequal segments, each of which contains a group of stars close to the ecliptic that are said to be part of the same *constellation.*

The line of celestial longitude that separates two segments of a zodiac may be referred to as a *cusp*. Because a cusp is a line of celestial longitude, the range of celestial longitude that it occupies is infinitesimally small (although a factor is sometimes referred to as being *on the cusp* if it is close to a cusp). Thus, the cusp between two signs is simultaneously exactly 30° of the sign to the west and exactly 0° of the sign to the east. As noted above, astrologers usually record the zodiacal position of a factor as a value between 0° and 30° of a particular zodiacal sign, referring to this as the factor's *zodiacal position.*

Sign/constellation	Abbreviation	Glyph
Aries	AR	♈
Taurus	TA	♉
Gemini	GE	♊
Cancer	CN	♋
Leo	LE	♌
Virgo	VI	♍
Libra	LI	♎
Scorpio	SC	♏
Sagittarius	SG	♐
Capricorn	CP	♑
Aquarius	AQ	♒
Pisces	PI	♓

Figure 1.4 The twelve zodiacal signs/constellations

With regard to the labelling of single degree increments, some words of caution are warranted. If the celestial longitude of a factor is 27°20' Gemini, then it occupies the 28th degree of Gemini rather than the 27th degree (just as the year 2020 occurs in the twenty-first century rather than the twentieth century). In books that give an account of the meaning of each degree increment – such as books on the Sabian Symbols – the 28th degree of Gemini is often listed simply as *Gemini 28.*

Where the celestial longitude of a factor is given as, for example, 8°00' Virgo, then it is not clear which degree increment the factor occupies. If this figure has been rounded up from, say, 7°59'48" Virgo, then the factor occupies the 8th degree of Virgo; and if the figure has been rounded down from, say, 8°00'20" Virgo, then the factor occupies the 9th degree of Virgo.

Unfortunately, some astrology books define the 9th degree of a zodiacal sign as the span between 8°00' and 8°59' inclusive, while others define it as the span between 8°01' and 9°00' inclusive.

Another important point concerns the distinction between the name of a degree increment and a value of celestial longitude rounded to the nearest degree. *27° Libra* may be used as an approximation of any value between exactly 26°30' and exactly 27°30' Libra. A factor may be said to be *in the 27th degree of Libra* – or *in Libra 27* – when its celestial longitude is between exactly 26° and exactly 27° Libra.

The Tropical Zodiac

The Aries node of the *tropical zodiac* (or *seasonal zodiac)* is the vernal point. Thus, tropical Aries begins at the line of 0° absolute celestial longitude and tropical Libra begins at the line of 180° absolute celestial longitude (which passes through the anti-vernal point). Figure 1.5 represents the tropical zodiac as a two-dimensional chart wheel. As noted above, each point on the chart wheel represents all points on a particular line of celestial longitude. The values inside the chart wheel show the absolute celestial longitude at which each tropical sign begins. The diagram is drawn as 'seen' from the north ecliptic pole (this being the conventional way to draw chart wheels), and so anticlockwise movement around the chart wheel corresponds to eastward motion around the celestial sphere.

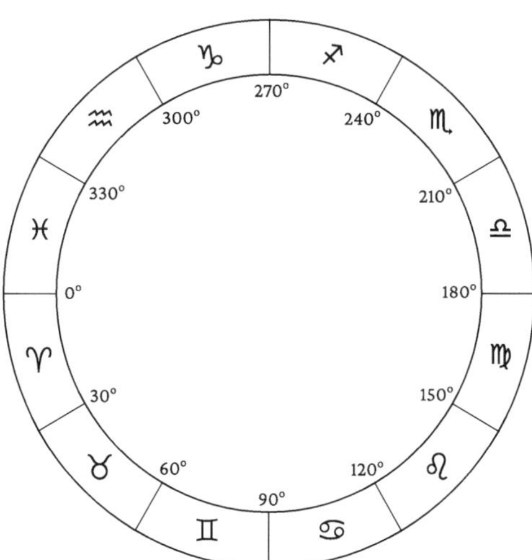

Figure 1.5 The tropical zodiacal signs with the absolute celestial longitude of each sign cusp

Thus, where the tropical zodiac is used, absolute celestial longitude 40°20' is equivalent to 10°20' Taurus (also written 10TA20 or 10♉20) because 40°20' = 30° + 10°20'. As another example, absolute celestial longitude 283°17' is equivalent to 13°17' Capricorn (also written 13CP17 or 13♑17) because 283°17' = 270° + 13°17'.

Figure 1.6 shows how the declination of the ecliptic varies with absolute celestial longitude through the tropical zodiacal signs. Note that declination equals zero at the first point of tropical Aries and the first point of tropical Libra, with northerly declination peaking at the first point of tropical Cancer and southerly declination peaking at the first point of tropical Capricorn.

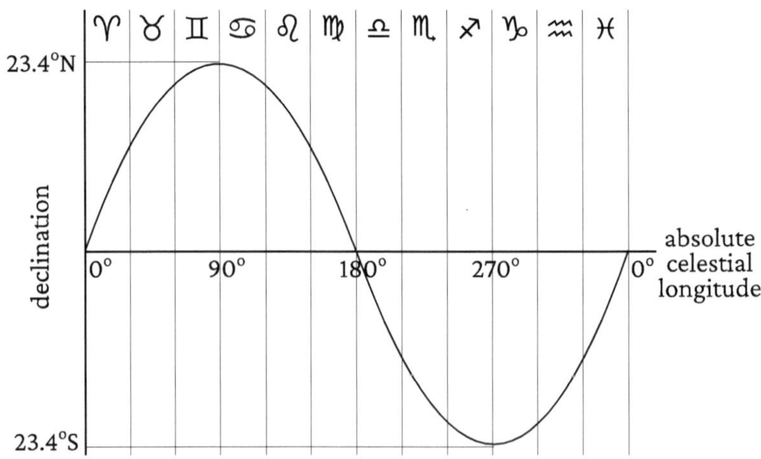

Figure 1.6 The declination of the ecliptic against absolute celestial longitude, with tropical sign cusps

The Annual Seasonal Cycle

As Earth orbits the Sun, the north and south geographic poles lean towards the Sun in turn, giving rise to the annual seasonal cycle. The period of this cycle/orbit is referred to as a *tropical year* or *solar year*. Figure 1.7 shows the changing relationship between Earth and the Sun geocentrically, with Earth at the centre of the celestial sphere and the Sun positioned at four points on the ecliptic. (Diagrams and animations showing this cycle from the *heliocentric* – or Sun-centred – viewpoint can be found online.)

Points 1 and 3 are the vernal and anti-vernal points, respectively, where the declination of the ecliptic is 0°. These points are called the *equinoctial points*, and a moment in time at which the Sun (i.e. the centre of the solar disc) occupies an equinoctial point is called an *equinox* (derived from *equinoxium*, which is Latin for *equal night*). On the day of an equinox, each location experiences twelve hours of daylight and twelve hours of darkness, except those locations that are close to a geographic pole (such locations are discussed below).

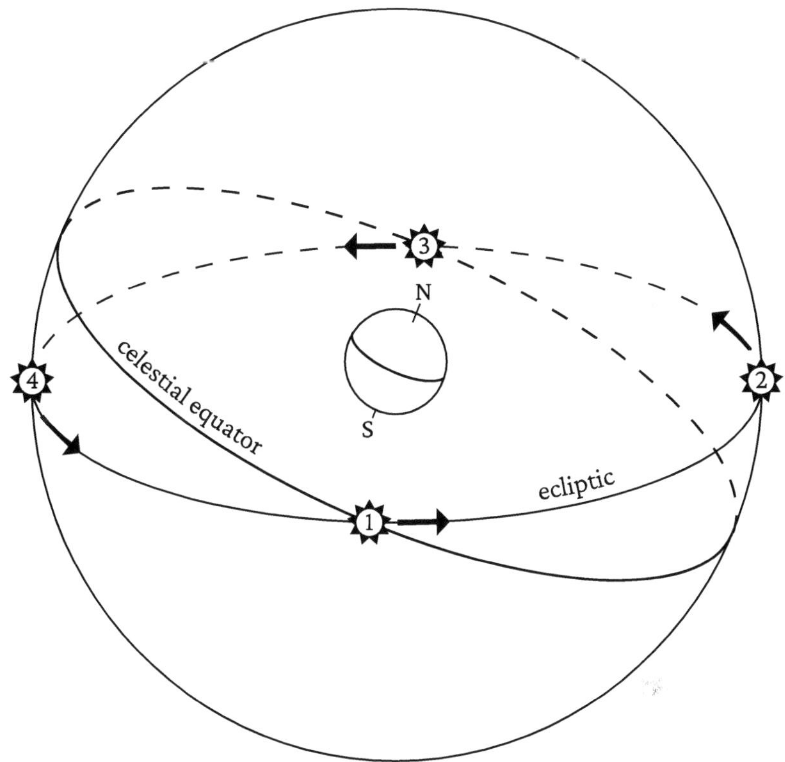

Figure 1.7 The annual seasonal cycle

Points 2 and 4 are the points at which the ecliptic has greatest northerly and southerly declination, respectively. These points are called the *solstitial points*, and a moment in time at which the Sun occupies a solstitial point is called a *solstice* (derived from *solstitium*, which is Latin for *sun standing*). On the day of a solstice, each location in one hemisphere experiences its 'shortest day' (shortest period of daylight), while each location in the other hemisphere experiences its 'longest day' (longest period of daylight), except for locations close to the equator (for which the duration of daylight varies only slightly throughout the seasonal cycle anyway) and locations close to a geographic pole.

Point 1 is the vernal point, where the Sun has absolute celestial longitude 0° as it moves northwards across the celestial equator and into tropical Aries. The moment at which the Sun occupies this point is the *March equinox* or *northward equinox*. In the northern hemisphere, this is the *spring equinox* or *vernal equinox*; for the following six months, the Sun will have northerly declination, shining more directly than average, and for more than half of each 24 hour period, on northern hemisphere locations (with the exception of those locations that are close to the equator). In the southern hemisphere, the March equinox is the *autumnal equinox*.

At point 2, the Sun has absolute celestial longitude 90° as it reaches its maximum northerly declination of 23.4° and enters tropical Cancer. The moment at which the Sun occupies this point is the *June solstice* or *northern solstice*. In the northern hemisphere, this is the *summer solstice*, and the day on which it occurs is the 'longest day' of the year. In the southern hemisphere, this is the *winter solstice*, and the day on which it occurs is 'shortest day' of the year. The line of terrestrial latitude 23.4° N is called the *Tropic of Cancer*.

Point 3 is the anti-vernal point, where the Sun has absolute celestial longitude 180° as it moves southwards across the celestial equator and into tropical Libra. The moment at which the Sun occupies this point is the *September equinox* or *southward equinox*. In the northern hemisphere, this is the autumnal equinox; for the following six months, the Sun will have southerly declination, shining less directly than average, and for less than half of each 24 hour period, on northern hemisphere locations. For southern hemisphere locations, this is the spring or vernal equinox.

At point 4, the Sun has absolute celestial longitude 270° as it reaches its maximum southerly declination of 23.4° and enters tropical Capricorn. The moment at which the Sun occupies this point is the *December solstice* or *southern solstice*. In the northern hemisphere, this is the *winter solstice*, and the day on which it occurs is the 'shortest day' of the year. In the southern hemisphere, this is the summer solstice, and the day on which it occurs is 'longest day' of the year. The line of terrestrial latitude 23.4° S is called the *Tropic of Capricorn*.

The solstitial points are sometimes referred to as the *tropical points*, from the Greek *tropo*, which means *turn*. The equinoctial and solstitial points are together referred to as the four *cardinal points*; and Aries, Cancer, Libra and Capricorn are generally referred to as the *cardinal signs*, even where a zodiac other than the tropical zodiac is used.

The *astronomical seasons* are defined by changes in the Sun's declination. The spring equinox marks the beginning of *astronomical spring* in the hemisphere concerned; the summer solstice marks the beginning of *astronomical summer*, and so on. The *meteorological seasons* are defined differently, with definitions varying from country to country. In many countries, *meteorological spring* begins on March 1st (northern hemisphere) or September 1st (southern hemisphere), meteorological summer begins on June 1st (northern hemisphere) or December 1st (southern hemisphere), and so on. In some countries, temperature changes are used to define the meteorological seasons, and so the timing of them varies from year to year.

Locations close to the north geographic pole are subject to perpetual daylight for part of the year either side of the June solstice, and to perpetual darkness for part of the year either side of the December solstice. The duration of these periods increases with proximity to the north geographic pole. At the north geographic pole, the Sun rises and sets just once each year, gradually rising above the horizon around the time of the March (northward) equinox and gradually setting below the horizon around the time of the September (southward) equinox. At locations close to the south geographic pole, the situation is reversed.

The Precession of the Equinoxes

The cardinal points move westwards along the ecliptic. This motion is traditionally referred to as the *precession of the equinoxes*, often shortened to *precession*. The *sidereal period* of a factor is the period between successive passages of the factor across a fixed line of celestial longitude. The sidereal period of a cardinal point is usually quoted as being just under 2,600 years, which corresponds to a movement of just over 50" of arc per year (or 1° of arc in approximately 72 years). Due to the precession of the equinoxes, a tropical year (the period between successive passages of the Sun across the vernal point) is approximately 20 minutes shorter than a sidereal year (the period between successive passages of the Sun across a fixed point on the ecliptic).

The consensus view is that precession is caused by a gradual and continuous change in the orientation of Earth's rotation axis. This type of motion is referred to as *axial precession*, and in the case of Earth, the main cause of this motion would be the gravitational pull of the Sun and Moon on Earth's equatorial bulge. Thus, this view is often referred to as *lunisolar theory*. Figure 1.8 shows the presumed axial precession of Earth. We can see that as the orientation of Earth's rotation axis and the equatorial plane change in tandem, each celestial pole traces a circle around an ecliptic pole, and the vernal and anti-vernal points move westwards along the ecliptic.

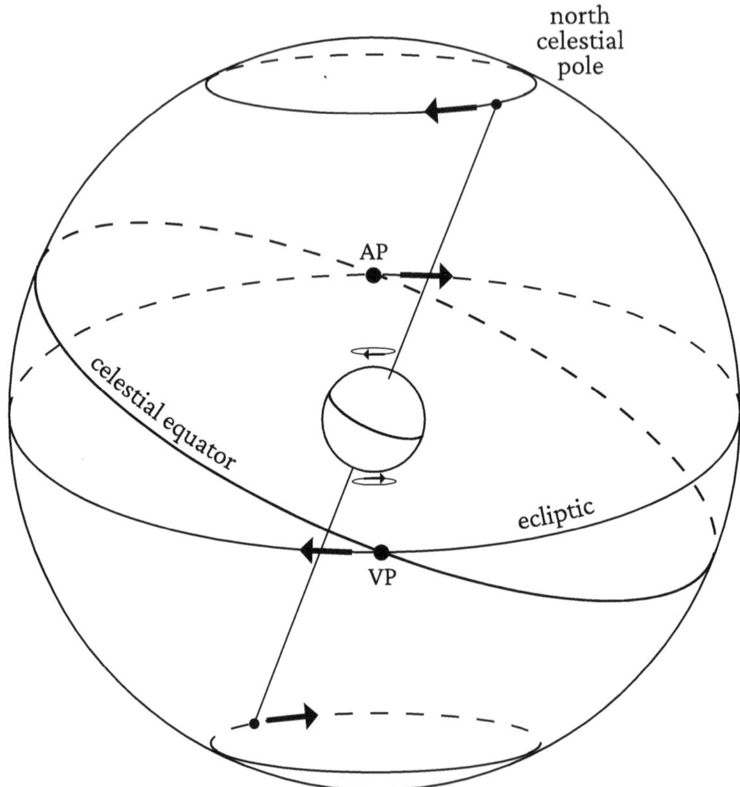

Figure 1.8 The axial precession of Earth

Some people believe that the motion of the cardinal points along the ecliptic is not a result of axial precession, but rather of the Sun being part of a binary system with another star. This being the case, the Sun's orbit around the system's centre of gravity – or *barycentre* – would cause the orientation of the solar system-as-a-whole to change, and with it the orientation of Earth's rotation axis relative to the background of stars. This is referred to as *binary theory* and is currently being promoted by Walter Cruttenden* and others.

* For more information, go to BinaryResearchInstitute.com

Sidereal Zodiacs

A number of sidereal zodiacs are in use; however, most sidereal astrologers believe that there can be only one valid sidereal zodiac. Thus, there is ongoing debate about where the true sidereal Aries point is located in relation to the stars. The *ayanamsa* of a sidereal zodiac is the arc-length measured eastwards along the ecliptic from the vernal point to the zodiac's Aries point. As the vernal point moves westwards along the ecliptic, the ayanamsa of each of sidereal zodiac increases accordingly.

It is thought that Babylonian astrologers – the first astrologers known to have used twelve zodiacal stages (first constellations, then signs) – positioned 15° Taurus and 15° Scorpio at the stars Aldebaran and Antares, respectively. (The celestial longitudes of these stars differed by approximately 179° 59' when this zodiac was first introduced, and differ by approximately 179° 57' today.)

In 1955, one sidereal zodiac was sanctioned as the official Indian zodiac by the Indian government in an attempt to synchronise the celebration of religious festivals across India. In this zodiac – which was named the *Lahiri zodiac* – the star Spica is positioned at 0° Libra. The Lahiri zodiac is by far the most commonly used zodiac in India today, although, for various reasons, many Indian astrologers do not accept its validity.

The Lahiri zodiac is also used by many western sidereal astrologers. However, the sidereal zodiac proposed by twentieth-century astrologers Cyril Fagan and Donald Bradley – referred to as the *Fagan/Bradley zodiac* – is also in common use in the West. In the Fagan/Bradley zodiac, Aldebaran and Antares are positioned at almost exactly 15° Taurus and 15° Scorpio respectively, and so this zodiac is almost exactly aligned with the zodiac thought to have been used by Babylonian astrologers.

Figure 1.9 shows the approximate current alignment of the tropical zodiac with the Fagan/Bradley and Lahiri zodiacs. (As usual, the zodiac wheels are shown as viewed from the north ecliptic pole, and so the westward motion of the tropical zodiac relative to the fixed sidereal zodiacs appears on the diagram as clockwise motion.)

As of January 1st 2020: the Lahiri ayanamsa was 24°08'11", with the vernal point positioned at 5°51'49" Lahiri Pisces; and the Fagan/Bradley ayanamsa was 25°01'11", with the vernal point positioned at 4°58'49" Fagan/Bradley Pisces. At any given moment in time, the Fagan/Bradley ayanamsa is 53' of arc larger than the Lahiri ayanamsa.

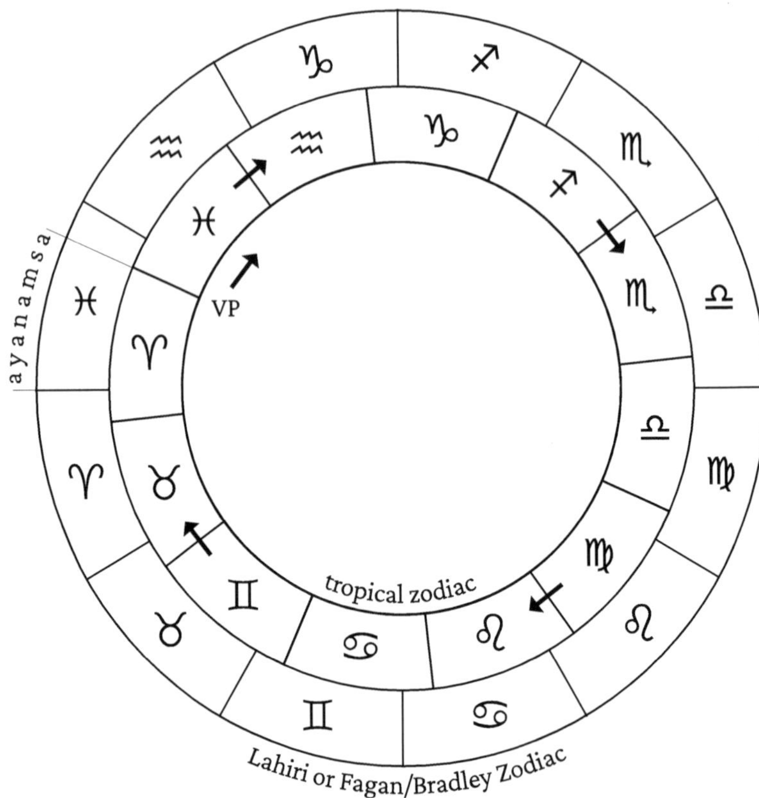

Figure 1.9 The approximate current alignment of the tropical zodiac with the Lahiri and Fagan/Bradley zodiacs

The Astrological Ages

The passage of the vernal point through the twelve signs or constellations of the sidereal zodiac (whichever sidereal zodiac is chosen) is thought by many to correspond to a sequence of twelve *Astrological Ages*. The vernal point will move from Lahiri Pisces to Lahiri Aquarius early in the twenty-fifth century CE, and from Fagan/Bradley Pisces to Fagan/Bradley Aquarius near the end of that century. According to other proposed sidereal zodiacs, the beginning of the *Age of Aquarius* may have been as early as the eighteenth century CE, or may be as late as the thirty-first century CE.*

Much attention has been given to the retrograde motion of the vernal point through one or another of the proposed sidereal zodiacs, and less to the

* *Mundane Astrology*, Baigent, Campion & Harvey (1995) pp. 497 to 500. (1st ed. 1984)

other consequence of this motion: the apparent direct motion of seemingly fixed factors – such as the galactic centre – through the tropical zodiac. This is discussed in Chapter 5.

Midpoints

The *midpoints* of two factors are the diametrically opposed points on the ecliptic that lie midway between the factors' lines of celestial longitude. The midpoint that is nearest to the two factors is referred to as the *direct midpoint* and the other is referred to as the *indirect midpoint*. For example, if the absolute celestial longitudes of two factors are 130° and 240°, one of their midpoints has celestial longitude 185°, because this is the mean of 130° and 240°. The other midpoint is found by adding or subtracting 180° to arrive at another value between 0° and 360°. In this case, we subtract 180° to give celestial longitude 5°. The midpoint with celestial longitude 185° is the direct midpoint because this midpoint is closer to the lines of celestial longitude of the two factors. The line between the direct and indirect midpoints of a pair of factors is referred to as the *midpoint axis* of those factors.

Aspects

Two factors are said to form a *perfect aspect* when their celestial longitudes differ by a factor* of 360° or a multiple of a factor of 360°. For example, 90° is 1/4 of 360°, and when the celestial longitudes of two factors differ by exactly 90°, they are said to form a perfect *square*. As another example, 30° is 1/12 of 360°, and when the celestial longitudes of two factors differ by exactly 150° (5 x 30°), they are said to form a perfect *quincunx*. Theoretically, a set of aspects could be derived by dividing the circle by any whole number, but for practical reasons, the astrologer must limit the number of types of aspect used in interpretation.

The *orb* of an aspect is the amount by which it deviates from perfection. For example, when the celestial longitudes of two factors differ by 87° or 93° they are said to be forming a square aspect with an orb of -3° or +3°, respectively. When deciding the maximum orb that should be allowed for a given aspect, the astrologer will generally take into account the interpretive weight given to the factors making the aspect and the number from which the aspect is derived. An aspect with an orb that is less than, say, one tenth

---

* In this book, the word *factor* is underlined when used as a mathematical term; for example, 2 is a factor of 4.

of the maximum allowable orb may be referred to as *exact*. An aspect with an orb that is less than, say, one third of the maximum allowable orb may be referred to as *close*. An aspect with an orb that is nearly as large as (or slightly larger than) the maximum allowable orb may be referred to as *wide*.* An aspect that is within the allowed orb and approaching perfection is said to be *applying*, while an aspect that is within the allowed orb having already been perfected is said to be *separating*. Aspect orbs are discussed further in Chapter 3.

Figure 1.10 shows the most commonly used aspect types and the abbreviation and glyph(s) used to denote each of them. The difference in celestial longitude at the perfection of the aspect is given in degrees and as a fraction of 360°.

Aspect	Abbreviation	Glyph	Fraction	Arc-length
Conjunction	CJN	☌	1	0° (360°)
Opposition	OPP	☍	$^1/_2$	180°
Trine	TRI	△	$^1/_3$	120°
Square	SQR	□	$^1/_4$	90°
Quintile	Q	Q	$^1/_5$	72°
Bi-quintile	BQ	± BQ Q^2	$^2/_5$	144°
Sextile	SXT	⚹	$^1/_6$	60°
Semi-square	SSQ	∠	$^1/_8$	45°
Sesquiquadrate	SES	⚼	$^3/_8$	135°
Semi-sextile	SSX	⚺	$^1/_{12}$	30°
Quincunx	QNX	⚻	$^5/_{12}$	150°

Figure 1.10 The most commonly used aspects

As the celestial longitude of a factor changes more quickly than that of another, the two factors form a sequence of aspects between successive

* Note that these figures are arbitrary.

conjunctions. Figure 1.11 shows the aspects listed in Figure 1.10 in the order in which they are formed. The larger dot represents the position of the slower-moving factor at any given moment in time, and each dot (including the larger dot) represents the position of the faster-moving factor relative to the slower-moving factor as each aspect is perfected. The sequence is shown unfolding anticlockwise because the celestial motions with which astrologers are concerned are mostly eastwards, appearing as anticlockwise motion when viewed from the north ecliptic pole. Note that each point on the circle shown in Figure 1.11 represents all points on a particular line of celestial longitude.

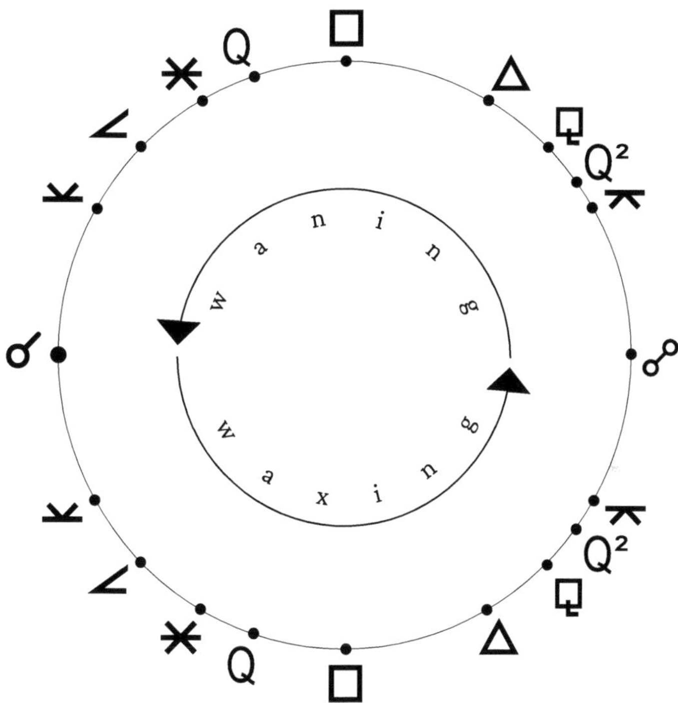

Figure 1.11 The most commonly used aspects in order of formation

The *waxing hemicycle* (half-cycle) begins at the perfection of the conjunction and ends at the perfection of the opposition, and the *waning hemicycle* begins at the perfection of the opposition and ends at the perfection of the conjunction. All aspects apart from the conjunction and opposition occur once during the waxing hemicycle and once during the waning hemicycle, and the astrologer may interpret an aspect differently according to whether it is a waxing or a waning aspect. As discussed below, Mercury, Venus and the Sun form only a limited range of aspects with one another because, from the geocentric viewpoint, they remain close to one another on the celestial sphere.

When noting aspects formed between a midpoint and a third factor, astrologers usually consider only those aspects that are derived by dividing the 360° circle by a power of two (1, 2, 4, 8...). In each case, the aspect to the direct midpoint is listed rather than to the indirect midpoint. Generally, a maximum orb of 2° is allowed for a conjunction or opposition between a direct midpoint and third factor, with proportionately smaller orbs allowed for aspects based on larger numbers (for example, 1° for a square, ½° for a semisquare or sesquiquadrate, and so on).

Parallels and Contraparallels

The interpretation of *parallels* and *contraparallels* is the only commonly used technique in which the declinations of two factors are compared. Two factors are said to be in parallel when – within the allowed orb – both factors have the same northerly declination, or both factors have the same southerly declination. Two factors are said to be in contraparallel when – within the allowed orb – the northerly declination of one body is equal to the southerly declination of the other. The glyphs used to denote parallels and contraparallels are *//* and *#* respectively.

To the extent that a factor is close to the ecliptic (the Sun and most nodes used by astrologers are on the ecliptic, and the Moon and the planets remain quite close to the ecliptic), they are more likely to be in parallel or contraparallel with one another when their celestial longitudes are related in certain ways. The likelihood of two such factors being in parallel is greater to the extent that their midpoints are close to the solstitial points, and also to the extent that their lines of celestial longitude are in proximity. (Interestingly, the meaning attributed to a parallel is similar to that attributed to a conjunction aspect.) The likelihood of two such factors being in contraparallel is greater to the extent that their midpoints are close to the equinoctial points, and also to the extent that their lines of celestial longitude oppose one another. (The meaning attributed to a contraparallel is similar to that attributed to an opposition aspect.)

Figure 1.6 (page 10) can be used to verify that these tendencies exist. For example, when two bodies have absolute celestial longitudes 145° and 215°, their midpoints occur at celestial longitudes 0° and 180°, which are the equinoctial points. Looking at Figure 1.6, we can see that if both bodies are close to the ecliptic, they are likely to be in contraparallel.

Factors on or close to the ecliptic tend to sustain parallels and contraparallels with other factors for shorter periods when closer to an equinoctial point, and for longer periods when closer to a solstitial point. This is because the declination of the ecliptic changes more quickly around the equinoctial points and more slowly around the solstitial points. For this reason, it has been suggested that the orbs allowed for parallels and contraparallels should be increased to the extent that the bodies concerned have celestial longitudes close to 90° and 270°, and/or decreased to the extent that the bodies concerned have celestial longitudes close to 0° (i.e. 360°) and 180°.*

Synodic Cycles

A *synodic cycle* is a cycle of change in the relative positions of three or more celestial bodies, and is usually measured between successive occurrences of a particular state of alignment – *synodic* being derived from the Greek for *meeting*. The period between successive alignments is referred to as the *synodic period* of the group of bodies concerned. In geocentric astrology, the unfoldment of a synodic cycle is measured between successive perfect conjunctions of two bodies, as 'seen' from the centre of Earth (which is thus the third body involved in the alignment).

One way to divide a synodic cycle into distinct stages is to divide the celestial sphere into equal segments using lines of celestial longitude. One line of celestial longitude passes through the slower-moving body, and as this body moves, the segments move in tandem with it. As the cycle unfolds, the faster-moving body moves through each segment in turn between successive perfect conjunctions. The Sun-Mercury, Sun-Venus and Mercury-Venus synodic cycles cannot be charted in this way because these bodies remain close to one another on the celestial sphere.

(The section *Direct and Retrograde Motion* (below) looks at an alternative method of charting a synodic cycle – a method that can only be used to chart the synodic cycle of the Sun and a body that orbits the Sun, including the Sun-Mercury and Sun-Venus cycles.)

As noted above, during the unfoldment of a zodiacal cycle, particularly significant shifts of meaning occur every 30° of celestial longitude beginning at the first point of Aries. Similarly, particularly significant shifts of meaning occur every 30° of celestial longitude during the unfoldment of a synodic cycle, but in this case, particularly significant shifts of meaning also occur

---

* See, for example, *Horoscope Symbols*, by Robert Hand (1981, 1st ed.) pp. 117 to 120.

every 45° of celestial longitude. Thus, when dividing the celestial sphere into equal segments for the purposes of interpreting synodic position, most astrologers focus on either the eight-fold or the twelve-fold division. As with a zodiacal cycle, however, a synodic cycle can be divided into various numbers of distinct stages.

The Lunation Cycle

The Moon's sidereal period is approximately 27 days and 8 hours, and is referred to as a *sidereal month.* The synodic cycle of the Sun and Moon is commonly known as the *lunation cycle,* and the period of this cycle is referred to as a *synodic month,* which averages approximately 29 days and 13 hours. A synodic month is longer than a sidereal month due to Earth's motion relative to the Sun, which appears to us as the movement of the Sun along the ecliptic. Approximately 27 days and 8 hours after the perfection of a Sun-Moon conjunction, the Moon has returned to the same line of celestial longitude, but it takes, on average, a further 2 days and 5 hours, approximately, for the Moon to catch up with the Sun. When Earth is furthest from the Sun, and the apparent motion of the Sun is slowest, the synodic month is approximately 29 days and 8 hours. When Earth is closest to the Sun, and the apparent motion of the Sun is quickest, the synodic month is approximately 29 days and 18 hours.

Astrologers usually divide the lunation cycle into eight stages using eight equally spaced lines of celestial longitude, one of which is that of the Sun. Figure 1.12 shows the position of the Moon in relation to Earth and the Sun as the Moon crosses each of these lines (as seen from the north ecliptic pole, with sunlight approaching from the left). Figure 1.13 shows how the Moon appears to an observer facing south (i.e. how it typically appears to a northern hemisphere observer) at each of these points. To see how the Moon appears to an observer facing north (i.e. how it typically appears to a southern hemisphere observer), turn the diagram upside down (keeping in mind that the sequence now runs from right to left).

The name of each of these eight points is also the name of the phase that begins at the point. The *new moon* (perfect conjunction) marks the beginning of the *new moon phase.* The *crescent moon* (perfect waxing semisquare) marks the beginning of the *crescent phase.* The *first quarter moon* (perfect waxing square) marks the beginning of the *first quarter phase.* The *gibbous moon* (perfect waxing sesquiquadrate) marks the beginning of the *gibbous phase.* These four phases make up the *waxing hemicycle.*

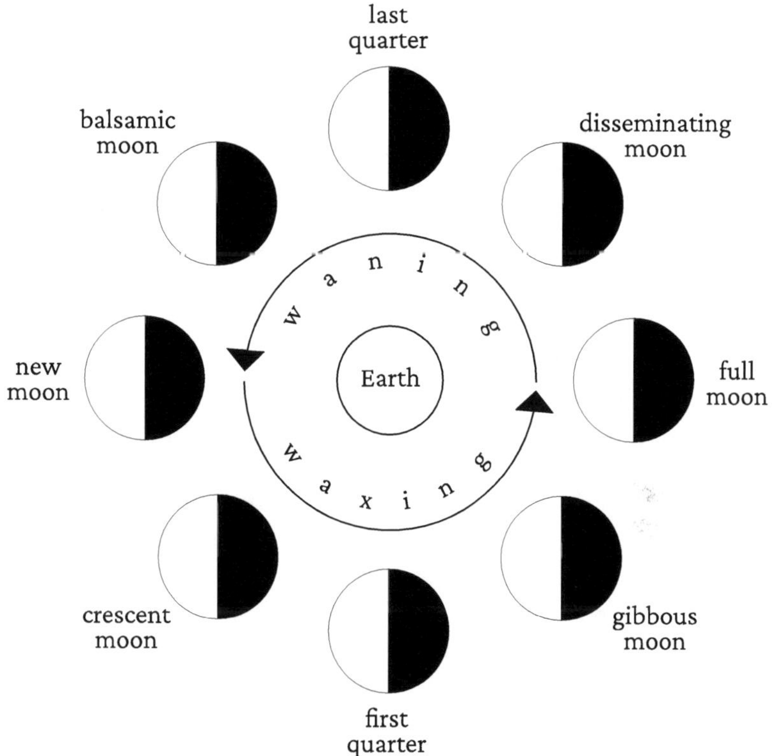

Figure 1.12 The lunation cycle

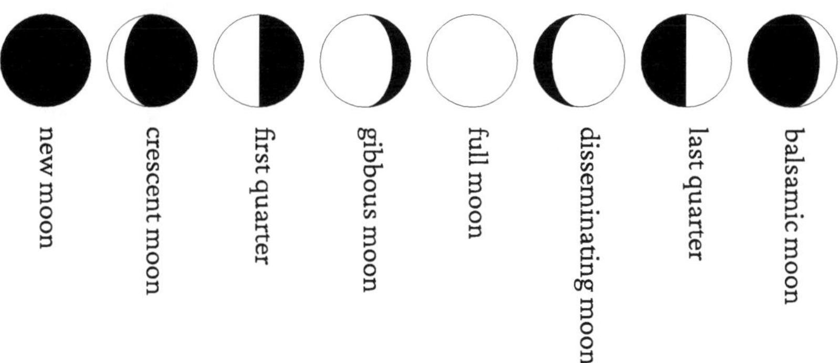

Figure 1.13 The Moon as seen from Earth

The *full moon* (perfect opposition) marks the beginning of the *full moon phase*. The *disseminating moon* (perfect waning sesquiquadrate) marks the beginning of the *disseminating phase*. The *last quarter moon* (perfect waning square) marks the beginning of the *last quarter phase*. The *balsamic moon* (perfect waning semisquare) marks the beginning of the *balsamic phase*. These four phases make up the *waning hemicycle*.

The crescent moon and the balsamic moon are sometimes referred to, respectively, as the *waxing crescent moon* and the *waning crescent moon*. The gibbous moon and the disseminating moon are sometimes referred to, respectively, as the *waxing gibbous moon* and the *waning gibbous moon*. The phases that begin at these points are named accordingly.

Many non-astrological sources divide the lunation cycle into four phases, referred to as the *waxing crescent phase* (new moon to first quarter), the *waxing gibbous phase* (first quarter to full moon), the *waning gibbous phase* (full moon to last quarter) and the *waning crescent phase* (last quarter to new moon).

The Lunar Nodes

The plane of the Moon's orbit around Earth is inclined to the ecliptic plane by approximately 5°. Because these planes both pass through Earth's centre, the nodal axis formed by their intersection also passes through Earth's centre, and meets the celestial sphere at diametrically opposed points called the *Moon's nodes* – or *lunar nodes*. The Moon's orbital plane meets the celestial sphere at a great circle. Following this circle eastwards around the celestial sphere, the ecliptic is crossed northwards at the *north lunar node* (also called the *ascending lunar node* or simply the *north* or *ascending node*) and southwards at *south lunar node* (also called the *descending lunar node* or simply the *south* or *descending node*).

The lunar nodes move westwards around the ecliptic (clockwise when viewed from the north ecliptic pole) due to the changing orientation of the Moon's orbital plane. The sidereal period of a lunar node is approximately 18.6 years. The movement of the lunar nodes along the ecliptic is unsteady, slowing to a virtual standstill for a two-month period during each six-month period. Rather than interpreting the actual positions of the lunar nodes, some astrologers interpret the positions of imaginary points that move steadily at the average speed of the lunar nodes. To avoid confusion, the former are referred to as the *true lunar nodes* (or simply the *true nodes*) and the latter are referred to as the *mean lunar nodes* (or simply the *mean nodes*).

The north lunar node is the Aries node of the *draconic zodiac*. Thus, the first points of draconic Aries and Libra, respectively, are the lines of celestial longitude that pass through the north and south lunar nodes. The astrologer might choose to define the position of the draconic zodiac using the true lunar nodes or the mean lunar nodes.

The orbital plane of each celestial body that orbits the Sun (other than Earth) forms its own nodal axis with the ecliptic plane. However, from the geocentric viewpoint, only the Moon's nodes are diametrically opposed, because only the Moon's orbital plane passes through Earth's centre.

Eclipses

A lunar eclipse occurs when, at a full moon, the Moon is close enough to the ecliptic for part of the Moon to pass through Earth's shadow. A solar eclipse occurs when, at a new moon, the Moon is close enough to the ecliptic for the Moon to hide at least some of the Sun from view for some locations on Earth. (This is how the term *ecliptic* originated.) As noted above, the Moon crosses the ecliptic at a true lunar node; thus, an eclipse is the result of a new or full moon sufficiently close to one of the true lunar nodes.

During a *partial lunar eclipse*, some of the lunar disc remains outside Earth's shadow and continues to receive direct sunlight throughout. For a period during a *total lunar eclipse*, no direct sunlight reaches any part of the Moon's surface. A lunar eclipse can be seen from any part of Earth's surface from which the Moon is visible at the time of the eclipse.

A solar eclipse is only visible from a limited area of Earth's surface. The area affected changes during the eclipse due to Earth's rotation and the ongoing change in the relative positioning of the Sun, Moon and Earth. The total area of Earth's surface for which the Sun is partly – but not completely – covered by the Moon at some point during the eclipse is referred to as the *partial eclipse path*. The total area of Earth's surface for which the solar disc is completely covered by the Moon at some point during the eclipse is referred to as the *total eclipse path*. During a *partial solar eclipse*, the solar disc is never completely covered for any location, and only a partial eclipse path forms. A *total solar eclipse* results in a total eclipse path surrounded by a partial eclipse path.

Diagrams portraying the different types of solar and lunar eclipse, and animations showing the formation of eclipse paths during past and future solar eclipses, can be found online.

Whether an eclipse will occur at a new or full moon, and if so whether it will be partial or total, depends not only on the proximity of the Sun and Moon to one or both lunar nodes, but also on the orbital radii of Earth and the Moon.* If the alignment of the Sun, Moon and Earth is very close at the time of a new moon, but the Moon appears smaller than the Sun, the outer edge of the solar disc is still visible at the point of closest alignment. This type of partial eclipse is called an *annular eclipse*.

A partial lunar eclipse is possible when a full moon occurs within 12°15' of a lunar node. When a full moon occurs between 6°00' and 9°30' of a lunar node, a partial lunar eclipse always occurs, but never a total lunar eclipse. When a full moon occurs between 3°45' and 6°00' of a lunar node, there is always a lunar eclipse, which may be partial or total. When a full moon occurs within 3°45' of a lunar node, a total lunar eclipse always occurs.

A partial solar eclipse is possible when a new moon occurs within 18°31' of a lunar node. When a new moon occurs between 11°15' and 15°21' of a lunar node, a partial solar eclipse always occurs, but never a total solar eclipse. When a new moon occurs between 9°55' and 11°15' of a lunar node, there is always a solar eclipse, which may be partial or total. When a new moon occurs within 9°55' of a lunar node, the eclipse is always either a total eclipse or an annular eclipse.

A period of time during which the Sun is within 18°31' of a lunar node – and thus close enough for an eclipse to be possible – is called an *eclipse season*. An eclipse season lasts approximately 5 weeks, and due to the westward motion of the lunar nodes, the average period between the beginnings of successive seasons is just under 6 months. During most eclipse seasons, there is one solar eclipse and one lunar eclipse, one of which is partial and the other total. If a new moon occurs very close to a lunar node, the preceding and succeeding full moons may be too far from the lunar nodes for a lunar eclipse to occur at either, in which case the eclipse season will contain one total (or annular) solar eclipse and no lunar eclipses. During some eclipse seasons the full moon occurs very close to the lunar nodal axis, resulting in two solar eclipses either side of a total lunar eclipse (sometimes

* The Moon's *apogee* is the point in its orbit at which it is furthest from Earth; its *perigee* is the point at which it is closest to Earth. Thus, the Moon appears smaller around its apogee and larger around its perigee. *Aphelion* refers to the point at which a celestial body orbiting a star is furthest from the star, while *perihelion* refers to the point at which the body is closest to the star. Thus, the Sun appears smaller when Earth is around its aphelion and larger when Earth is around its perihelion.

one solar eclipse is total (or annular), but never both).

Saros Series

A *draconic month* is the average period between two successive perfect conjunctions of the Moon and the north lunar node (or between two successive perfect conjunctions of the Moon and the south lunar node). Because the lunar nodes move westwards along the ecliptic, a draconic month is slightly shorter than a sidereal month.

A *Saros* is equal to the period of 223 synodic months, which is less than one hour shorter than the period of 242 draconic months. Both periods approximate to 18 years, 11 days and 8 hours (or 18 years, 10 days and 8 hours if this period contains 5 leap years) when rounded to the nearest hour. In other words, over a period of one Saros, the Sun-Moon synodic cycle and the Moon's draconic cycle each unfold a whole number of times.

A *lunar Saros series* is a series of lunar eclipses that occur at intervals of one Saros; and a *solar Saros series* is a series of solar eclipses that occur at intervals of one Saros. All eclipses within a given Saros series occur with the Moon positioned close to the same lunar node (because a Saros is equal to a whole number of draconic months). At an eclipse, the position of the Moon relative to the lunar node concerned is always slightly west of its position at the previous eclipse of the same Saros series. This is because the 242nd draconic month is not quite complete as the new or full moon marks the end of the 223rd synodic month. Consequently, in a Saros series in which eclipses occur with the Moon close to the north lunar node, the Moon's celestial latitude is slightly more southerly with each successive eclipse; and in a Saros series in which eclipses occur with the Moon close to the south lunar node, the Moon's celestial latitude is slightly more northerly with each successive eclipse.

The first eclipse in a solar Saros series occurs with the Moon just within 18°31' east of the lunar node concerned. If this is the north lunar node, this (partial) solar eclipse will be visible from the region of Earth's surface that is furthest north of the ecliptic plane. (At any given moment in time, the location on Earth's surface that is furthest north of the ecliptic plane is that which has terrestrial latitude 66.6° N and whose line of terrestrial longitude to the south lies beneath the line of celestial longitude 0° tropical Capricorn.) If this is the south lunar node, this (partial) solar eclipse will be visible from the region of Earth's surface that is furthest south of the ecliptic plane. (At any given moment in time, the location on Earth's surface that is furthest south of the ecliptic plane is that which has terrestrial latitude 66.6°

S and whose line of terrestrial longitude to the north lies beneath the line of celestial longitude 0° tropical Cancer.)

During the first half of a solar Saros series, the alignment of the Sun, the Moon and Earth becomes more precise with each eclipse; non-annular partial eclipses give way to total (or annular) eclipses, and eclipse paths get closer to the tropics. During the second half of a solar Saros series, the alignment becomes less precise; total (or annular) eclipses give way to non-annular partial eclipses, and eclipse paths get further from the tropics.

Each Saros series is given a number. In the case of a Saros series associated with the north lunar node, this is an odd number; and in the case of a Saros series associated with the south lunar node, this is an even number. At present, approximately 40 solar Saros series and 40 lunar Saros series are in progress. A Saros series lasts between approximately 1200 and 1600 years (typically around 1300 years). The shortest Saros series consist of around 69 eclipses and the longest series consist of around 89 eclipses (with a typical series consisting of around 71 eclipses).

It is believed that a unique thread of meaning runs through each Saros series, and the series to which an eclipse belongs may be taken into account during interpretation.

Direct and Retrograde Motion

From the geocentric viewpoint, a body that orbits the Sun alternates between eastward and westward motion. Eastward geocentric motion* is usually referred to by astrologers as *direct motion* and by astronomers as *prograde motion*. Westward geocentric motion is referred to as *retrograde motion*.

Direct and retrograde motion are denoted by the glyphs **D** and ℞ respectively. In an ephemeris, **D** appears next to the first zodiacal position given for a factor after the factor turns direct, and ℞ appears next to the first zodiacal position given for a factor after the factor turns retrograde. On an astrological chart, ℞ appears next to any factor whose motion was (or will be) retrograde at the moment for which the chart is cast.

A celestial body that orbits the Sun inside Earth's orbit is referred to as an *inferior body*, while a celestial body that orbits the Sun outside Earth's orbit is referred to as a *superior body*. Synodic cycles involving the Sun and an

* *Geocentric motion* is apparent motion, as 'seen' from Earth's centre.

inferior body follow a particular pattern, while synodic cycles involving the Sun and a superior body follow a different pattern. We will look at each pattern in turn, using Mercury and Jupiter as examples.

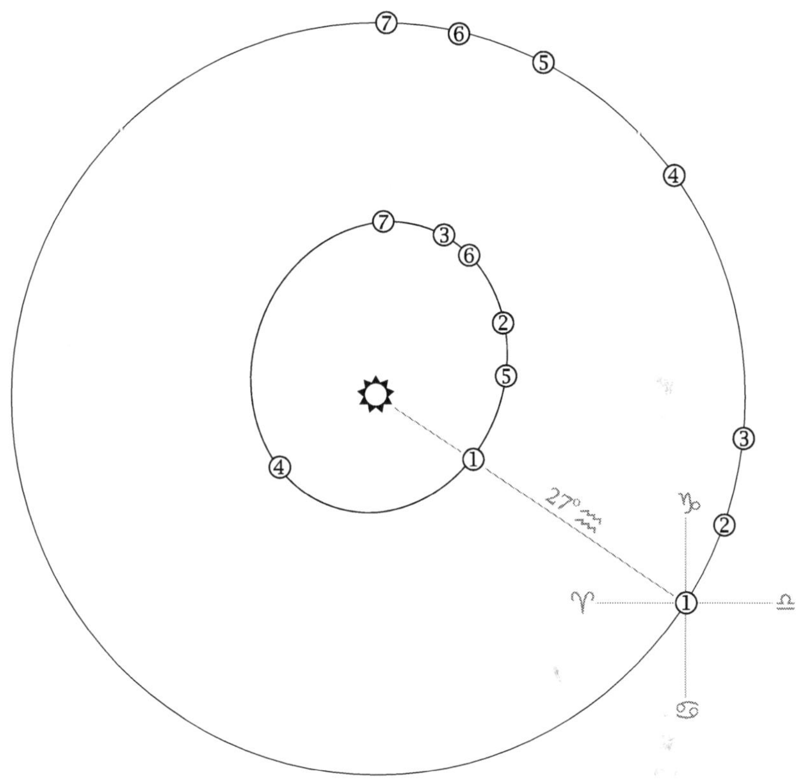

Figure 1.14 The synodic cycle of Mercury and the Sun

Figure 1.14 shows the highly elliptical orbital path of Mercury within the more circular orbital path of Earth. The numbered circles show the positions of Mercury and Earth at seven key points of an unfoldment of the synodic cycle of Mercury and the Sun that occurred in 2014. The cross at Earth's position at point 1 shows the directions of the cardinal points. The orientation of this cross on the page remains the same for all points on Earth's orbit. Figure 1.15 shows points 1 to 6 as they appear on a chart wheel. Figure 1.16 is a graphic ephemeris showing changes in the celestial longitudes of Mercury (the curved line) and the Sun (the straight line). Note that celestial longitude increases down the vertical axis, this being the conventional way of drawing graphic ephemerides.

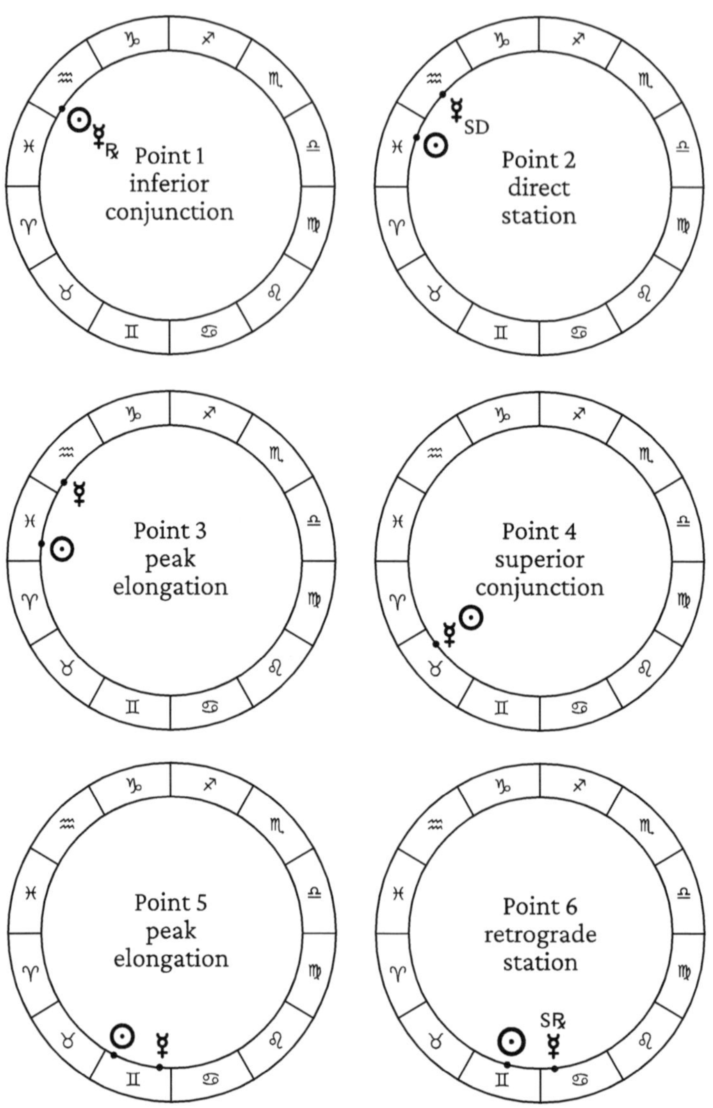

Figure 1.15 The synodic cycle of Mercury and the Sun, as seen on the chart wheel

Figure 1.17 shows the cycle from the geocentric viewpoint, with Mercury orbiting the Sun while the Sun follows its apparent path around the celestial sphere. (Earth would be positioned approximately 8cm directly below the Sun.) In Figure 1.17, point 1 is also point 7. Figure 1.18 gives the date and the celestial longitude (rounded to the nearest whole degree) of Mercury and the Sun at each point.

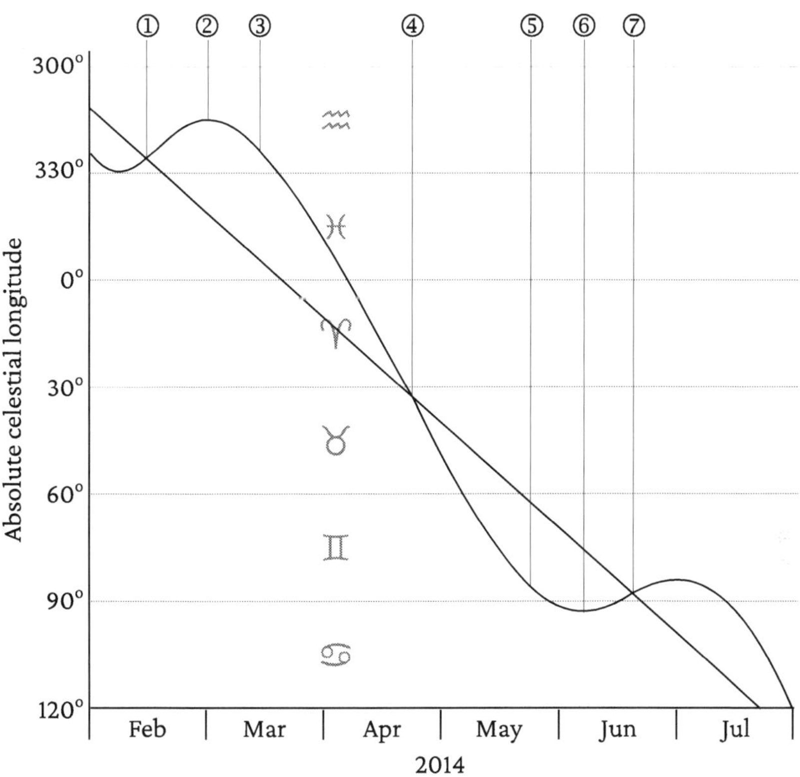

Figure 1.16 Graphic ephemeris - Mercury and the Sun

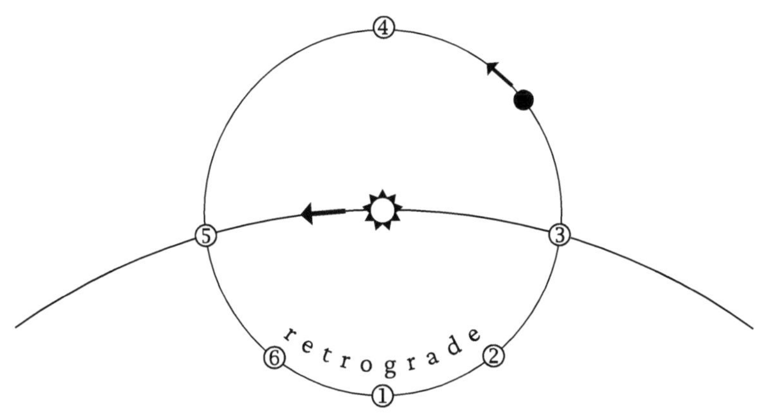

Figure 1.17 The geocentric view of the synodic cycle of Mercury and the Sun

Point in the cycle	Date (2014)	Celestial longitude of the Sun	Celestial longitude of Mercury	Event in Mercury's direct-retrograde cycle
1	Feb 15th	327° (27°♒)	327° (27°♒)	Inferior conjunction. Retrograde speed peaks.
2	Feb 28th	340° (10°♓)	318° (18°♒)	Direct station.
3	Mar 14th	354° (24°♓)	326° (26°♒)	Speed equals that of Sun. Elongation peaks at 28°.
4	Apr 26th	036° (6°♉)	036° (6°♉)	Superior conjunction. Direct speed peaks.
5	May 24th	063° (3°♊)	086° (26°♊)	Speed equals that of Sun. Elongation peaks at 23°.
6	Jun 7th	077° (17°♊)	093° (3°♋)	Retrograde station.
7	Jun 19th	089° (29°♊)	089° (29°♊)	Inferior conjunction. Retrograde speed peaks.

Figure 1.18 Dates and positions at points 1 to 7

At point 1, Mercury's retrograde speed peaked as Mercury and the Sun perfected a conjunction with Mercury between Earth and the Sun. A conjunction of the Sun and an inferior body that occurs with the body between Earth and the Sun (i.e. with the body at its perigee) is referred to as an *inferior conjunction.*

Between points 1 and 2, Mercury appeared to slow down, until at point 2, Mercury appeared to stop moving as its motion changed from retrograde to direct. A point at which a celestial body appears to stop as its geocentric motion changes is referred to as a *station.* Geocentric motion changes from retrograde to direct at a *direct station* (denoted by **SD**) and from direct to retrograde at a *retrograde station* (denoted by **S℞**).

Between points 1 and 3, the Sun appeared to be pulling away from Mercury as the difference between their celestial longitudes increased. At point 3, Mercury's speed – which had been gradually increasing since the direct station at point 2 – equalled the speed of the Sun (note that the lines in Figure 1.16 have the same gradient at this point). Thus, at point 3, Mercury's westerly elongation (distance from the Sun in celestial longitude) peaked, and from here Mercury began to catch up with the Sun.

Between points 3 and 4, Mercury caught up with the Sun. At point 4, Mercury's direct motion peaked as Mercury and the Sun formed a perfect conjunction with Mercury behind the Sun. A conjunction of the Sun and an inferior body that occurs with Earth and the body on opposite sides of the Sun (i.e. with the body at its apogee) is referred to as a *superior conjunction*.

Between points 4 and 6, Mercury's apparent speed decreased, until at point 6, the retrograde station was reached. Mercury's direct motion remained greater than that of the Sun until point 5, after which Mercury appeared to move more slowly than the Sun. Thus, Mercury's easterly elongation peaked at point 5. From the retrograde station at point 6, Mercury's retrograde motion quickened until it peaked at the inferior conjunction (point 7).

At point 3, Mercury's elongation peaked at approximately 28° of arc, while at point 5 it peaked at approximately 23° of arc. This is because Mercury happened to be very close to its aphelion at point 3, and closer to its perihelion at point 5. Mercury's peak elongation, which is also affected by the orbital radius of Earth, varies between 18° and 28° of arc.

Mercury's orbital period is just 88 days, while that of Venus is 225 days. Consequently, the synodic period of Mercury and the Sun (approximately 4 months) is much shorter than that of Venus and the Sun (approximately 19 months), because Mercury takes less time to catch up with Earth between successive inferior conjunctions. Venus' peak elongation varies between 45° and 47° of arc. This is greater than that of Mercury because the orbital path of Venus is further from the Sun, and varies by a much smaller margin than that of Mercury because Venus' orbital path is much more circular.

Figure 1.19 shows the positions of Jupiter and Earth at five key points during the unfoldment of the synodic cycle of Jupiter and the Sun that occurred during 2014/15. Figure 1.20 shows the points 1 to 5 as they appear on a chart wheel.

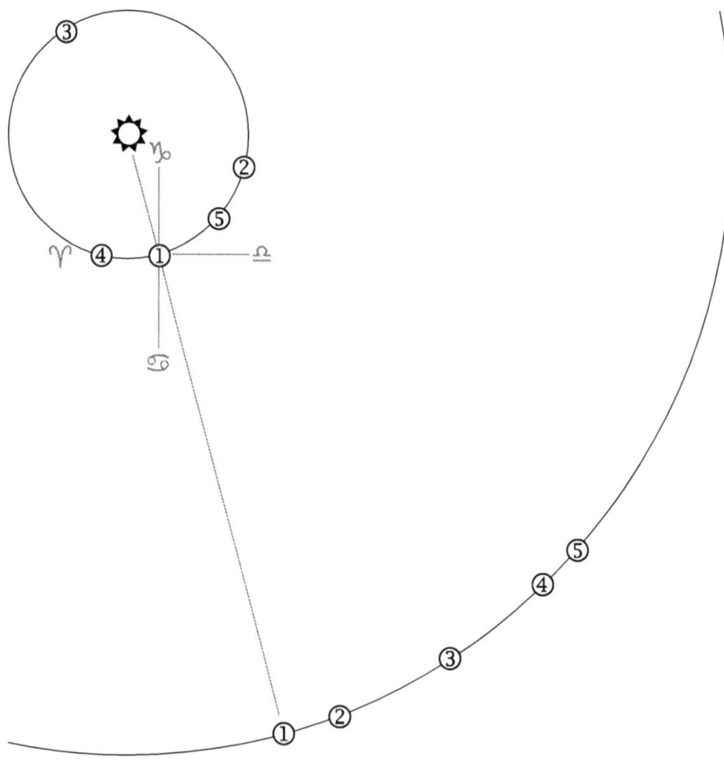

Figure 1.19 The synodic cycle of Jupiter and the Sun

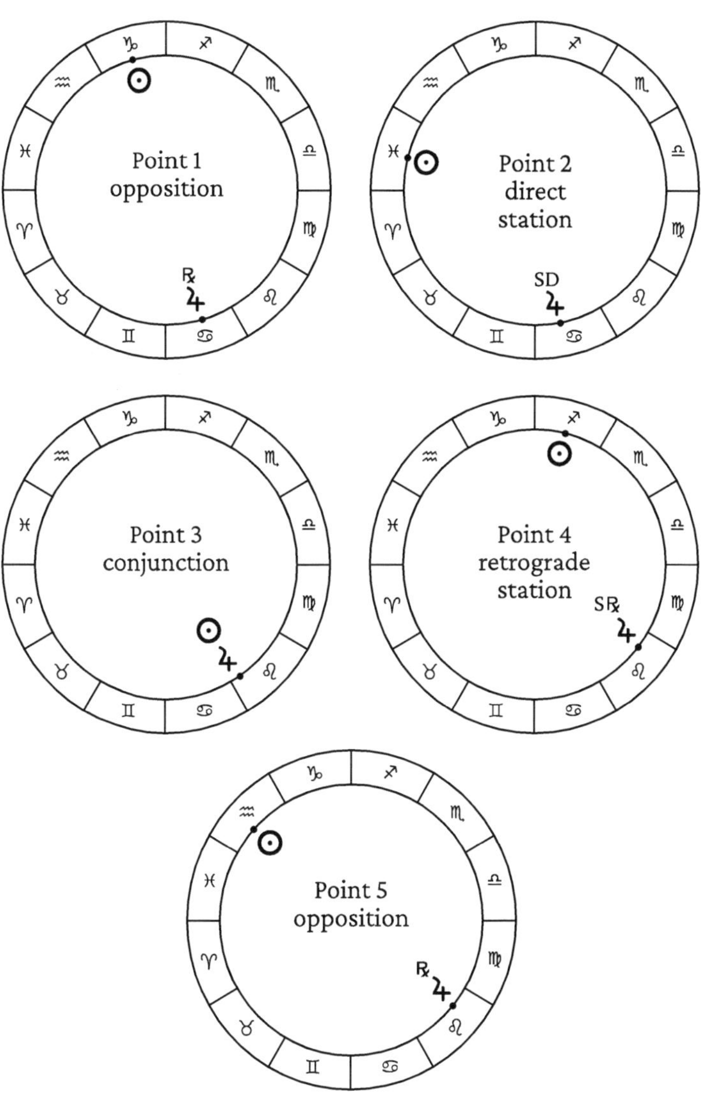

Figure 1.20   The synodic cycle of Jupiter and the Sun, as seen on the chart wheel

Figure 1.21 shows changes in the celestial longitudes of Jupiter and the Sun. Figure 1.22 (not drawn to scale) shows the cycle from the geocentric viewpoint. The lower part of the diagram shows the geocentric motion of the Sun, while the upper part shows the two components of Jupiter's geocentric motion: that which arises by virtue of Jupiter's actual orbit of the Sun (shown by the arrow to the left) and that which occurs in tandem with the Sun's geocentric motion (shown by the arrow on the circle). (Note that from the geocentric viewpoint, the solar system-as-a-whole moves in tandem with the Sun's geocentric motion.) Figure 1.23 gives the date and the celestial longitudes (rounded to the nearest degree) of Jupiter and the Sun at each point.

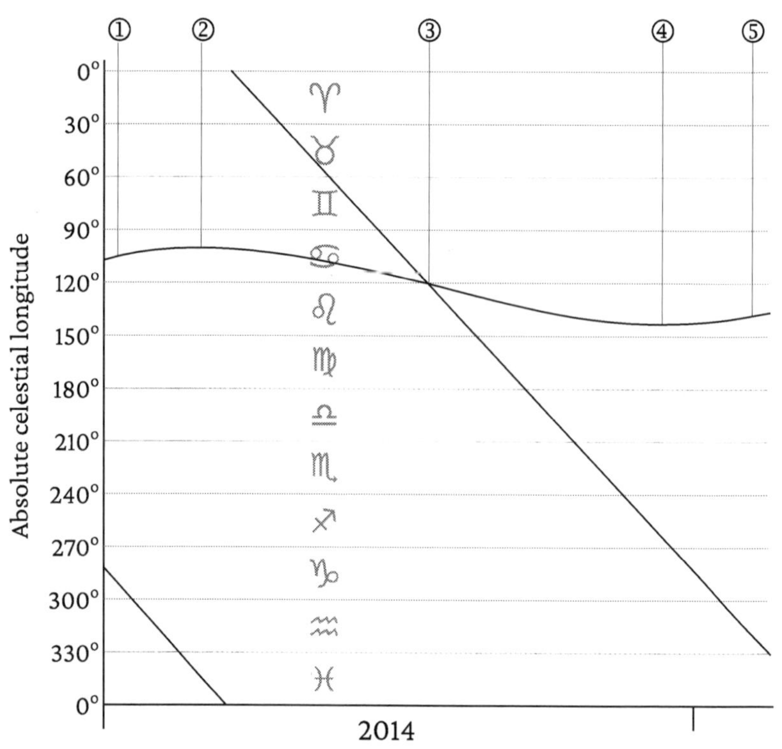

Figure 1.21 Graphic ephemeris - Jupiter and the Sun

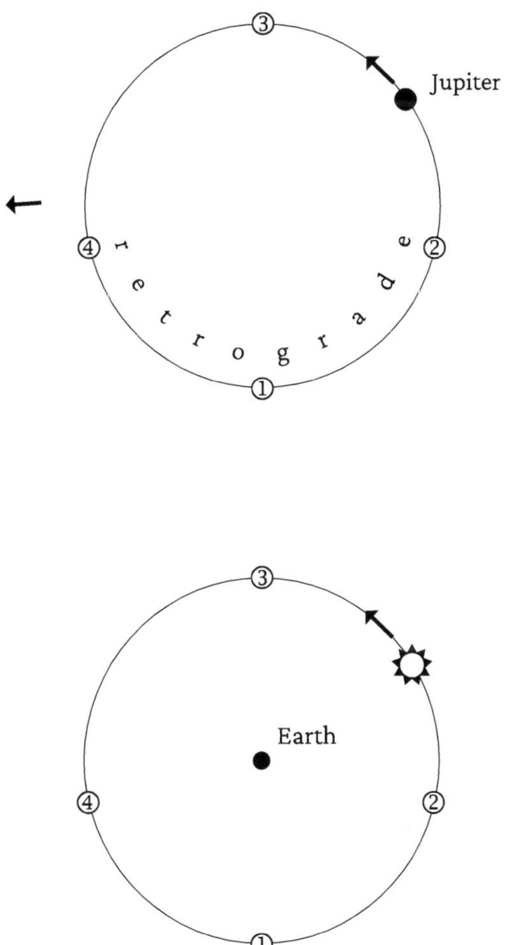

Figure 1.22 The geocentric view of the synodic cycle of Jupiter and the Sun

We have seen that the retrograde speed of an inferior body peaks as the body reaches its perigee and perfects an inferior conjunction with the Sun. The retrograde speed of a superior body also peaks at its perigee, at which point the body and the Sun form a perfect opposition (as in point 1).

Between points 1 and 2, Jupiter's retrograde motion slowed until the direct station was reached at point 2. Between points 2 and 3, Jupiter's direct motion quickened, peaking as Jupiter perfected a conjunction with the Sun at point 3. Between points 3 and 4, Jupiter's direct motion slowed until the retrograde station was reached at point 4. Jupiter's retrograde motion then quickened, peaking at the perfect opposition (point 5).

Point in the cycle	Date 2014/15	Celestial longitude of the Sun	Celestial longitude of Jupiter	Event in Jupiter's direct-retrograde cycle
1	Jan 5th	285° (15°♑)	105° (15°♋)	Sun opposite Jupiter. Retrograde speed peaks.
2	Mar 6th	346° (16°♓)	100° (10°♋)	Direct station
3	Jul 24th	122° (2°♌)	122° (2°♌)	Sun conjunct Jupiter. Direct speed peaks.
4	Dec 8th	257° (17°♐)	143° (23°♌)	Retrograde station
5	Feb 6th	318° (18°♒)	138° (18°♌)	Sun opposite Jupiter. Retrograde speed peaks.

Figure 1.23 Dates and positions at points 1 to 5

Figure 1.24 gives data for the planets of our solar system and Pluto. Apart from the orbital periods, all of the values given are mean values, because these values vary from one synodic cycle with the Sun to the next due to variation in the body's orbital radius. We can see that synodic period and proportion of time spent in retrograde motion are related to the difference between the body's orbital radius and Earth's orbital radius. As this difference increases from one orbiting body to the next (Venus to Mercury; and Mars to Jupiter to Saturn, etc.), the period of a body's synodic cycle with the Sun decreases, and the proportion of time that the body spends in retrograde motion increases.

We saw in the above example that a superior body is retrograde for a period of time before and after it forms an opposition aspect with the Sun. Figure 1.24 shows that Mars is typically stationary when elongated from the Sun by approximately 138°, and is therefore typically retrograde when within approximately 42° of perfecting an opposition with the Sun (because 138° + 42° = 180°). Saturn is typically stationary when elongated from the Sun by approximately 108°, and is therefore retrograde when within approximately 72° of perfecting an opposition with the Sun.

Celestial Body	Orbital period	Synodic period with Sun	Period of retrograde motion	Proportion of time retrograde	Elongation at station (approx.)
Mercury ☿	88 days	116 days	22 days	19%	-
Venus ♀	225 days	584 days	42 days	7%	-
Mars ♂	687 days	780 days	73 days	9%	138°
Jupiter ♃	11.9 yrs.	399 days	121 days	30%	116°
Saturn ♄	29.5 yrs.	378 days	138 days	37%	108°
Uranus ♅	84.0 yrs.	370 days	152 days	41%	103°
Neptune ♆	164.8 yrs.	368 days	158 days	43%	101°
Pluto ♇	248.5 yrs.	367 days	161 days	44%	99°

Figure 1.24 Orbital and retrograde periods, and elongation at stations, for the planets and Pluto

In Figure 1.25, the dot represents the line of celestial longitude of any of the superior bodies shown on the diagram at any given moment in time, and the circle represents the path of the Sun around the ecliptic relative to the body's line of celestial longitude. Each arc above the circle shows where the Sun is located relative to the body concerned while that body's motion is retrograde. We can see that each body turns retrograde during the waxing hemicycle as the Sun moves away from the body, and turns direct during the waning hemicycle as the Sun moves towards the body. During the Sun-Mars synodic cycle, Mars turns retrograde between the waxing trine and waxing quincunx, and turns direct between the waning quincunx and the waning trine. The other bodies – whose orbital paths are further from that of Earth – turn retrograde between the waxing square and the waxing trine, and turn direct between the waning trine and the waning square.

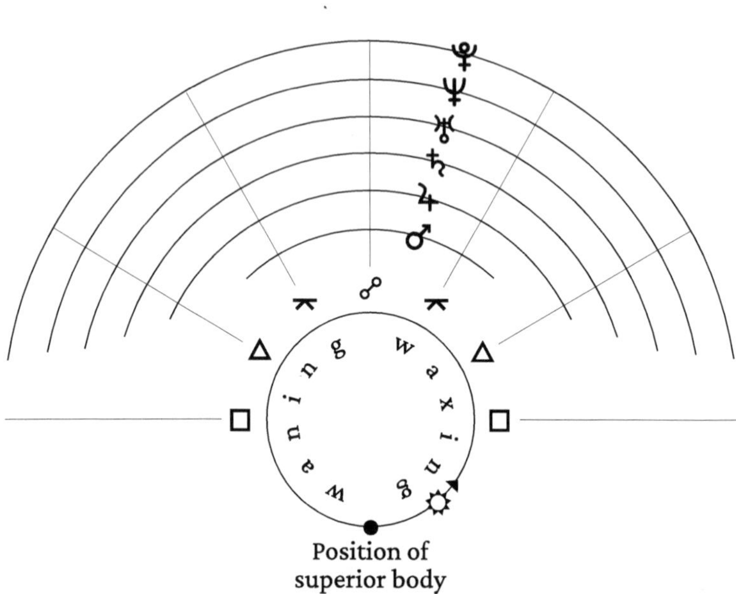

Figure 1.25 The relationship of the Sun to each superior planet and Pluto during retrogression

The synodic cycle of the Sun and a body that orbits the Sun may be divided into four phases, using the stations and perfect conjunctions in the case of an inferior body, and using the stations and the perfect conjunction and opposition in the case of a superior body. (Some astrologers use the points of peak elongation rather than the stations.) These phases are described in Figure 1.26 (inferior bodies) and Figure 1.27 (superior bodies).

A celestial body is considered stationary for a period of time either side of its actual station. A body is usually deemed stationary while its speed is below a certain percentage of its average speed – the percentage used tending to vary between 3% and 10%. Alternatively, the body may be deemed stationary for a set period before and after its station. Whether a body should be interpreted as stationary at a given moment in time can be judged more intuitively by looking at a graphic ephemeris.

Phase	Appearance on the chart wheel	Appearance in the sky
Inferior conjunction to direct station. Body is west of the Sun and has retrograde motion.	Body is clockwise of the Sun (Sun is further along the zodiac).	Body rises and sets before the Sun and is visible just before sunrise once it moves far enough from the Sun.
Direct station to superior conjunction. Body is west of the Sun and has direct motion.	Body is clockwise of the Sun (Sun is further along the zodiac).	Body rises and sets before the Sun and is visible just before sunrise until it moves too close to the Sun.
Superior conjunction to retrograde station. Body is east of the Sun and has direct motion.	Body is anticlockwise of the Sun (body is further along the zodiac).	Body rises and sets after the Sun and is visible just after sunset once it moves far enough from the Sun.
Retrograde station to inferior conjunction. Body is east of the Sun and has retrograde motion.	Body is anticlockwise of the Sun (body is further along the zodiac).	Body rises and sets after the Sun and is visible just after sunset until it moves too close to the Sun.

Figure 1.26 The division of the synodic cycle of the Sun and an inferior body into four phases using the conjunctions and stations

Some astrologers also place significance on the *shadow phases* of celestial bodies. A shadow phase begins as a body crosses the line of celestial longitude that it will occupy at the next direct station, and ends as it crosses the line of celestial longitude that it occupied at the previous retrograde station. For example, looking at Figure 1.16 (page 31) we can see that Mercury began a shadow phase some time on May 23rd 2014 (UT) as it crossed the line of 24° 22′ GE – the line that it would later occupy at the direct station of July 1st 2104. This shadow phase ended some time on July 16th 2014 as it crossed the line of 3° 10′ CN – the line that it had previously occupied at the retrograde station of June 7th 2014.

Phase	Appearance on the chart wheel
Opposition to direct station (retrograde motion).	First part of waning hemicycle.
Direct station to conjunction (direct motion).	Second part of waning hemicycle.
Conjunction to retrograde station (direct motion).	First part of waxing hemicycle.
Retrograde station to opposition (retrograde motion).	Second part of waxing hemicycle.

Figure 1.27 The division of the synodic cycle of the Sun and a superior body into four phases using the conjunction, opposition and stations

The apparent speed of a body may also be taken into account during interpretation, and for a body that orbits the Sun, the primary influence on this is the point reached in the body's synodic cycle with the Sun. As discussed above, the apparent direct speed of an inferior body peaks at the superior conjunction, while its apparent retrograde speed peaks at the inferior conjunction; and the apparent direct speed of a superior body peaks at the conjunction, while its apparent retrograde speed peaks at the opposition. The Moon's geocentric motion varies much less, but many astrologers consider this in interpretation. On average, the Moon's celestial longitude changes by just over 13° per day, changing by less than 12° per day around the its apogee and by more than 15° per day around its perigee.

Diurnal Position

In order to interpret the significance of celestial events for particular locations on Earth's surface, astrologers use frames of reference that take location into account.

In Figure 1.28, the black dot on Earth's surface is a northern hemisphere location. The north geographic pole is shown as a grey dot on Earth's surface, and the north celestial pole is shown as a grey dot on the celestial sphere. In Figure 1.29, the black dot is a southern hemisphere location, and the grey dots show the south geographic pole and the south celestial pole. In each of these diagrams, three great circles are shown on the celestial sphere, along with the nodal axes formed where the planes of these circles intersect. Part of the location's line of terrestrial longitude is shown as a line on

Earth's surface, and N, E, S and W refer, respectively, to the north, east, south and west points on the rational horizon. The explanations of these terms given below are valid for all locations on Earth's surface.

The vertical line that passes through Earth's centre and a location on Earth's surface meets the celestial sphere at the location's *zenith* (above) and the location's *nadir* (below). The *horizon plane* of a location passes through the centre of Earth and is perpendicular to the zenith-nadir axis. The horizon plane meets the celestial sphere at a great circle that may be referred to as the *rational horizon*, the *celestial horizon* or the *astronomical horizon*.

If you imagine that you are 'on top' of the world, the rational horizon divides the celestial sphere into the half that is above Earth's centre (which appears to you as the sky) and the half that is below Earth's centre (which is hidden from view and appears to you as the ground). (If the view of the observer is not obstructed, slightly more than half of the celestial sphere is visible due to the curvature of Earth's surface.)

The *meridian plane* of a location passes through the location, Earth's rotation axis (including Earth's centre and the geographic poles), all points on the location's line of terrestrial longitude, and all points on the opposite line of terrestrial longitude. The meridian plane meets the celestial sphere at a great circle called the *celestial meridian*, which passes through the zenith and nadir, the celestial poles, and the north and south points on the rational horizon. Thus, the horizon plane and the meridian plane are perpendicular to one another. All locations on a particular line of terrestrial longitude, and all locations on the opposite line of terrestrial longitude, share the same celestial meridian.

If you face directly north or south, the celestial meridian divides the celestial sphere into the half to the right of you and the half to the left.

The rational horizon always has 0° declination at its east and west points, for this is where the rational horizon and celestial equator intersect. The rational horizon always has maximum northerly and southerly declination, respectively, at its north and south points. (The rational horizon of a geographic pole coincides with the celestial equator and therefore has 0° declination throughout.)

The celestial equator has been omitted from Figure 1.28 and Figure 1.29 to avoid cluttering the diagrams, but can be envisaged passing through the east and west points on the rational horizon. For a northern hemisphere location (Figure 1.28), the celestial equator intersects the celestial meridian above the rational horizon to the south and below the rational horizon to the north. For a southern hemisphere location (Figure 1.29), the celestial equator intersects the celestial meridian above the rational horizon to the north and below the rational horizon to the south.

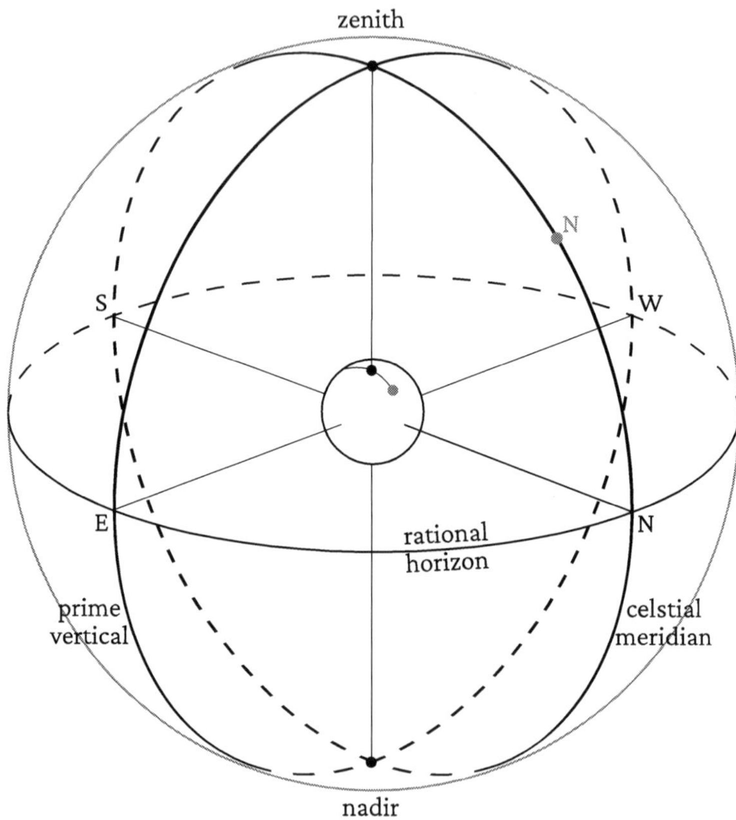

Figure 1.28 Great circles defined by the observer's location (northern hemisphere observer)

The *prime vertical* of a location is the great circle that intersects the celestial meridian at the zenith and nadir, and intersects the rational horizon at the east and west points. The points of intersection of the prime vertical and the ecliptic are called the *vertex* (to the west) and the *anti-vertex* (to the east). The plane of the prime vertical is perpendicular to both the horizon plane and the meridian plane.

If you face either north or south, the prime vertical divides the celestial sphere into the half that is in front of you and the half that is behind you.

Any circle that passes through the zenith and nadir is perpendicular to the rational horizon and is referred to as a *vertical circle*. Thus, the celestial meridian and prime vertical are vertical circles. Because the zenith-nadir axis passes through Earth's centre, all vertical circles are great circles.

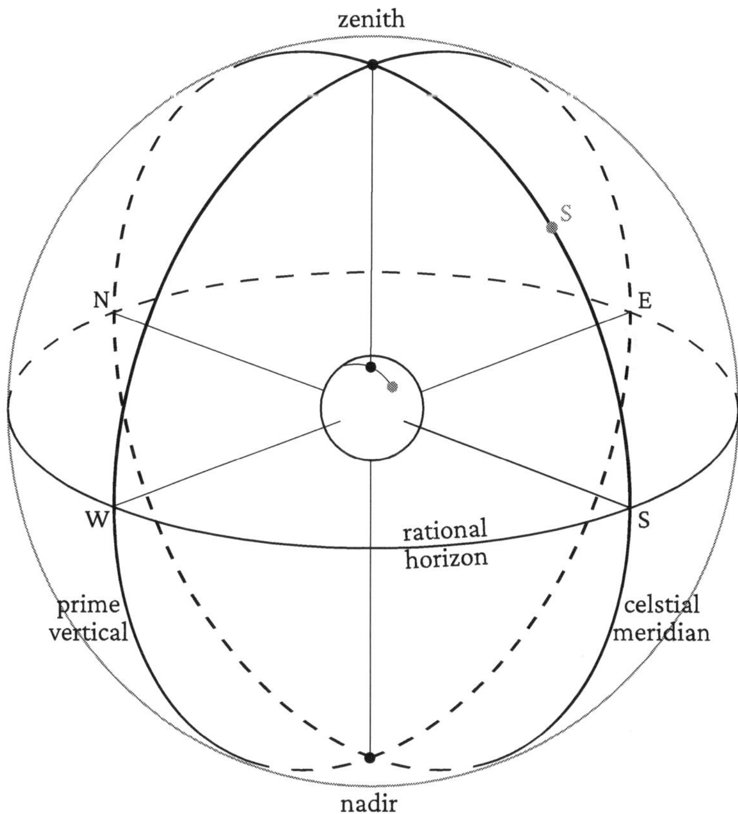

Figure 1.29 Great circles defined by the observer's location (southern hemisphere observer)

The Topocentric Coordinate System

The *topocentric coordinate system* – also called the *horizontal coordinate system* – uses the same principles as the ecliptic and equatorial coordinate systems. However, the topocentric coordinates of a given point on the celestial sphere show where the point is in relation to Earth's centre, as 'seen' from a particular location on Earth's surface at a given moment in time.

In the topocentric coordinate system, a line of *azimuth* is a great semicircle on the celestial sphere that runs perpendicular to the location's rational horizon from the zenith to the nadir. Each line of azimuth takes its name from the arc-length measured clockwise (as viewed from the zenith) along the rational horizon from 0° azimuth to the line. The line of 0° azimuth is usually (but not always) taken to be the line of azimuth that passes through the north point on the rational horizon, in which case: the line of 90° azimuth passes through the east point on the rational horizon; the line of 180° azimuth passes through the south point; and the line of 270° azimuth passes through the west point. (To move east or west along Earth's surface is to follow a particular line of terrestrial latitude, but when an observer faces east or west, they face the line of azimuth that passes through the east or west point on the rational horizon.)

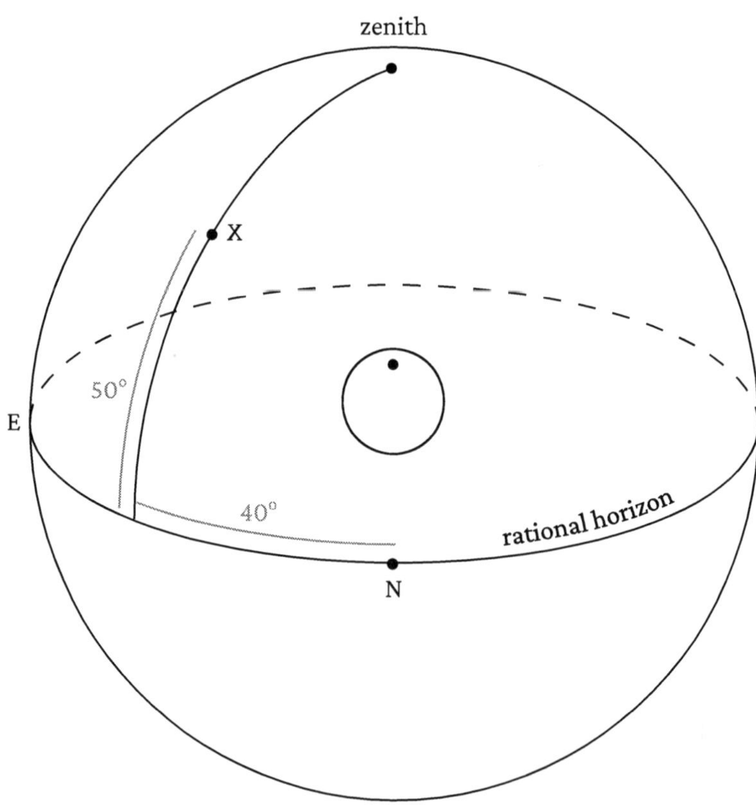

Figure 1.30 The Topocentric coordinate system

Also in the horizontal coordinate system, a line of *altitude* – also called a line of *elevation* – is a circle on the celestial sphere that lies in a plane that is parallel to the rational horizon. A line of altitude takes its name from the arc-length measured upwards or downwards along any line of azimuth from the rational horizon to the line. The rational horizon is the line of 0° altitude, and altitude is measured from 0° to 90° upwards from the rational horizon and from 0° to –90° downwards from the rational horizon. The zenith and nadir have altitude 90° and –90° respectively. With the exception of the rational horizon, each line of altitude is a small circle.

In Figure 1.30, the black dot on Earth represents any given location on Earth's surface, and the north and east points on the rational horizon are marked N and E, respectively. The diagram shows the line of 40° azimuth and the line of 50° altitude. We can see that at this location, at this moment in time, the topocentric coordinates of point X are 40°, 50°.

The Apparent Rotation of the Celestial Sphere

As a given location revolves around Earth's rotation axis, each point on the location's rational horizon, celestial meridian and prime vertical moves eastwards, parallel with the celestial equator. Since these great circles are stationary in the experience of the observer, each point on the celestial sphere appears to move westwards parallel with the celestial equator (i.e. appears to move along a particular line of declination). The apparent motion of a factor resulting from the rotation of the observer's location around Earth's rotation axis is referred to as *diurnal motion*.

Figure 1.32 and Figure 1.33 (pages 58 and 59) show the celestial meridian and the rational horizon of observer O. In order to simplify the diagrams, the prime vertical has been omitted and the celestial meridian lies in the plane of the page. The observer's line of terrestrial latitude is shown in black, with the observer's eastward motion around Earth's rotation axis shown by the small arrow. One large arrow shows the eastward motion of a point on the celestial meridian and the other shows the eastward motion of a point on the rational horizon.

A point or factor is said to *rise* as it crosses the horizon plane in an upward direction, *culminate* as it crosses the celestial meridian above the horizon plane, *set* as it crosses the horizon plane in a downward direction, and *anti-culminate* as it crosses the celestial meridian below the rational horizon.

The arc that a point or factor traces during its diurnal motion above the rational horizon is referred to as its *diurnal arc*. This diurnal arc consists of two *semi-diurnal arcs*, one of which is traced between rising and culminating, and one of which is traced between culminating and setting. A given point on the celestial sphere takes the same amount of time to complete each of its semi-diurnal arcs. The arc that a point or factor traces during its diurnal motion below the rational horizon is referred to as its *nocturnal arc*. This nocturnal arc consists of two *semi-nocturnal arcs*, one of which is traced between setting and anticulminating, and one of which is traced between anticulminating and rising. A given point on the celestial sphere takes the same amount of time to complete each of its semi-nocturnal arcs.

The Measurement of Time

The period of a complete rotation of Earth is referred to as a *sidereal day*. During this period, each point on a given location's celestial meridian moves once around the celestial sphere; and to the observer, the celestial sphere appears to undergo one revolution. During a sidereal day, the Sun appears to move approximately 1° of arc along the ecliptic due to Earth's orbital motion around the Sun. Consequently, the period between successive culminations of the Sun at a given location – referred to as a *solar day* – is one sidereal day plus approximately four minutes. At a given location, a moment at which the Sun culminates is referred to as *noon solar time* – also called *true solar time* or *apparent solar time*.

The *civil day* measured by our clocks is an average solar day. The length of a solar day undergoes an annual cycle of change due to two phenomena that affect the time taken for the celestial meridian to catch up with the Sun between successive culminations. First, the Sun's apparent speed along the ecliptic undergoes an annual cycle of change because Earth's orbital speed varies with its distance from the Sun. Second, while the right ascension of each point on the celestial meridian changes at a steady rate, the Sun's right ascension changes relatively quickly when the Sun is nearer to a solstitial point (where the ecliptic runs parallel with the celestial equator) and relatively slowly around the equinoctial points (where the ecliptic and celestial equator are most steeply inclined).

Universal Time (UT) – also called *Greenwich Mean Time* (GMT) – is mean solar time at the Greenwich Observatory (or any other location on the prime meridian). In other words, noon UT is the time at which a theoretical 'mean sun' culminates at the Greenwich Observatory. The difference between UT and true solar time at Greenwich is called the *equation of time* (EqT). The equation of time is recorded as a negative value when true solar time at Greenwich occurs after noon UT and as a positive value when true solar time at Greenwich occurs before noon UT. The equation of time reaches its maximum values of approximately –14 minutes in mid-February each year, and approximately +16 minutes in early November each year. Because the length of the solar day is influenced by two factors (Earth's elliptical orbit and the obliquity of the ecliptic, as noted above), EqT peaks and troughs twice each year. Graphs showing the rise and fall of EqT during the year can be found online. The way in which EqT varies throughout the year is changing very gradually as Earth's points of perihelion and aphelion move very slowly in relation to the cardinal points.

An *ephemeris* gives data for either noon or midnight on each calendar date. Some ephemerides refer to noon or midnight UT, while others use *ephemeris time* (ET). Ephemeris time is a form of *dynamical time* – a way of measuring time that, unlike UT, is unaffected by the long term gradual slowing of Earth's rotation. The amount by which ET is fast of UT – called *Delta T* (ΔT) – is currently just over 1 minute, and so 15:00 UT is equivalent to approximately 15:01 ET. The value of Delta T is gradually increasing, and its value at a given time is given in ephemerides that use ET.

Just as the civil day is divided into 24 civil hours, so the sidereal day is divided into 24 sidereal hours. The *local sidereal time* (LST) at a given location is 00:00 as the vernal point culminates. Thus, local sidereal time is equivalent to the right ascension of the location's celestial meridian, and all locations on a given line of terrestrial longitude share the same LST at any given moment. The local sidereal time at Greenwich is called *Greenwich sidereal time* (GST) – usually shortened to *sidereal time* (ST). Thus, the sidereal time is 00:00 as the vernal point passes over the line of 0° terrestrial longitude.

Earth rotates eastwards at a rate of 360° per 24 sidereal hours, or 1° per 4 sidereal minutes. Thus, at locations with terrestrial longitude 10° east, the local sidereal time is always 40 sidereal minutes ahead of sidereal time; and at locations with terrestrial longitude 15° west, local sidereal time is always 60 sidereal minutes behind sidereal time. The difference between sidereal time and the local sidereal time on a given line of terrestrial longitude is referred to as the *longitude equivalent in time*; in the above examples, this would be expressed as +40 minutes and -60 minutes, respectively.

The Julian and Gregorian Calendars

Two different standardised calendars have been in use, and the date attributed to a given day is different under each. The *Julian calendar* – often now referred to as the *Old Style calendar* – was introduced by Julius Caesar in

45 BCE. A *Julian year* is defined as a period of exactly 365.25 days, and so in order that each Julian year may contain a whole number of days, each Julian year which is a multiple of 4 is designated a *leap year*, containing 366 days, and each other Julian year contains 365 days. Because a tropical year is approximately 11 minutes shorter than 365.25 days, the Julian calendar drifts out of sync with the seasonal cycle by three days in every four hundred years.

On October 5th 1582 (Old Style), Pope Gregory introduced the *Gregorian calendar* (or *New Style calendar*), which is still in use today. In order that the (northern hemisphere) spring equinox would fall on March 21st in the Gregorian calendar, October 5th 1582 Old Style was referred to as October 15th 1582 New Style. In order to prevent the Gregorian calendar from drifting out of sync with the seasonal cycle, the number of leap years in the Gregorian calendar was reduced to 97 in every 400 years. Thus, in the Gregorian calendar, a leap year is any year that is a multiple of 4, except that a century year is only a leap year if it is a multiple of 400. (For example, 2000 and 2400 CE are designated as leap years, but 2100, 2200 and 2300 CE are not.)

Although many Catholic countries adopted the Gregorian calendar immediately, most countries took longer, with some not changing from the Julian calendar to the Gregorian calendar until the early part of the twentieth century. Thus, for over 300 years, dates were recorded using the Julian calendar in some countries and the Gregorian calendar in others.

Initially, the Gregorian calendar was 10 days ahead of the Julian calendar. However, because the years 1700, 1800 and 1900 were designated as leap years in the Julian calendar but not in the Gregorian calendar, the Gregorian calendar was 13 days ahead of the Julian calendar by the time the Gregorian calendar became the sole calendar in use around the world (see Figure 1.31).

Another issue is that while the number of the Gregorian year has always changed on Gregorian January 1st, the number of the Julian year changed on different Julian dates from country to country. In England and the United States, for example, the Julian year number would change on March 25th; thus, a Julian date in England or the United States between January 1st and March 24th is traditionally accompanied by two consecutive Julian year numbers – the lower number referring to the actual Julian year and the higher number referring to Julian year that it would have been if the year number had changed on January 1st.

Old Style Date	New Style Date	Difference
February 28th 1700	March 10th 1700	10 days
February 29th 1700	March 11th 1700	11 days
March 1st 1700	March 12th 1700	11 days
February 28th 1800	March 11th 1800	11 days
February 29th 1800	March 12th 1800	12 days
March 1st 1800	March 13th 1800	12 days
February 28th 1900	March 12th 1900	12 days
February 29th 1900	March 13th 1900	13 days
March 1st 1900	March 14th 1900	13 days

Figure 1.31 The continuing divergence of the Julian and Gregorian calendars during the gradual introduction of the Gregorian calendar

When casting a chart, it is important to know whether the date given is of the Julian or Gregorian calendar. Modern ephemerides and chart calculation software use Gregorian dates, so a Julian date must be converted. This conversion can be performed on various internet sites. In order to simplify matters, each day is given a *Julian Day number* (JD), which is the number of days that have passed since January 1st 4713 BCE (noon), and a *Modified Julian Day number*, which is the number of days that have passed since November 17th 1858 CE (midnight). (To convert between the two: MJD = JD – 2,400,000.5) The JD and MJD number for any given day can be found in ephemerides and online.

The Angles of the Astrological Chart

The nodal axis at the intersection of the ecliptic plane and the meridian plane is referred to as the *meridian axis*. Thus, the nodes of the meridian axis are the diametrically opposed points at which the ecliptic and celestial meridian intersect. The node above the rational horizon may be labelled using the Latin term *medium coeli* (usually abbreviated to MC) or the English translation *midheaven*, and the node below the rational horizon may be labelled using the Latin term *imum coeli* (usually abbreviated to IC) or the

English translation *lower heaven*. For northern hemisphere locations outside the Arctic circle, the midheaven is always closer to the south point on the rational horizon; and for southern hemisphere locations outside the Antarctic circle, the midheaven is always closer to the north point on the rational horizon. (Locations within the Arctic and Antarctic circles are discussed below.) The meridian axis may be represented on an astrological chart by a straight line between the midheaven and lower heaven.

The nodal axis at the intersection of the ecliptic plane and the horizon plane is referred to as the *horizon axis*. Thus, the nodes of the horizon axis are the diametrically opposed points at which the ecliptic and rational horizon intersect. The node at which the ecliptic moves upwards across the rational horizon is referred to as the *ascendant* (abbreviated to AS or ASC), and the node at which the ecliptic moves downwards across the rational horizon is referred to as the *descendant* (abbreviated to DS or DES). For locations outside the Arctic and Antarctic circles, the ascendant is always the node closest to the east point on the rational horizon, and the descendant is always the node closest to the west point on the rational horizon. The horizon axis may be represented on an astrological chart by a straight line between the ascendant and the descendant.

The ascendant, descendant, midheaven and lower heaven are referred to as the *angles* of the astrological chart. As do various other types of node, the angles form aspects and midpoint configurations with other factors.

Calculating the Positions of the Angles

The time of an event is usually recorded as the time shown on a clock. Clocks in a particular *time zone* are set to show the *standard time* used in that zone, unless *daylight saving time* is in use, in which case they are set one or two hours ahead of standard time. Each standard time has a particular name and is slow or fast of *Coordinated Universal Time* – also called *Universal Time Coordinated* (UTC) – by a fixed amount. UTC is a form of dynamical time that is adjusted regularly to prevent it from drifting more than 1 second from UT. Thus, for astrological purposes, UTC can be taken to be identical with UT. Standard times vary from -12:00 (12 hours slow of UTC), as used on Baker Island (terrestrial longitude 176° W) and +14:00 (14 hours fast of UTC), as used on the Line Islands (terrestrial longitude 150° to 160° W).*

---

* The Line Islands are part of the Republic of Kiribati. Most of the Republic's population inhabits the Gilbert Islands, which have terrestrial longitude 173° E to 177° E and use +12:00. Because the Line Islands use +14:00 rather than -10:00, all of

By checking which standard time was in use at the event location at the time of the event, and whether or not daylight saving time was in use at the time, the astrologer can convert clock time to UT. Note that at any given moment in time, the calendar date in one time zone may be different to that at Greenwich. For example, since Eastern Standard Time (EST) is five hours behind UT, when it is 10:00pm on June 2nd EST, it is 3:00am on June 3rd UT.

As noted above, if the ephemeris uses ET, ΔT must be added to the event time in UT to give the event time in ET. The astrologer then notes the difference between the time of the event and the time of day for which data is given in the ephemeris. For example, if the event time is 14:30 ET and a noon ET ephemeris is used, it is noted that the event time is 2½ civil hours later than the time used in the ephemeris. The zodiacal positions of celestial bodies can then be found by noting the change of position of each body between noon on the UT date of the event and noon on the following date, and calculating how far each body moves during the first 2½ hours of that 24-hour period.

The next step in calculating the positions of the angles is to convert the time of the event in UT or ET to sidereal time. Suppose that a chart is being cast for 2:30pm ET, and the sidereal time at noon ET on the date of the event is given in the ephemeris as 23:08:22. A period of 2½ civil hours must be added to the sidereal time of 23:08:22, but this period must first be converted into sidereal hours, minutes and seconds. Since a sidereal day is approximately 4 minutes shorter than a solar day, a sidereal hour is approximately 10 seconds (more precisely, 9.86 seconds) shorter than a civil hour. The difference between the number of civil minutes and the number of sidereal minutes in this period is referred to as the *acceleration on the interval.*

2½ hours of civil time is equivalent to 2½ hours + 25 seconds of sidereal time (because 2½ hours x 10 seconds per hour = 25 seconds). Thus, in this case, the sidereal time of the event is 23:08:22 + 2:30:25 = 25:38:47. Since sidereal time is measured from 0 to 24 hours, it is necessary to subtract 24 sidereal hours from the result to arrive at a value within these limits. In this case, 25:38:47 - 24:00:00 = 01:38:47.

As another example, if the event time is 08:45 ET, then 3 civil hours and 15 civil minutes will be subtracted from the sidereal time at noon ET to find the sidereal time of the event. 3 hours 15 minutes of civil time is equivalent to 3 hours 15 minutes and 32.5 seconds of sidereal time, so this is subtracted

---

the islands of the Republic are on the same side of the International Date Line as one another and the many neighbouring nations that lie to the west.

from the sidereal time at noon ET to give the sidereal time of the event.

The sidereal time of the event is then converted to local sidereal time by adding or subtracting the longitude equivalent in time. Suppose that in the example used above, the chart is being cast for a location with terrestrial longitude 150°20'W. In this case, the longitude equivalent in time is found as follows: 150°20' x 4 sidereal minutes per degree = 601 sidereal minutes and 20 sidereal seconds (or 10 sidereal hours, 1 sidereal minute and 20 sidereal seconds).

Because this location has westerly terrestrial longitude, the longitude equivalent in time is actually -10:01:20. Thus, 10:01:20 is subtracted from the sidereal time of the event to give the local sidereal time of the event at the event location: 01:38:47 -10:01:20 = -08:22:33. 24:00:00 must be added to give a value between 00:00 and 24:00, giving a local sidereal time of 15:37:27. (Alternatively, to make the calculation easier, 24:00:00 could have been added to 01:38:47 before 10:01:20 was subtracted.)

A *table of houses* is used to look up the zodiacal positions of the angles (and any other house cusps in the house system* for which the tables have been compiled). Typically, such a table gives these positions for a particular line of northerly terrestrial latitude at each local sidereal time at which the midheaven enters a new degree increment. Usually the terrestrial latitude of the location for which the chart is being cast will fall between the latitudes used in the available tables, and the exact local sidereal time of the event will fall between those listed in the tables. Thus, accurate zodiacal positions are found using the two closest sidereal times for each of the two closest latitudes.

The zodiacal positions of the angles and other house cusps for a location with southerly latitude can be found using tables calculated for northerly latitudes, but this requires a little additional work. Such tables can be used for this purpose because for every southern hemisphere location, there is a northern hemisphere location that has both the same celestial meridian (and thus the same meridian axis) and the same rational horizon (and thus the same horizon axis). These two locations always occupy exactly opposite points on the globe; therefore, they have equivalent northerly and southerly terrestrial latitudes, and have local sidereal times that differ by exactly 12 sidereal hours.

The local sidereal time of the event at the event location is converted to the

---

* House systems are discussed below.

local sidereal time of the event at the opposite point on the globe by adding or subtracting 12 sidereal hours to give a time between 0:00:00 and 24:00:00. Tables are then used to find the angles and other house cusps for this new local sidereal time. Because the view of the celestial sphere at the southern hemisphere location is 'upside down' compared to that at the northern hemisphere location: the ascendant of one location is the descendant of the other; the midheaven of one location is the lower heaven of the other; the 2nd house cusp of one location is the 8th house cusp of the other, and so on. Thus, the final step is to switch each sign to its opposite; for example, 10° 25' Pisces ascends at a given northern hemisphere location as 10° 25' Virgo ascends at the opposite southern hemisphere location.

(Further examples of chart calculations can be found online.)

The Motion of the Angles along the Ecliptic

For all locations on Earth, the meridian plane is perpendicular to the equatorial plane. Consequently, as Earth rotates, the celestial meridian spins without wobbling, and the points of intersection of the celestial meridian and the celestial equator move along the celestial equator at a steady rate of 1° of arc per 4 sidereal minutes.

Due to the inclination of the celestial equator to the ecliptic, the rate at which the midheaven and lower heaven (the points of intersection of the celestial meridian and the ecliptic) move along the ecliptic undergoes a cycle of change with each rotation of Earth. This motion is slowest around the solstitial points (where the ecliptic runs parallel with the celestial equator) and quickest around the equinoctial points (where the ecliptic is most steeply inclined to the celestial equator), but deviates by only 8% from its average of 1° of arc per 4 sidereal minutes.

For locations on the equator, the ascendant and descendant move along the ecliptic in the same manner, because at these locations, the horizon plane remains perpendicular to the equatorial plane as Earth rotates; but as the observer moves away from the equator, the horizon plane begins to wobble.

To demonstrate this motion,* a piece of string or elastic can be tied around a globe to mark the circle at which the horizon plane of a given location meets Earth's surface. For a location with longitude 000° and latitude 50°N, for example, the string will pass through the locations with the following

---

* Antony Milner has mentioned to me that a growing number of smartphone and computer apps are available that can replicate this motion.

terrestrial coordinates: 000° 40°S, 090°W 00°, 180° 40°N and 090°E 00°. These points are directly below the south, west, east and north points, respectively, on the rational horizon. A ring of card can be positioned parallel with the surface on which the globe stands – and level with the centre of the globe – to represent the ecliptic plane. (This ring must be freestanding and independent of the globe so that the ring remains stationary as the globe rotates.)

If we now imagine that the globe is the celestial sphere: the observer's location on the globe becomes the observer's zenith; the terrestrial equator becomes the celestial equator; each line of terrestrial latitude becomes a line of declination; the elastic or string that has been added to the globe becomes the location's rational horizon; and the location's line of terrestrial longitude and the opposite line of terrestrial longitude become the location's celestial meridian. The two diametrically opposed points at which the rational horizon and the ecliptic intersect are now the ascendant and the descendant, the ascendant being the point on the ecliptic that is ascending across the rational horizon at any given moment in time as the globe rotates eastwards (anticlockwise when viewed from the north). The two diametrically opposed points at which the celestial meridian intersects the ecliptic are the midheaven (above the rational horizon) and the lower heaven (below the rational horizon).

As the globe rotates eastwards, the point on the ecliptic at which the equator descends below the ecliptic plane is the vernal point (0° tropical Aries), and the point on the ecliptic at which the equator ascends above the ecliptic plane is the anti-vernal point (0° tropical Libra). The ecliptic has maximum northerly declination at 0° tropical Cancer, and maximum southerly declination at 0° tropical Capricorn. It may be useful to mark these four points - the cardinal points of the tropical zodiac – on the ring.

Rotating the globe eastwards reveals that: the inclination of the horizon plane to the equatorial plane remains constant, but the inclination of the horizon plane to the ecliptic plane undergoes a cycle of change during each rotation; the declination of a given point on the rational horizon or celestial meridian remains constant; and the ascendant and descendant move back and forth along the rational horizon either side of the east and west points, respectively.

Figure 1.32 and Figure 1.33 show two points in Earth's rotation. As noted above, in these diagrams, the celestial meridian lies in the plane of the page, the location's line of terrestrial latitude is shown in black, and the direction of the location's motion around Earth's rotation axis is shown by the small arrow on Earth.

Figure 1.32 shows the approximate position of the rational horizon at 18:00 LST – the local sidereal time at which the midheaven passes the first point of tropical Capricorn. At 18:00 LST, the ascendant is at the vernal point (the first point of tropical Aries) and the inclination of the horizon plane to the ecliptic plane reaches its minimum value.

Figure 1.33 shows the approximate position of the rational horizon at 06:00 LST – the local sidereal time at which the midheaven passes the first point of tropical Cancer. At 06:00 LST, the ascendant is at the anti-vernal point (the first point of tropical Libra) and the inclination of the horizon plane to the ecliptic plane reaches its maximum value.

At all locations between the Tropic of Cancer and the Arctic circle, the inclination of the rational horizon to the ecliptic reaches its minimum value at 18:00 LST and its maximum value at 06:00 LST. At all locations between the Tropic of Capricorn and the Antarctic circle, the situation is reversed: the inclination of the rational horizon to the ecliptic reaches its minimum value at 06:00 LST (as the first point of tropical Libra rises) and reaches its maximum value at 18:00 LST (as the first point of tropical Aries rises).

For all locations, at 06:00 and 18:00 LST, the celestial meridian passes through the first points of tropical Cancer and Capricorn, and the rational horizon passes through the first points of tropical Aries and Libra. Only at these local sidereal times do the ascendant and descendant coincide with the east and west points, respectively, on the rational horizon; and only at these local sidereal times are the angles equally spaced along the ecliptic.

Figure 1.34 shows the tropical zodiacal positions of the horizon and meridian axes at four local sidereal times for any location with terrestrial latitude 50°N. As a further visual aid to understanding the following account of this sequence, the reader may wish to refer to a globe set up in the manner described above.

At 18:00 LST, the inclination of the horizon plane to the ecliptic plane reaches its minimum value, and so the anticlockwise motion of the ascendant and descendant along the rational horizon is at its quickest. Consequently, the anticlockwise motion of these points along the ecliptic is also at its quickest. Between 18:00 and 21:56 LST, the anticlockwise motion of the ascendant and descendant along the rational horizon slows down, and consequently, so does the motion of these points along the ecliptic. At 21:56 LST, the ascendant and descendant stop moving along the rational horizon, with the ascendant as close to the north point on the rational horizon, and the descendant as close to the south point, as they can be for this terrestrial latitude. Note that at this point, the ascendant is at 0° tropical Cancer (where the northerly declination of the ecliptic peaks) and the descendant is at 0° tropical Capricorn (where the southerly declination of the ecliptic peaks). At 21:56 LST, the speed of the ascendant and descendant along the ecliptic is equal to that of the midheaven and lower heaven, and the difference between the celestial longitudes of the ascendant and midheaven reaches its maximum value of 123°.

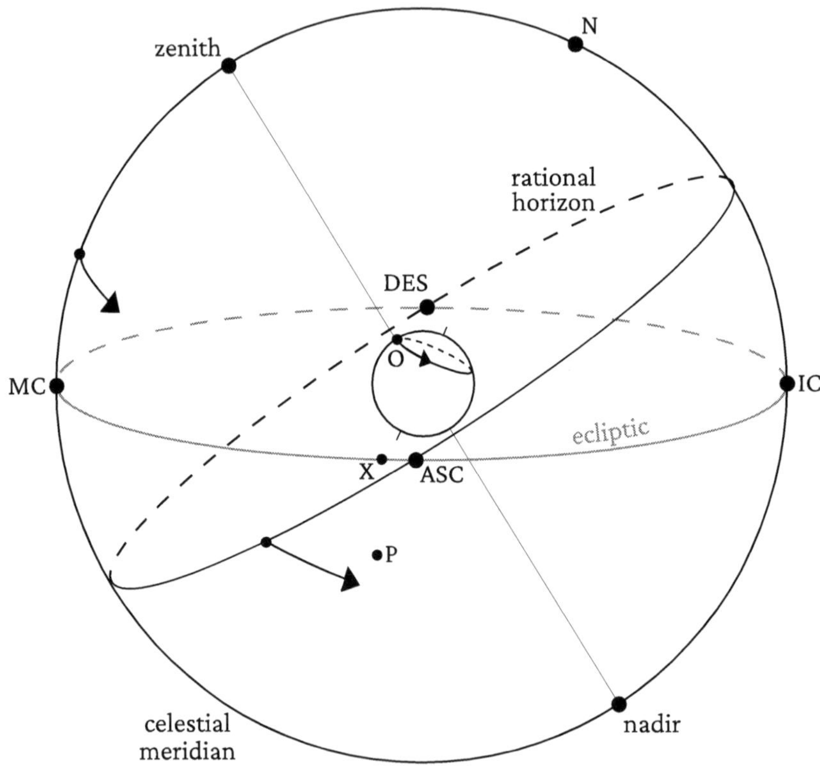

Figure 1.32 The approximate position of the rational horizon for any location with latitude 50°N at the rising of the vernal point (18:00 LST)

Between 21:56 and 06:00 LST, the ascendant and descendant accelerate clockwise along the rational horizon towards the east and west points respectively, and so the anticlockwise motion of these points along the ecliptic continues to slow down. At 06:00 LST, as the inclination of the rational horizon to the ecliptic peaks, the clockwise motion of the ascendant and descendant along the rational horizon is at its quickest, and so the anticlockwise motion of the ascendant and descendant along the ecliptic is at its slowest. Between 06:00 and 14:04 LST, the clockwise motion of the ascendant and descendant along the rational horizon slows, and so the anticlockwise motion of these points along the ecliptic quickens. At 14:04 LST, the ascendant and descendant stop moving along the rational horizon, the ascendant as close to the south point on the rational horizon and the descendant as close to the north point as they can be for this terrestrial latitude. Note that at this point, the ascendant is at 0° tropical Capricorn (where the southerly declination of the ecliptic peaks) and the descendant is at 0° tropical Cancer (where the northerly declination of the ecliptic peaks). At 14:04 LST, the speed of the ascendant and descendant along the ecliptic is equal to that of the midheaven and lower heaven, and the difference between the celestial longitudes of the ascendant and midheaven reaches a minimum value of 53°.

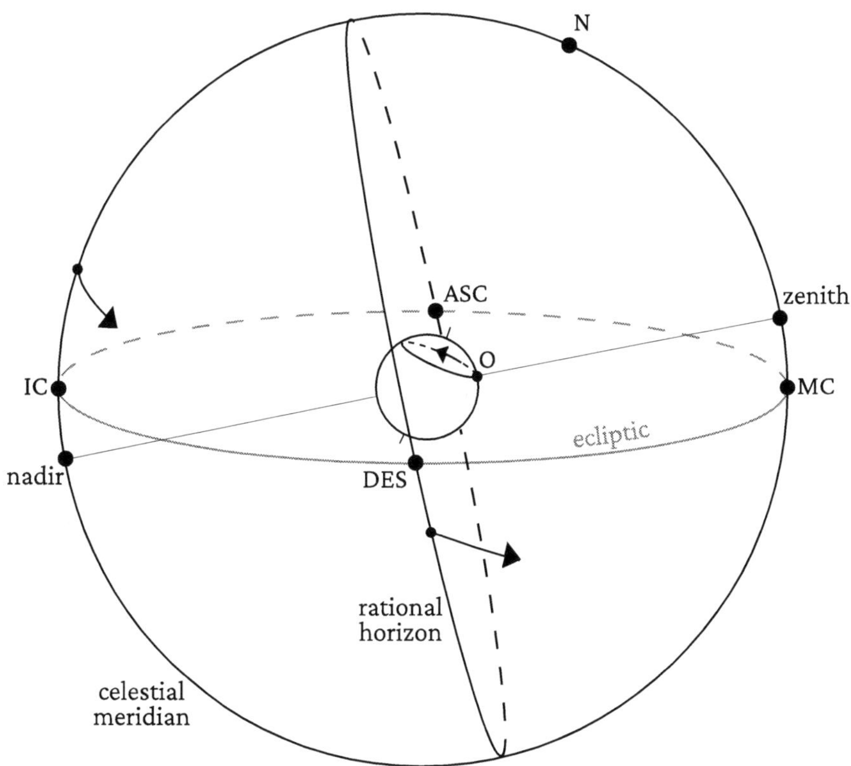

Figure 1.33 The approximate position of the rational horizon for any location with latitude 50°N at the rising of the anti-vernal point (06:00 LST)

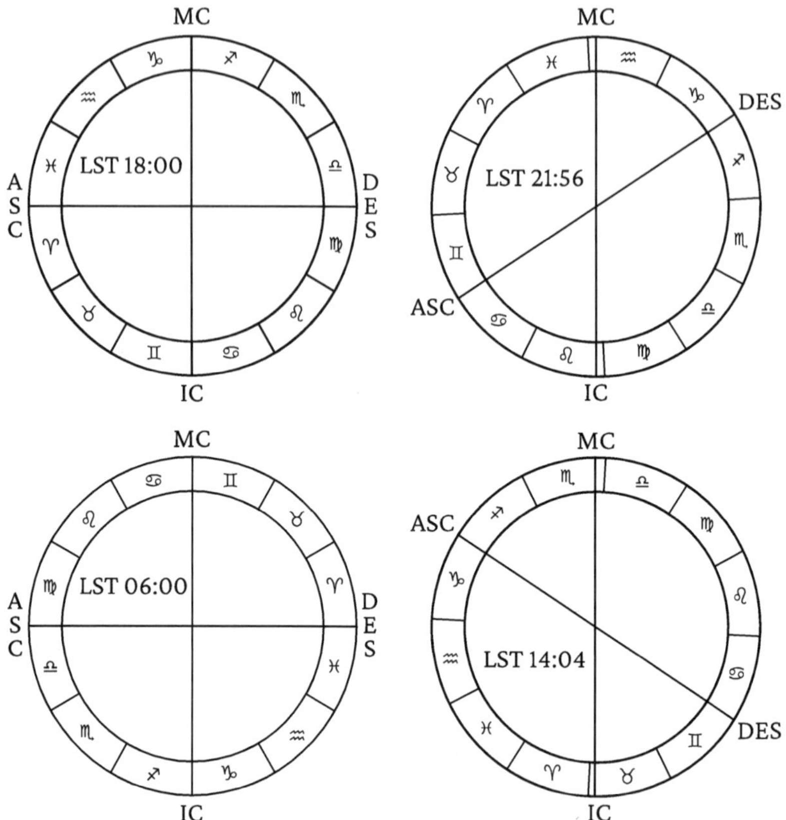

Figure 1.34 Positions of the angles at four local sidereal times for locations with latitude 50°N

Between 14:04 and 18:00 LST the ascendant and descendant accelerate anticlockwise along the rational horizon towards the east and west points, respectively, and so the motion of these points along the ecliptic quickens. As noted above, the speed of the ascendant and descendant along the ecliptic peaks at 18:00 LST as the ascendant and descendant pass the east and west points on the rational horizon.

Note that the maximum and minimum differences between the celestial longitudes of the ascendant and midheaven given in the above example are specific to locations with terrestrial latitude 50°N, as are the local sidereal times at which these extremes are reached.

Signs of Long and Short Ascension

Figure 1.35 shows the time taken for each tropical zodiacal sign to rise at a number of different terrestrial latitudes. The periods are given in civil hours and minutes, and are rounded to the nearest minute. The first row shows the time taken for tropical Aries to rise at each of a number of northerly terrestrial latitudes and for tropical Libra to rise at each of the equivalent southerly terrestrial latitudes. We can see that tropical Aries rises over a period of 1 hour 25 minutes at terrestrial latitude 30°N, and tropical Libra rises over the same period at terrestrial latitude 30°S. Note that for any given terrestrial latitude, the ascension period of tropical Pisces is equal to that of Aries, and the same may be said of the tropical sign pairings: Taurus and Aquarius; Gemini and Capricorn; Cancer and Sagittarius; Leo and Scorpio; and Virgo and Libra.

At locations on or close to the equator, the signs either side of an equinoctial point (tropical Pisces, Aries, Virgo and Libra) rise relatively quickly, while the signs either side of a solstitial point (tropical Gemini, Cancer, Sagittarius and Capricorn) rise relatively slowly. By terrestrial latitude 20°N, approximately, each point on the ecliptic between 0° tropical Capricorn and 0° tropical Cancer rises more quickly than any point between 0° tropical Cancer and 0° tropical Capricorn. This difference is further accentuated as the northerly terrestrial latitude of the observer increases. For locations south of the equator, this situation is reversed.

Thus, for terrestrial latitudes between 20°N (approximately) and 66.6°N, the tropical signs Capricorn through Gemini are the *signs of short ascension*, and the tropical signs Cancer through Sagittarius are the *signs of long ascension*. And for terrestrial latitudes between 20°S (approximately) and 66.6°S, the tropical signs Cancer through Sagittarius are the signs of short ascension, and the tropical signs Capricorn through Gemini are the signs of long ascension.

The above comments on the diurnal motion of points on the ecliptic relate to the earlier account of the annual seasonal cycle. For a given location, a given point on the ecliptic always rises and sets at the same points on the rational horizon, and spends the same amount of time above the rational horizon during each rotation of Earth. Figure 1.34 shows that for a location with terrestrial latitude 50°N, the first point of tropical Cancer rises at approximately 21:56 LST and sets at approximately 14:04 LST, remaining above the rational horizon for approximately 16 sidereal hours and 8 sidereal minutes. Thus, on the day of the June solstice, this is the period over which the centre of the solar disc is above the rational horizon of a location with terrestrial latitude 50°N (and below the rational horizon of a location with terrestrial latitude 50°S).

N	S	0°	10°	20°	30°	40°	50°	60°
♈	♎	1:51	1:43	1:34	1:25	1:12	0:56	0:29
♉	♏	1:59	1:53	1:46	1:37	1:27	1:12	0:44
♊	♐	2:08	2:06	2:03	1:59	1:55	1:48	1:32
♋	♑	2:08	2:11	2:14	2:17	2:22	2:29	2:45
♌	♒	1:59	2:06	2:13	2:21	2:32	2:47	3:15
♍	♓	1:51	2:00	2:08	2:18	2:30	2:47	3:13
♎	♈	1:51	2:00	2:08	2:18	2:30	2:47	3:13
♏	♉	1:59	2:06	2:13	2:21	2:32	2:47	3:15
♐	♊	2:08	2:11	2:14	2:17	2:22	2:29	2:45
♑	♋	2:08	2:06	2:03	1:59	1:55	1:48	1:32
♒	♌	1:59	1:53	1:46	1:37	1:27	1:12	0:44
♓	♍	1:51	1:43	1:34	1:25	1:12	0:56	0:29

Figure 1.35 Time taken for each tropical zodiacal sign to rise at various terrestrial latitudes (in civil hours and minutes)

The Motion of the Angles at Locations within the Arctic and Antarctic Circles

The rational horizon of a geographic pole coincides with the celestial equator. Thus, at the north geographic pole, the half of the ecliptic that has northerly declination remains permanently above the rational horizon, the half of the ecliptic that has southerly declination remains permanently below the rational horizon, and no points on the ecliptic rise or set. For an observer at the south geographic pole, this situation is reversed.

At locations with terrestrial latitude between 66.6°N and 66.6°S, the north and south points on the rational horizon have sufficient northerly and southerly declination for all points on the ecliptic to rise and set – and thus for all points on the ecliptic to both culminate and anti-culminate – during each rotation of Earth. At terrestrial latitudes between 66.6° and 90° (north or south) – where some but not all points on the ecliptic rise and set – the angles cannot complete a circuit of the ecliptic.

At locations with terrestrial latitude 70°N*, for example, the south point on the rational horizon has declination 20°S, and so points on the ecliptic with southerly declination greater than 20° (the tropical signs Sagittarius and Capricorn, approximately) cannot rise above the rational horizon and culminate; and the north point on the rational horizon has declination 20°N, and so points on the ecliptic with northerly declination greater than 20° (the tropical signs Gemini and Cancer) cannot set below the rational horizon and anti-culminate. As the midheaven moves into tropical Cancer, the ascendant moves into tropical Libra. At this moment, the ascendant is moving clockwise along the rational horizon and therefore moves more slowly along the ecliptic than does the midheaven. As the ascendant approaches the end of tropical Scorpio, the midheaven has almost caught up with it, and the ascendant is almost at the south point on the rational horizon. As the two points of intersection of the celestial meridian and the ecliptic move into tropical Gemini and Sagittarius, the midheaven and the lower heaven switch places, so that the midheaven is now at the north point on the rational horizon (at the end of tropical Taurus) and the lower heaven is at the south point on the rational horizon. This happens because the midheaven, by definition, is the point at which the celestial meridian intersects the ecliptic above the rational horizon, and tropical Sagittarius and Capricorn do not rise above the rational horizon for an observer with this terrestrial latitude. The ascendant and descendant switch places at the same moment. From this point, the midheaven moves through tropical Gemini and Cancer, while the ascendant moves so quickly clockwise along the rational horizon that it moves westwards along the ecliptic through tropical Taurus, Aries, Pisces and Aquarius. As the ascendant approaches 0° Aquarius, it almost reaches the south point of the rational horizon (and thus the lower heaven). At this point, the midheaven jumps back to the south point on the rational horizon at the beginning of tropical Aquarius, and the ascendant jumps to the beginning of tropical Leo close to the north point on the rational horizon. From here, the ascendant moves anticlockwise along

---

* On a globe set up in the manner described above to represent the rational horizon for a location with geocentric coordinates 000°, 70°N, the string or elastic passes through: 000° 20°S, 90°E 0°, 180° 20°N and 90°W 0°. The movement of the angles along the ecliptic can also be observed on a 360° graphic ephemeris covering a 24-hour period.

the ecliptic, arriving at the first point of tropical Libra and the east point on the rational horizon as the midheaven arrives at the first point of tropical Cancer.

Thus, for locations with terrestrial latitude 70°N, during each rotation of Earth, the points on the ecliptic that correspond, approximately, to tropical Sagittarius and Capricorn anti-culminate twice, but never culminate; and the points on the ecliptic that correspond approximately to tropical Gemini and Cancer culminate twice but never anti-culminate. Consequently, during the part of the year when the Sun moves through tropical Gemini and Cancer, the centre of the solar disc does not set below the rational horizon; and during the part of the year when the Sun moves through tropical Sagittarius and Capricorn, the centre of the solar disc does not rise above the rational horizon.

Although the midheaven is defined as the point on the ecliptic that is culminating above the rational horizon, some astrological software gives the option of keeping the midheaven above the rational horizon – i.e. to the south for a location within the Arctic circle and towards the north for a location within the Antarctic circle. If this approach is adopted, the midheaven and lower heaven each complete a circuit of the ecliptic during each rotation of Earth, with the midheaven remaining in the upper hemisphere of the chart and the lower heaven remaining in the lower hemisphere. In this case, the ascendant and descendant still behave in the same manner; thus, the ascendant jumps to the lower heaven rather than the midheaven, and the descendant jumps to the midheaven.

The Reliability of the Angles on the Astrological Chart

Because the angles move so quickly, a small error in the timing of an event can have a relatively large effect on the positions of the angles on an astrological chart. As discussed above, the meridian axis moves along the ecliptic at 1° of arc per 4 minutes +/- 8% (approximately) at all locations, as does the horizon axis for locations on the equator; but as northerly or southerly terrestrial latitude increases, so does the variation in the speed of the horizon axis during each rotation of Earth.

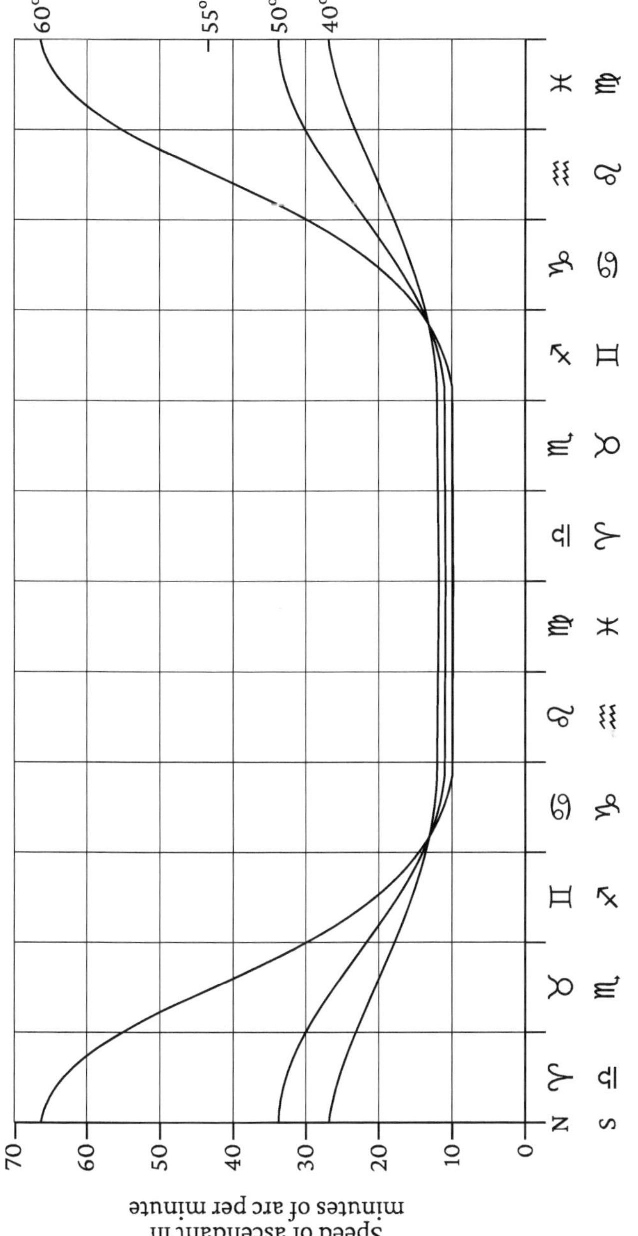

Figure 1.36 Variation in the speed of the ascendant around the tropical zodiac

Figure 1.36 shows how the speed of the ascendant varies with celestial longitude at three northerly and southerly terrestrial latitudes. A speed of 15' of arc per minute is equivalent to 1° of arc per 4 minutes. For 40°, 50° and 60° north use the sign glyphs in the row marked N, and for the equivalent southerly terrestrial latitudes use the sign glyphs in the row marked S. The speed of the ascendant as it passes the first points of tropical Aries and Libra for locations with terrestrial latitude 55°N and 55°S, respectively, is included to help the reader to visualise the curve for these latitudes.

We can see that when judging the possible margin of error in the position of the ascendant and descendant, the astrologer cannot simply assume that these points move along the ecliptic at approximately 1° of arc every 4 minutes. If the time is assumed to fall within a specific margin of, for example, between 6pm and 7pm, the astrologer can use a chart cast for 6:30pm, but also refer to the charts cast for 6pm and 7pm to see the range of movement of the angles during this period.

Representing Diurnal Position on an Astrological Chart

As noted above, each point on a conventional chart wheel represents all points on a particular line of celestial longitude. Consequently, while a conventional chart accurately shows the difference between the celestial longitude of a celestial body and the celestial longitude of an angle, it does not accurately show the position of a body relative to the horizon and meridian planes. In Figure 1.32 (page 58), for example, planet P is well below the rational horizon of observer O; however, on a chart wheel, P would be positioned at point X, implying that P is close to and just above the horizon plane. In *The Elements of House Division*, Ralph William Holden refers to this type of discrepancy as *latitude error*.

Figure 1.37 is a simplified version of a diagram from Holden's book.* Each of the concentric circles represents a different line of celestial latitude, and the straight lines crossing these circles represent sections of the twelve lines of celestial longitude used to divide the celestial sphere into the tropical zodiacal signs. The diagram shows the positions of the rational horizon and celestial meridian between celestial latitudes 10°N and 10°S for a location with terrestrial latitude approximately 51°N at 15:12 LST on any given day. The line of 0° celestial latitude is the ecliptic.

We can see that the ascendant and descendant are positioned at approximately 15° tropical Capricorn and 15° tropical Cancer, respectively,

* *The Elements of House Division* (1977, 1st ed.) Appendix 3.

and that the midheaven and lower heaven are positioned at approximately 20° tropical Scorpio and 20° tropical Taurus, respectively. Body A, with celestial longitude 15° tropical Capricorn and celestial latitude 10°N, rose above the rational horizon over an hour earlier, but is forming a perfect conjunction with the ascendant. A conventional chart would show body A at the same point on the chart wheel as the ascendant, implying that this body is in the horizon plane. Body B, with celestial longitude 27° tropical Sagittarius and celestial latitude 8°S, is in the horizon plane, but the celestial longitudes of the body and the ascendant differ by 18°. A conventional chart would imply that body B is elevated above the horizon plane.

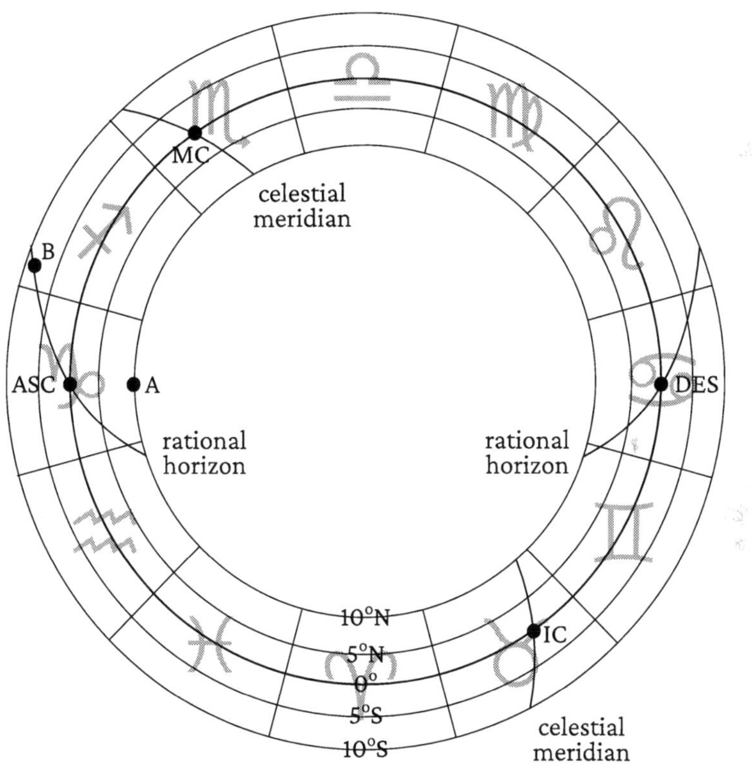

Figure 1.37 The tropical zodiacal positions of the rational horizon and celestial meridian between celestial latitudes 10°N and 10°S at terrestrial latitude 51°N at 15:12 LST

In order to simplify discussion of latitude error, we will define a further two planes. The lines of celestial longitude of the ascendant and descendant lie in the same plane, which will be referred to here as the *plane of ASC DES celestial longitude*. The lines of celestial longitude of the midheaven and lower heaven lie in the same plane, which will be referred to as the *plane of MC IC celestial longitude*.

The potential for latitude error increases with the celestial latitude of the body concerned, with such discrepancy never arising for a body positioned on the ecliptic. In addition, the potential for latitude error around the rational horizon increases with the inclination of the horizon plane to the plane of ASC DES celestial longitude; and the potential for latitude error around the celestial meridian increases with the inclination of the meridian plane to the plane of MC IC celestial longitude.

For all locations, the inclination of the meridian plane to the plane of MC IC celestial longitude is zero as the meridian plane crosses the solstitial points and reaches a maximum of 23.4° as the meridian plane crosses the equinoctial points.

For any given northern hemisphere location, as the first point of tropical Aries rises, the inclination of the horizon plane to the plane of ASC DES celestial longitude is equal to the terrestrial latitude of the location plus the obliquity of the ecliptic; and as the first point of tropical Libra rises, the inclination of the horizon plane to the plane of ASC DES celestial longitude is equal to the difference between the terrestrial latitude of the location and the obliquity of the ecliptic. These relationships are shown in graph form in Figure 1.38. We can see, for example, that at terrestrial latitude 23.4°N, the plane of ASC DES celestial longitude is parallel with the horizon plane as the first point of tropical Libra rises (23.4° - 23.4° = 0°), but the inclination is 46.8° as the first point of tropical Aries rises (23.4° + 23.4° = 46.8°). For any given southern hemisphere location the situation is reversed, and so Figure 1.38 shows the results for southern latitudes if the black line is assumed to the refer to the rising of the first point of tropical Libra and the grey line is assumed to refer to the rising of the first point of tropical Aries.

As noted above, for a location on the equator (0° terrestrial latitude), the rational horizon is perpendicular to the celestial equator. Consequently, the inclination of the rational horizon to the plane of ASC DES celestial longitude peaks at 23.4° as each equinoctial point rises, and is zero as each solstitial point rises. But with increasing northerly terrestrial latitude, a new pattern emerges in which this inclination peaks with the rising of the first point of tropical Aries and reaches its minimum with the rising of the first point of tropical Libra (and vice versa for increasing southerly terrestrial latitude). This, of course, is directly related to the above discussion of the signs of short and long ascension.

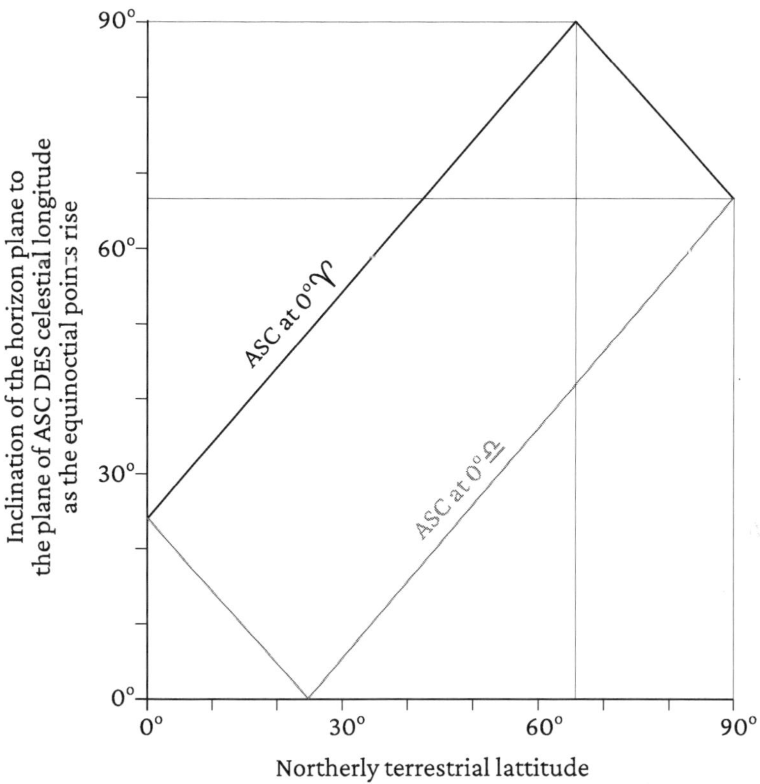

Figure 1.38 The inclination of the horizon plane to the plane of ASC DES celestial longitude as the equinoctial points rise, at different northerly terrestrial latitudes

Charting the Diurnal Cycle

The lines of celestial longitude that pass through the angles figure strongly in chart interpretation. A function is assumed to operate with added strength when the corresponding celestial body is *angular* (conjunct an angle within an allowable orb of around 8° to 10°). Other aspects to the angles are also considered significant, as are midpoints involving one or both angles.

Also observed to be significant is the proximity of a celestial body to the horizon plane or the meridian plane. The technique used to determine such proximity is referred to as *astro-mapping* (or using the trademark under which the technique was originally introduced: *astro*carto*graphy*). Astro-mapping is a feature of many astrological software programs and free to use on some astrology websites.

An *astro-map* is a map of an area of Earth's surface on which are drawn a number of lines. Each line passes through those locations at which a particular relationship exists – at the moment for which the map is drawn – between a particular celestial body and a feature of the diurnal wheel. When the *zodiacal* mode is used, each line passes through locations at which a particular celestial body is making a particular aspect to either the ascendant or midheaven at that moment. When the *in mundi* mode is used, each line passes through locations at which a particular celestial body is in the horizon or meridian plane.

In the in mundi mode, each celestial body represented on the map has two lines: a rational horizon line and a celestial meridian line. A body's rational horizon line is divided into two parts: one part passes through those locations at which the body is rising, and one part passes through those locations at which the body is setting. A body's celestial meridian line is also divided into two parts: one part passes through those locations at which the body is culminating, and one part passes through those locations at which the body is anti-culminating. These lines are usually labelled with the familiar abbreviations for the angles. For example, "♀MC" is used to label the section of Venus' celestial meridian line that passes through locations at which Venus is culminating. (This is perhaps unfortunate given that these lines pass through those locations at which the body is rising, culminating, setting or anticulminating – not those locations at which the body has a particular relationship to an angle.)

Two celestial bodies are said to be in *paranatellonta* – or *paran* for short – when, at the location concerned, both bodies are in the horizon plane, both bodies are in the meridian plane, or one body is in each plane. When two bodies are both in the meridian plane of a location, they are in paran not only for this location, but for all locations on the same line of terrestrial longitude and all locations on the opposite line of terrestrial longitude. When two bodies are in paran and at least one of them is in the horizon plane, the paran is observed from only two points on Earth's surface; and as Earth rotates eastwards, each of these points drifts westwards along its line of terrestrial latitude. Each of these lines of terrestrial latitude is referred to as a *paran line*.

Relocational astrology is based on the idea that if an entity moves away from its birthplace, it will – to some extent – begin to operate as if it had been born at its actual birth time but at the new location. A *relocated chart* is a chart cast for the moment of birth of an entity, for a location other than the birthplace. The same UT (or ET) time and date, and the same sidereal time, are used in the calculation of both the original birth chart and the relocated chart, but the local sidereal time used is different (unless the new location is on the same line of terrestrial longitude as the birthplace). In the relocated chart, the celestial longitudes of celestial bodies and the lunar nodes remain the same as in the birth chart, but the zodiacal wheel is oriented differently with respect to the horizon and meridian axes.

Astro-maps – in both the zodiacal mode and the in mundi mode – may be used alongside relocated charts to show the implications of spending time at a location other than the birthplace.

Dividing the Diurnal Cycle – House Systems

For the purposes of interpreting diurnal position, the celestial sphere is divided into twelve *houses* or *lunes*. Many methods of division – or *house systems* – have been proposed. In most house systems, the celestial sphere is divided into twelve segments by six great circles that mutually intersect at diametrically opposed points on the celestial sphere. In other systems, the celestial sphere is divided using one great circle and a number of parallel small circles. Whichever house system is used, the lines that separate the houses are referred to as *house cusps*.

On a standard astrological chart, each house cusp is represented by the point at which it intersects the ecliptic. In some house systems, the celestial sphere is divided by six great circles that mutually intersect at the ecliptic poles; thus, each house cusp is a line of celestial longitude, and the house position of each celestial body is accurately shown on a conventional astrological chart. In most house systems, the house cusps are not lines of celestial longitude, and so latitude error arises; however, in these cases, the astrologer may decide that it is valid to redefine the house cusps as the lines of celestial longitude that meet the original house cusps at the ecliptic.

Typically, the houses are numbered from 1 to 12 in an easterly direction around the celestial sphere (anticlockwise around the chart wheel). The house cusp that separates the twelfth and first houses is referred to as the *first house cusp*; the cusp that separates the first and second houses is referred to as the *second house cusp*, and so on. In house systems that use great semicircles as cusps, the first and seventh house cusps are always two halves of the same great circle, and whichever house system is used, these cusps meet the ecliptic at diametrically opposed points. The same is true of the second and eighth cusps, the third and ninth cusps, the fourth and tenth cusps, the fifth and eleventh cusps, and the sixth and twelfth cusps (see Figure 1.39).

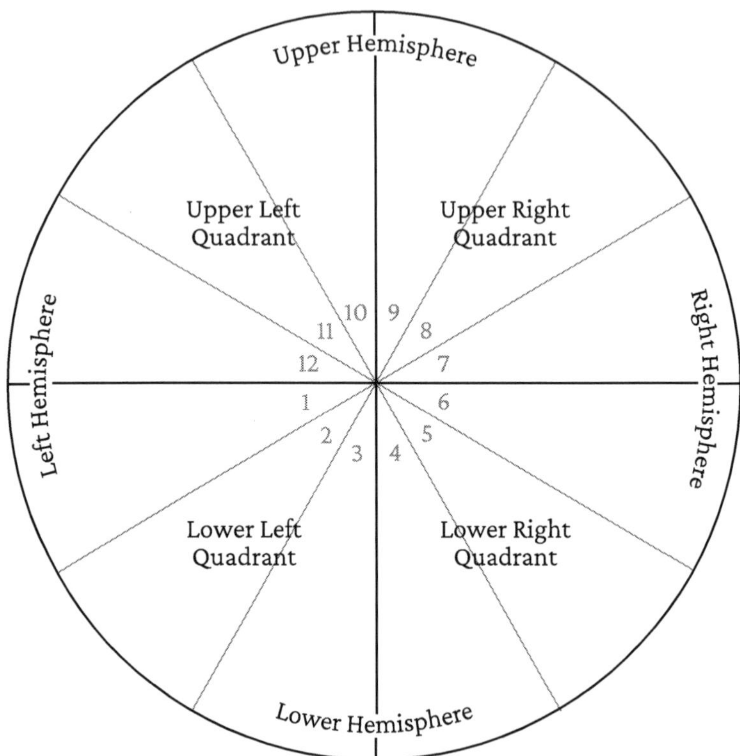

Figure 1.39 The hemispheres, quadrants and houses of the astrological chart

Whichever house system is used, the half of an astrological chart comprised of houses 1 through 6 is referred to as the *lower hemisphere*, and the half comprised of houses 7 through 12 is referred to as the *upper hemisphere*. The half of the chart that is comprised of houses 1 through 3 and 10 through 12 is referred to as the *left hemisphere*, and the half that is comprised of houses 4 through 9 is referred to as the *right hemisphere*. (For a location outside the Arctic and Antarctic circles, the ascendant is always the more easterly node of the horizontal axis, and so the left and right hemispheres may be referred to, respectively, as the *eastern* and *western* hemispheres.) Thus, the chart is divided into four quadrants: houses 1 through 3 make up the *lower left quadrant*, houses 4 through 6 make up the *lower right quadrant*, houses 7 through 9 make up the *upper right quadrant*, and houses 10 through 12 make up the *upper left quadrant*.

As Earth rotates, each point on each house cusp moves eastwards around the celestial sphere (anticlockwise around a chart wheel). Thus, if the revolving diurnal wheel is treated as a static frame of reference – as in the experience of an observer on Earth – the celestial bodies and zodiacal signs appear to move westwards around the diurnal wheel, passing through the houses in reverse numerical order. However, on a chart cast for a particular time and place, the house cusps are actually static; thus, when the eastward (direct) motion of a factor is superimposed onto such a chart, the factor moves through the houses in numerical order.

On pages 265 and 266 can be found the same astrological chart presented in two formats. On page 265, 1° of arc on the chart wheel corresponds to 1° of celestial longitude, and each zodiacal sign occupies 30° of arc on the chart wheel. On page 266, each house occupies 30° of arc on the chart wheel, and 1° of arc on the chart wheel does not correspond to 1° of celestial longitude. In both cases, each point on the chart wheel represents all points on a particular line of celestial longitude.

Commonly Used House Systems

In the *Equal House* system, the cusps are equally spaced lines of celestial longitude that cross the ecliptic at twelve equally spaced points. The first and seventh cusps cross the ecliptic at the ascendant and descendant, respectively. Thus, if the ascendant is positioned at 14♊30, the second house cusp is the line of celestial longitude 14♋30, the third house cusp is at 14♌30, and so on. The position of the meridian axis is often indicated by the inclusion of the midheaven on the chart, but it plays no part in defining the house cusps.

The *M-House* system is like the Equal House system except that the 4th and 10th cusps cross the ecliptic at the lower heaven and upper heaven, respectively. Thus, if the midheaven is positioned at 14♊30, for example, then the 11th cusp is the line of celestial longitude 14♋30, the 12th house cusp is at 14♌30, and so on. The position of the horizon axis is often indicated by the inclusion of the ascendant on the chart, but it plays no part in defining the house cusps.

As with the Equal House and M-House systems, the cusps of the *Whole Sign* system are equally spaced lines of celestial longitude that cross the ecliptic at twelve equally spaced points. In this system, the first house cusp crosses the ecliptic at the first point of the zodiacal sign of the ascendant. Thus, if the ascendant is positioned at 14♊30, the first house cusp is the line of celestial longitude 0♊00, the second house cusp is at 0♋00, and so on.

The ascendant and midheaven may be included on the chart.

A *quadrant house system* is a system in which the cusps of the first, fourth, seventh and tenth houses cross the ecliptic at the ascendant, lower heaven, descendant and midheaven, respectively. The *Porphyry* system is a quadrant system in which each cusp is a line of celestial longitude. In this system, the lower left quadrant is divided into three equal segments by the second and third cusps, the lower right quadrant is divided into equal segments by the fifth and sixth cusps, and so on.

Like the Porphyry system, the *Natural Graduation* system is a quadrant system in which each cusp is a line of celestial longitude. In this system, the 2nd, 3rd, 5th, 6th, 8th, 9th, 11th, and 12th cusps are positioned so that: the opposing houses that lie in the middle of the largest quadrants are the largest houses; the opposing houses that lie in the middle of the smallest quadrants are the smallest houses; house size increases from one house to the next between a smallest and largest house; and house size decreases from one house to the next between a largest house and a smallest house.

The *Campanus* system uses six great circles that mutually intersect at the north and south points on the rational horizon. One of the great circles is the rational horizon itself and another is the celestial meridian; thus, this is a quadrant system because these great circles intersect the ecliptic at the angles. These great circles are perpendicular to the prime vertical and intersect it at twelve equally spaced points. Thus, these circles divide the celestial sphere into twelve equal segments, but do not divide the ecliptic into equal arcs (except for locations on the equator).

The *Regiomontanus* system also uses six great circles that are perpendicular to the prime vertical and that mutually intersect at the north and south points on the rational horizon, two of which are the rational horizon and the celestial meridian (making this a quadrant system). However, these six great circles intersect the celestial equator at equally spaced points, and so do not divide the celestial sphere into equal segments.

The *Placidus* system also uses six great circles that mutually intersect at the north and south points on the rational horizon, two of which are the rational horizon and celestial meridian (making this a quadrant system). The first house cusp crosses the ecliptic at the point that is just beginning it's diurnal arc (the ascendant); the twelfth house cusp crosses the ecliptic at the point that is $^1/_6$ through the period of its diurnal arc; the eleventh house cusp crosses the ecliptic at the point that is $^2/_6$ ($^1/_3$) through the period of its diurnal arc; the tenth house cusp crosses the ecliptic at the point that is $^3/_6$

($^1/_2$) through the period of its diurnal arc (the midheaven), and so on. Note that the point on the ecliptic that is $^1/_6$ through the period of its diurnal arc (the twelfth cusp) is always diametrically opposed to the point on the ecliptic that is $^1/_6$ through the period of its nocturnal arc (the sixth cusp), and so on.

The *Topocentric* system is based on the Placidus system; however, the geometry used in the former is more complex. For a given chart, each Topocentric cusp is within 1° of arc of the equivalent Placidus cusp at the ecliptic.

Like the Placidus system, the *Alcabitus* system is a time-based quadrant system that uses six great circles that mutually intersect at the north and south points on the rational horizon, two of which are the rational horizon and celestial meridian. In this system, the period of the semi-diurnal arc of the rising point on the ecliptic is noted. The twelfth cusp crosses the point on the ecliptic that will reach the celestial meridian in $^2/_3$ of that period, and the eleventh cusp crosses the point on the ecliptic that will reach the celestial meridian in $^1/_3$ of that period. Also noted is the period of the semi-nocturnal arc of the anticulminating point on the ecliptic. The third cusp crosses the ecliptic at the point that will reach the rational horizon in $^2/_3$ of that period, and the second cusp crosses the ecliptic at the point that will reach the rational horizon in $^1/_3$ of that period.

Like the Placidus and Alcabitus systems, the *Birthplace* system – also called the *Koch* system – is a time-based quadrant system. However, in this system the celestial sphere is divided into six slices by planes that are parallel to the horizon plane. The twelfth and seventh houses share the slice that sits immediately above the rational horizon, the eleventh and eighth houses share the slice above, and the tenth and ninth houses share the slice above that. Similarly, the first and sixth houses share the slice that sits immediately below the rational horizon, the second and fifth houses share the slice below, and the third and fourth houses share the slice below that. To find the altitude of each dividing plane that sits above the rational horizon, the period of the semi-diurnal arc of the culminating point on the ecliptic is noted. One plane crosses the ecliptic at the point that rose $^2/_3$ of this period earlier and the other crosses the ecliptic at the point that rose $^1/_3$ of this period earlier. To find the altitude of each dividing plane that sits below the rational horizon, the period of the semi-nocturnal arc of the rising point on the ecliptic is noted. One plane crosses the ecliptic at the point that anti-culminated $^2/_3$ of this period earlier and the other plane crosses the ecliptic at the point that anti-culminated $^1/_3$ of this period earlier.

The final house system that we will look at was named the *Poli-Equatorial* system by its proponent, twentieth-century astrologer, Charles Carter.* This system uses six great circles that mutually intersect at the celestial poles and divide the celestial equator into equal arcs (and thus divide the celestial sphere into equal segments). In other words, in this system, the house cusps are equally spaced lines of right ascension. This system places more emphasis on Earth's rotation than do the house systems outlined above. The first and seventh house cusps cross the ecliptic at the ascendant and descendant respectively, but this is not a quadrant system because the fourth and tenth house cusps are independent of the lower heaven and midheaven.

Interestingly, if the Poli-Equatorial system is adapted so that the fourth and tenth cusps coincide with the celestial meridian, but the cusps are still equally spaced lines of right ascension, the first and seventh house cusps now pass through the east and west points on the rational horizon rather than the ascendant and descendant. This gives a house system in which: the celestial sphere is divided into equal segments; the ecliptic – and thus the chart wheel – is divided fairly evenly by these cusps for all locations; each body or point moves through all of the houses during each rotation of Earth for any given location; and each point or body reaches its highest altitude as it crosses the tenth cusp, its lowest altitude as it crosses the fourth cusp, and its average altitude as it crosses the first and seventh cusps. Such a house system might be called the *Relative Elevation* system.

No one can say for sure whether there is a particular house system that always gives the best results, or whether the best system to use varies according to culture, geographical region, the astrological techniques used and/or the approach and goal of the astrologer. Amongst the issues that prevent clarity in this area are: 1) inaccuracy in the timing of events (especially births); 2) the misrepresentation of diurnal positions on the astrological chart when certain house systems are used; 3) confirmation bias on the part of the astrologer; 4) the widespread belief that – unlike zodiacal signs – houses blur into one another over several degrees; 5) the apparent limitations of statistical research as a tool for studying the meanings of discrete stages of celestial cycles. (Note that the second, third and fourth of these issues tend to exacerbate one another.)

---

* *Essays on the Foundations of Astrology* (1978) p. 158. (1st ed. 1947)

CHAPTER TWO

INTERPRETING CELESTIAL MOTIONS

The first part of this chapter explores the general principles of astrology, including the introduction of a new idea concerning the relevance of harmonics to astrology. The second part of the Chapter focuses on the relevance of these principles to psychological astrology.

Polarity and Cyclicity

> All life is based on the operation of two opposite trends in constant dynamic interrelationship and interdependence.... Polarity is not something which is secondary to existence; it is the very basis of existence. (Rudhyar*)

Two trends that unfold in opposite directions along the same continuum are said to be *polarised* with respect to one another. Typically, polar-opposite trends operate in turn, giving rise to a recurring pattern of change, or *cycle*. For example, inhalation and exhalation occur in opposite directions along the continuum that lies between the lungs' fullest and emptiest states. The alternation of inhalation and exhalation is the breathing cycle.

During each unfoldment of a cycle, four pivotal points can be identified: two *points of equilibrium* and two *points of maximum disequilibrium*, or *poles*. At a point of equilibrium, the polar-opposite trends cancel one another out; and at a pole, the effect of one trend peaks and there is a reversal of the direction of change. To illustrate this, Figure 2.1 shows the pivotal points of the cycle of changing displacement of a swinging pendulum. The polar-opposite trends operating in this cycle (considered from the vantage point adopted in Figure 2.1) are clockwise motion and anticlockwise motion.

---

* *Cycles of Life: The Structure and Unfoldment of Cyclic Processes in Astrology* (1975) RudhyarAudioArchives.com

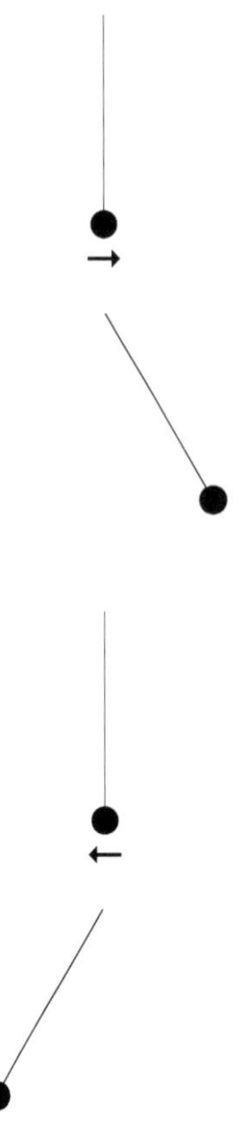

Figure 2.1a This is a point of equilibrium, with no displacement in either direction. The motion of the pendulum is anticlockwise, so at this point, clockwise displacement gives way to anticlockwise displacement.

Figure 2.1b This is the anticlockwise pole. The pendulum is momentarily stationary as anticlockwise displacement peaks and begins to decrease – as anticlockwise motion gives way to clockwise motion.

Figure 2.1c This is the point of equilibrium that follows the anticlockwise pole. The motion of the pendulum is clockwise, so at this point, anticlockwise displacement gives way to clockwise displacement.

Figure 2.1d This is the clockwise pole. The pendulum is momentarily stationary as clockwise displacement peaks and begins to decrease – as clockwise motion gives way to anticlockwise motion. The clockwise pole is followed by the point of equilibrium shown in Figure 2.1a.

Figure 2.1 The pivotal points of the cycle of changing displacement of a swinging pendulum

Figure 2.2 represents one complete unfoldment of the cycle, showing the position of each of the points illustrated above. We can see that at each point of equilibrium (a and c), the direction in which the pendulum is displaced changes, and at each pole (b and d), the trend of increasing displacement in a particular direction is reversed.

Figure 2.2 shows the cycle divided into distinct quarters* by its pivotal points. Throughout the first quarter, displacement is anticlockwise and the

* The terms *quarter* and *half* are used figuratively. The pivotal points are equally spaced over time in some cycles, but not in others.

pendulum continues to move in an anticlockwise direction. Throughout the second quarter, displacement is anticlockwise but the motion of the pendulum is clockwise. Throughout the third quarter, displacement is clockwise and the pendulum continues to move in a clockwise direction. Throughout the fourth quarter, displacement is clockwise but the motion of the pendulum is anticlockwise.

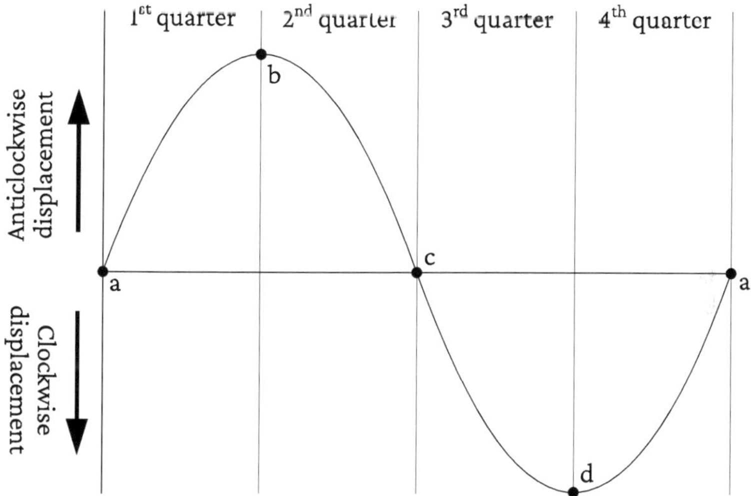

Figure 2.2 The cycle of changing displacement of a swinging pendulum

If we wish to divide the cycle into distinct halves – or *hemicycles* – we have two options. Using one option, each hemicycle begins at a point of equilibrium, with one hemicycle consisting of the first and second quarters (throughout which displacement is anticlockwise) and the other consisting of the third and fourth quarters (throughout which displacement is clockwise). Using the other option, each hemicycle begins at a pole, with one hemicycle consisting of the fourth and first quarters (throughout which motion is anticlockwise) and the other consisting of the second and third quarters (throughout which motion is clockwise).

Multiplicity, Unity and Wholeness

During the twentieth century, the physicist's view of the universe came to resemble that of the mystic, and there is now broad agreement that the universe is a single, undivided unity. Each phenomenon is simply this unity manifesting in a particular form – a transient set of conditions with no enduring essence of its own. Yet because phenomena can be distinguished from one another, the universe in which we live is also a multiplicity. Rudhyar[*] saw the dual nature of existence as being the result of the operation of two polar-opposite principles: the *principle of multiplicity* (a yang principle) and the *principle of unity* (a yin principle).

For the purposes of this discussion, a *whole* is defined as "an organised system of activity within definite limits" (Rael[†]). The principles of multiplicity and unity are "inherent and coactive in wholeness" (Rael[‡]), for each whole is comprised of a number of discrete parts operating as a unified system. Much of the mass of the universe is arranged into wholes such as atoms, solar systems, galaxies and galaxy clusters. In a biological whole – such as a cell, plant, animal or colony – constituent parts operate in synthesis with one another to sustain, regenerate and replicate the whole.

The organised activity that characterises wholeness is always comprised of one or more cycles. A whole such as an atom, a solar system or a galaxy only exists by virtue of orbital cycles, and a biological whole only exists by virtue of various biochemical and behavioural cycles. Alan Watts[§] points out that due to the nature of our language, we are conditioned to distinguish between objects (labelled using nouns) and the characteristic activities of those objects (labelled using verbs). When we speak of 'the activity that arises within a whole', this distinction is particularly flawed; and rather than speaking of an atom in which electrons orbit a nucleus, for example, or an animal that engages in various biochemical and behavioural cycles, it would be more accurate to speak of an occurrence of *atom-ing* or *animal-ing*.

The defining boundary that circumscribes a whole allows that whole to function as a distinct constituent part of larger wholes, and indeed the manifest universe is arranged into a "hierarchy of wholes within wholes within wholes – cycles within cycles within cycles" (Rael[**]). A solar system is an organised group of celestial bodies; a galaxy is an organised group of solar systems; a galaxy cluster is an organised group of galaxies; and a super cluster is an organised group of galaxy clusters. Even the whole that we call

---

[*] See, for example, *The Fullness of Human Experience* (1985) Khaldea.com/rudhyar/

[†] *The Essential Rudhyar – An Outline and an Evocation* (1983) Khaldea.com/rudhyar/ Pt. 2, Section 8.

[‡] Ibid Pt. 2, Section 9.

[§] Recorded lecture on You Tube. (Unable to find title.)

[**] *The Essential Rudhyar – An Outline and an Evocation* (1983) Khaldea.com/rudhyar/ Pt. 2, Section 5.

the universe is now believed to be a constituent part of a still larger whole, which has been labelled the *multiverse*. Similarly, a cell is an organised group of smaller components; a plant or animal is an organised group of cells; and an ecosystem is an organised group of animals, plants and other biological organisms.

For the purposes of this discussion, a *collective* is defined as a whole that exists by virtue of the coordinated activity of two or more individuals – for example, a one-to-one relationship, a family, an interest group, a community or a nation state. An individual's motivation for participating in a given collective may be, for example, biological, recreational, financial, vocational, ideological, political and/or spiritual. Human collectives are arranged into hierarchies; for example, one-to-one relationships within families within communities within nation states within international alliances, or departments within shops and factories within businesses within corporations.

The health of a biological whole or a biological-cultural whole (i.e. a collective) is dependent upon the health and integration of its constituent 'organs' and 'cells' (using these terms in their widest sense) and upon its successful integration into the encompassing wholes of which it is a constituent part.

The Cycle of Being

> For Rudhyar, unity is no more 'real' than multiplicity; reality is the cyclic interplay between them. (Rael*)

The dynamic interrelatedness of the principles of multiplicity and unity is expressed as a cyclical shift of emphasis back and forth between them, which Rudhyar† refers to as the *cycle of being*. Figure 2.3 represents one complete unfoldment of the cycle of being. We can see that the cycle has two points of equilibrium (one at which the principle of multiplicity becomes dominant and one at which the principle of unity becomes dominant) and two poles (one at which emphasis on multiplicity peaks and one at which emphasis on unity peaks).

The changing displacement of the curve above and below the horizontal axis

---

* *The Essential Rudhyar – An Outline and an Evocation* (1983) Khaldea.com/rudhyar/ Pt. 2, Section 11.

† See, for example, *The Fullness of Human Experience* (1985) Khaldea.com/rudhyar/

shows the movement of dominance back and forth between the principles of multiplicity and unity, respectively. At a pole, the strength of one principle peaks while the effect of the other principle is at a minimum (though still present); and at a point of equilibrium, neither principle is dominant. The gradient of the line upwards or downwards shows the rate at which the dominance of the principle of multiplicity or unity, respectively, is increasing. The rate of change in favour of one principle or the other peaks at a point of equilibrium, and is zero at a pole.

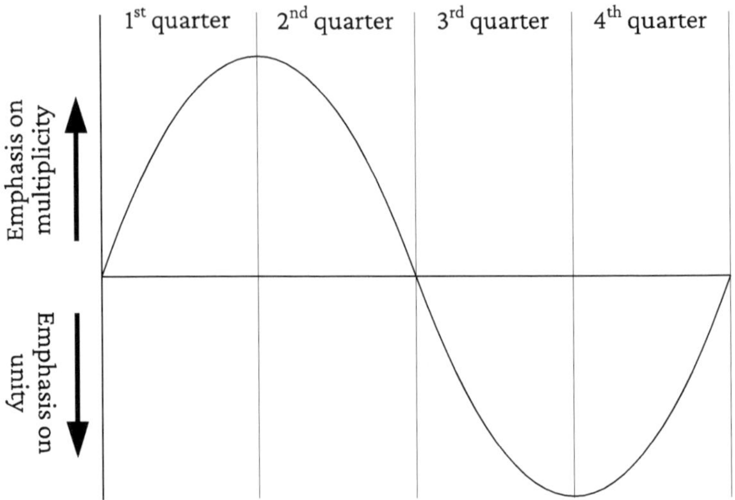

Figure 2.3 The cycle of being

Figure 2.3 shows the cycle divided into distinct quarters. Throughout the first quarter, the principle of multiplicity is dominant and becoming stronger. Throughout the second quarter, the principle of multiplicity is dominant but becoming weaker. Throughout the third quarter, the principle of unity is dominant and becoming stronger. Throughout the fourth quarter, the principle of unity is dominant but becoming weaker.

The points of equilibrium divide the cycle into a hemicycle consisting of the first and second quarters (throughout which the principle of multiplicity is dominant) and a hemicycle consisting of the third and fourth quarters (throughout which the principle of unity is dominant). The poles divide the cycle into a hemicycle consisting of the fourth and first quarters (throughout which there is increasing emphasis on multiplicity) and a hemicycle consisting of the second and third quarters (throughout which there is increasing emphasis on unity).

Macrocosm and Microcosm

Having discussed the nature and interrelatedness of the principles of polarity, cyclicity, multiplicity, unity and wholeness, we can explore their relevance to astrology. First, let us consider what astrology is.

The health of a biological whole or a biological-cultural whole is dependent upon the performance of certain vital functions by its constituent parts. According to astrological lore, each such function corresponds to a celestial body, with those functions that have the greatest significance in the life of the whole corresponding to the Sun, Moon, planets (including Earth) and Pluto.* Certain planes† associated with these bodies, and the nodal axes formed where two such planes intersect, are also seen to be astrologically significant. Astrology is the study of correlations between changes in the positions of these factors on the celestial sphere, and changes in the functioning of terrestrial wholes.

Astrologers have observed that for a human-based whole – such as an individual, a relationship, an organisation or a nation state – the arrangement of factors on the celestial sphere is significant in a number of ways, the most important of which are as follows.

The Birth Moment

The arrangement of factors on the celestial sphere at the moment of a whole's birth – as 'seen' from the birthplace – reflects the whole's basic predisposition and may be referred to as the whole's *birth*, *natal*, *radix* or *root pattern*. In the case of a whole that is spread over a wide area – such as a nation state, or a group or business that occupies a number of sites – the location of the parliament, capital city or headquarters, etc. is used.

If a whole moves away from its birthplace, it will, to some extent, begin to operate as if it had been born at the new location. The arrangement of factors at the moment of birth – as 'seen' from a location other than the birthplace – may be referred to as a *relocated birth pattern*.

---

* Each of these functions/archetypes is also given a place on the Kabbalistic Tree of Life. See, for example, *Tree of Life*, by Z'ev ben Shimon Halevi.

† Orbital planes, Earth's plane of rotation, and those planes that are defined by the observer's position relative to Earth's centre.

Following Birth

Following the birth of a whole, changes in the positions of factors on the celestial sphere reflect changes in the way the whole is predisposed to operate.

The position of a factor at a given moment in time is referred to as its *transiting* position. The transiting pattern at a given moment in time – as 'seen' from a whole's location at that moment – may be superimposed onto the whole's birth pattern and/or a relocated birth pattern to give insight into how the whole will be (or was) predisposed to operate at that time and place.

The transiting pattern at a significant moment may remain relevant for some time afterwards. This could be, for example, the moment at which a transiting factor perfects a significant aspect to another transiting factor or a natal factor, or the moment at which a factor passes from one distinct stage of a cycle (such as a zodiacal sign) to the next. The transiting pattern at such a moment may be superimposed onto the birth pattern, a relocated birth pattern and/or the transiting pattern at a later moment.

For a given whole, each factor has a number of continuously changing *progressed* positions, each derived using a different progression technique. At the moment of birth of the whole, all of the progressed positions of a given factor coincide with that factor's transiting position. Following birth, each of the factor's progressed positions changes in the same manner as the factor's transiting position, but over a longer timescale. In each progression technique, the ratio of the progressed timescale to real time is equal to *the period of one celestial cycle* divided by *the period of a shorter celestial cycle*. (It is as though the transiting motion of the factor is recorded on a medium revolving once with each unfoldment of the shorter celestial cycle and played back on a medium revolving once with each unfoldment of the longer celestial cycle, with both the recording and the playback beginning at birth.) For example, *secondary progression* – the most commonly used progression technique – is based on the ratio of *the period of the tropical year* to *the period of the solar day*. Thus, for example, the position of a whole's secondary progressed Mercury twenty years after the whole's birth is the position of transiting Mercury twenty days after the whole's birth. (The secondary progressed midheaven is assumed to move at the same rate as the secondary progressed Sun, and the secondary progressed ascendant is taken to be the ascendant that coincides with the secondary progressed midheaven at the location concerned.)

For a given whole, each factor also has a number of continuously changing *directed* positions, each derived using a different direction technique. At the moment of birth of the whole, all of the directed positions of a given factor coincide with that factor's transiting position. In each direction technique, the celestial longitude of each factor changes in the same manner as that of a particular progressed factor. For example, in *solar arc direction* – the most commonly used direction technique – the celestial longitude of each factor (including the ascendant and midheaven) changes at the same rate as that of the secondary progressed Sun. *One-degree direction* is a less popular direction technique in which the celestial longitude of each factor changes at the slightly faster rate of exactly one degree per year.

A progressed or directed pattern gives additional insight into how the whole is predisposed to function at a given time. It may be interpreted in isolation or superimposed onto the patterns mentioned above.

A whole's progressed and directed positions prior to birth can be found by working backwards in time from the birth moment. Pre-birth transiting patterns, and the pre-birth progressed and directed patterns of the whole, may be superimposed onto the whole's birth pattern, etc. to show the significance for the whole of events that occurred before its birth.

Relationships to Other Wholes

The comparison of the patterns of two or more wholes is referred to as *synastry*. The birth, progressed, directed and/or relocated patterns of a whole can be superimposed upon those of another whole to gain insight into how those wholes will affect one another. One of the wholes involved in the comparison may be a constituent part of the other (as, for example, when an individual's patterns are superimposed onto those of their nation state or a company they work for).

Other patterns commonly used in synastry are the *composite pattern* and the *Davison pattern*. The composite position of a factor is charted as the direct midpoint of its position in the natal pattern of one whole and its position in the natal pattern of the other. (Since midpoints come in opposing pairs, a composite position is essentially an axis rather than a point, but only the direct midpoint is shown on the composite chart.) A Davison pattern is the transiting pattern formed at the moment in time midway between the birth moments of the wholes, as 'seen' from the point on Earth's surface midway between the birthplaces of the wholes. A relationship involving more than two wholes also has a composite pattern and a Davison pattern. A composite or Davison pattern reflects the predisposition of the relationship-as-a-whole; it can be superimposed onto that of another relationship, onto a transiting pattern or onto the birth, progressed and directed patterns of any whole (including a whole that is part of the relationship).*

To some extent, a whole may operate as if it were visiting a particular location while interacting with a whole that was born at that location.†

Astrology and the Cycle of Being

Rudhyar‡ realised that as a celestial cycle unfolds in synchrony with a cycle of change in the functioning of terrestrial wholes, what is unfolding is a cycle of being. For example, the tropical zodiacal cycle of Mars is the cycle of changing declination of the point at which Mars' line of celestial longitude meets the ecliptic. This cycle is observed to coincide with a cycle of change in the way the martial function operates in certain terrestrial wholes, with increasing northerly declination coinciding with increasing emphasis on multiplicity, and increasing southerly declination coinciding with increasing emphasis on unity.

Figure 2.4 shows a zodiacal cycle as a cycle of being, with multiplicity and unity emphasised during the zodiac's first and second hemicycles, respectively. Viewing a zodiacal cycle in this way explains why the first six signs are traditionally referred to as the *personal* or *individual signs*, and the last six signs are referred to as the *social* or *collective signs*. It does not explain, however, why meaning is also observed to be subject to patterns of change that unfold multiple times during each unfoldment of a zodiacal cycle, such as the element cycle and the mode cycle (which unfold four and three times, respectively, during each unfoldment of a zodiacal cycle).

We may be able to go some way towards solving this mystery by referring to *harmonics*. Harmonics is concerned with the way that a cycle can unfold at different frequencies simultaneously. Where this occurs, the slowest unfoldment of the cycle is referred to as the *1st harmonic* or *fundamental*, and

---

* Perhaps also significant are the composite and/or Davison patterns formed between a whole's natal pattern (or perhaps the relocated natal pattern if the whole has changed location since birth) and the current transiting pattern (as 'seen' from the whole's current location); these patterns might be referred to as the whole's *composite clock* and *Davison clock*, respectively.

† I came across this idea in *Working with Astrology*, by Michael Harding and Charles Harvey (1990, 1st ed.) p. 311 and have found it to work. I highly recommend this book, which looks at the use of harmonic charts, midpoints and astro-mapping.

‡ References are given in later chapters.

the other unfoldments are referred to as *higher harmonics*. The frequency of each higher harmonic is a multiple of the frequency of the 1st harmonic. The *2nd harmonic* unfolds twice during each unfoldment of the 1st harmonic, the *3rd harmonic* unfolds thrice during each unfoldment of the 1st harmonic, and so on. From this point onwards, in the main text of this book, *1st harmonic* is abbreviated to *1H*, *2nd harmonic* is abbreviated to *2H*, and so on.

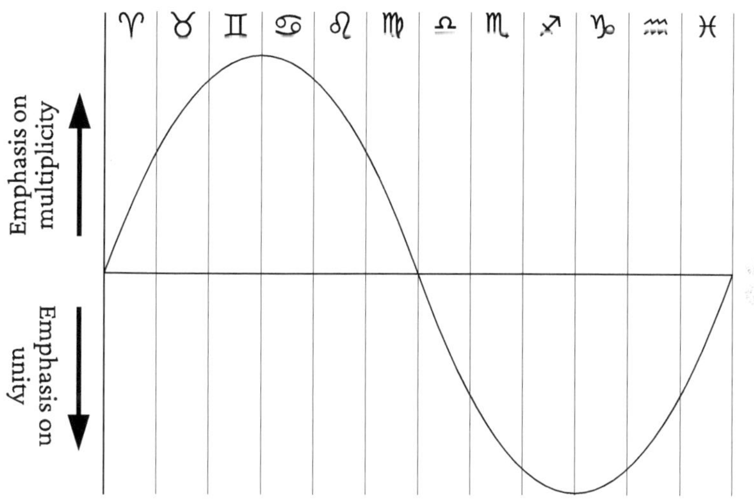

Figure 2.4 A zodiacal cycle as a cycle of being

The distance covered by a single unfoldment of a cycle is referred to as its *wavelength*. Over a given period, each higher harmonic covers the same distance as the 1H. Thus, because one unfoldment of the 1H coincides with two unfoldments of the 2H, one unfoldment of the 1H covers the same distance as two unfoldments of the 2H. In other words, the wavelength of the 2H is one-half that of the 1H; and similarly, the wavelength of the 3H is one-third that of the 1H, and so on.

Suppose that as a celestial cycle unfolds, the cycle of being unfolds not only at the same frequency as the celestial cycle, but also at higher harmonic frequencies. The cycle of being shown in Figure 2.4 has a wavelength of 360° of celestial longitude. If we take this to be the 1H, then the wavelength of the 2H would be 180° of celestial longitude, the wavelength of the 3H would be 120° of celestial longitude, and so on. Just as the pivotal points of the 1H occur at intervals of 90° of celestial longitude, so those of the 2H would occur at intervals of 45° of celestial longitude, those of the 3H at intervals of 30°, and so on.

The supposition of higher harmonic unfoldments of the cycle of being is the basis of the 'harmonic model of segmentation' that is explored in this book. Figure 2.5 shows the 1H and 3H* of a zodiacal cycle according to this model. We can see that the waveforms are aligned in such a way that there is a point at which the principle of multiplicity becomes dominant in both the 1H and 3H simultaneously. In later chapters, we will see that the model only reflects the empirically observed meanings of the stages of a celestial cycle when it is assumed that as the principle of multiplicity becomes dominant in the 1H, it does so simultaneously in all higher harmonics.

In Figure 2.5, the letters F, E, A and W refer to the elements fire, earth, air and water, respectively. We can see, for example, that at the 1H frequency, the principle of multiplicity is dominant and becoming stronger throughout Aries, Taurus and Gemini; and at the 3H frequency, the principle of multiplicity is dominant and becoming stronger throughout each fire sign.

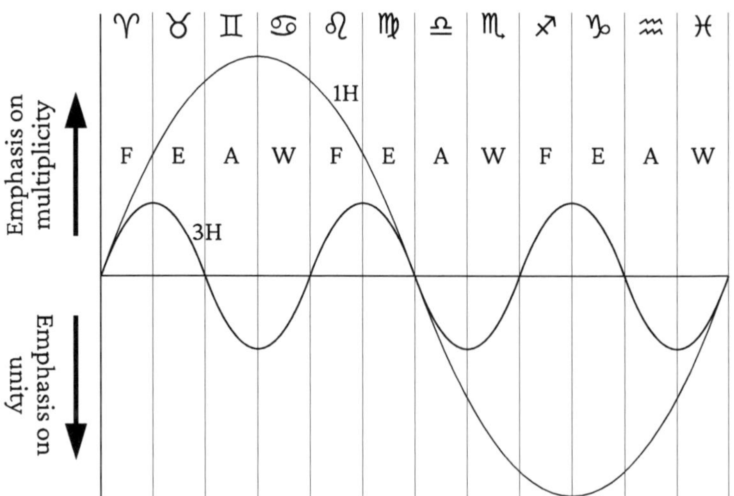

Figure 2.5 The 1H and 3H of a zodiacal cycle

Later chapters explore the model in greater depth, looking at how the cycle of being unfolds in the individual psyche in synchrony with different types of celestial cycle, how each harmonic frequency of unfoldment is imbued with the quality of the number concerned, and how each way of dividing a cycle into distinct stages brings certain harmonics into focus while excluding others from consideration.

---

* It is suggested that *1H and 3H* be read as *1st and 3rd harmonics.*

The Rebirth of a Cycle

Each celestial cycle (for example, the tropical zodiacal cycle of Venus, or the synodic cycle of the Sun and Moon) has a general meaning that incorporates the meaning of each factor involved in the cycle, and that is common to all unfoldments of the cycle. In addition, each unfoldment of a cycle is imbued with a unique quality that distinguishes it from other unfoldments of that cycle – a quality that is largely reflected by the transiting pattern at the beginning of the unfoldment. It is as though the entities involved in the cycle form a whole in their own right by virtue of this organised activity – a whole that is reborn with a new natal pattern as each new unfoldment begins.

Similarly, a particular stage in the unfoldment of a celestial cycle (for example, Venus in tropical Gemini, or the Sun and Moon in the full moon phase) has a general meaning that is common to all occurrences of it; and in addition, each occurrence of the stage has a unique meaning that reflects the unique quality of the unfoldment in which it occurs.

Any point of a cycle can be viewed as the end of one unfoldment and the beginning of another, but if the principles outlined in the previous two paragraphs are valid, there must be one particular point at which a cycle is born anew. With regard to the synodic cycle, there is broad agreement amongst astrologers that this point is the perfection of the conjunction – a consensus that is illustrated by the widespread use of the solar return chart. A solar return chart depicts the transiting pattern for the moment at which the transiting Sun perfects a conjunction to a whole's natal Sun, as 'seen' from the whole's location at that time. A solar return pattern is thought to be significant until the subsequent solar return, when the synodic cycle of the transiting Sun and the whole's natal Sun is reborn again.

As noted above, Rudhyar realised that when a celestial cycle unfolds in synchrony with a cycle of change in the functioning of terrestrial wholes, what is unfolding is a cycle of being. While not necessarily thinking in terms of the cycle of being, many astrologers believe that these cycles of changing functionality unfold according to a common structure or pattern – that the same core themes are expressed at the equivalent pivotal point or stage of each type of celestial cycle.

There seems to be universal agreement amongst astrologers that the first points of Aries and Libra are the points of equilibrium of a zodiacal cycle, and the first points of Cancer and Capricorn are the poles (see Figure 2.4). However, there are two main schools of thought regarding which pivotal points of the synodic cycle are points of equilibrium and which are poles, and thus how the synodic and zodiacal cycles correlate with one another.

According to one school of thought,* the perfect conjunction and opposition are the points of equilibrium of the synodic cycle, correlating with the first points of Aries and Libra, respectively; and the perfect waxing and waning squares are the poles of the synodic cycle, correlating with the first points of Cancer and Capricorn, respectively (see Figure 2.6). Thus, if the synodic cycle is viewed as a cycle of being, the perfect conjunction is taken to be the point at which the principle of multiplicity becomes dominant, and this is taken to be the point at which the cycle of being begins anew. This approach implies a tendency to view the spring equinox as the beginning of the seasonal cycle.

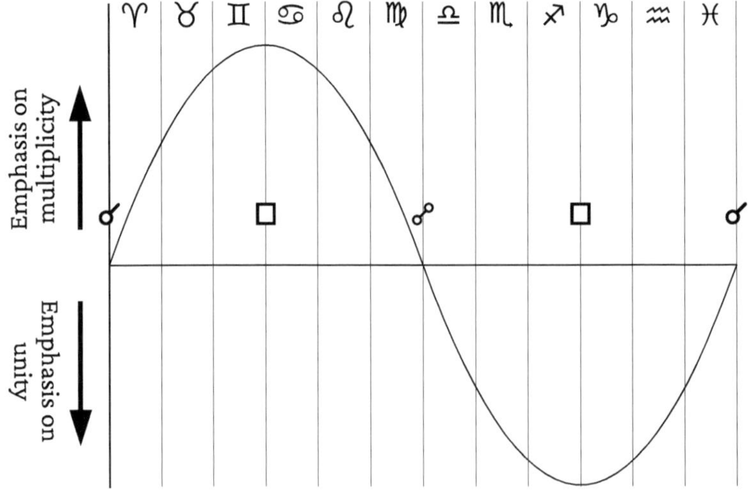

Figure 2.6 Correlating the first point of Aries with the perfect conjunction

According to the other school of thought, the perfect conjunction and opposition are taken to be the poles of the synodic cycle, correlating with the first points of Capricorn and Cancer, respectively; and the perfect waxing and waning squares are taken to be the points of equilibrium, correlating with the first points of Aries and Libra, respectively (see Figure 2.7). Thus, if the synodic cycle is viewed as a cycle of being, the perfect conjunction is taken to be the point at which the principle of unity peaks in strength and the principle of multiplicity begins to grow stronger, and this is

* Examples of proponents of each school of thought are given in Chapter 7.

taken to be the point at which the cycle of being begins anew. This approach implies a tendency to view the winter solstice as the beginning of the seasonal cycle.

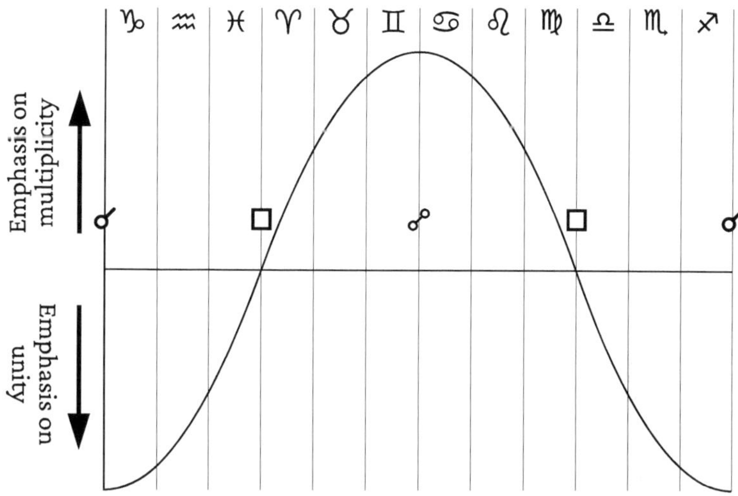

Figure 2.7 Correlating the first point of Capricorn with the perfect conjunction

We can see that the astrologer's preference for one school of thought or the other is influenced by their intuitive sense of what it means to begin anew, and by their sense of which pivotal points of the synodic cycle are points of equilibrium and which are poles. The definition of the pivotal points of the synodic cycle is discussed further in Chapter 7.

It is interesting to note that in each school of thought, the cycle of being is assumed to begin at a point at which the principle of unity gives way to the principle of multiplicity, thus paving the way for the emergence of new particularised forms. This is not surprising given that the experience of being a separate individual is more immediate than the experience of being an inseparable part of an encompassing whole.

Like Rudhyar, I correlate the perfect conjunction with the first point of Aries, taking these to be the points at which the principle of multiplicity becomes dominant in the synodic and zodiacal cycles. My view is that only when this approach is adopted do the stages and pivotal points of the different types of celestial cycle correlate with one another (see Chapters 5 through 8).

Taking the point at which the principle of multiplicity becomes dominant to be the point of rebirth of the cycle of being is consistent with the insight afforded by the proposed 'harmonic model of segmentation'. As noted above, the model only accounts for the empirically observed meanings of stages if it is assumed that as the principle of multiplicity becomes dominant in the 1H, it does so simultaneously in all higher harmonics. This means that as the principle of multiplicity becomes dominant in any given harmonic, it does so simultaneously in each sub-harmonic[*] of that harmonic. It seems fitting that the rebirth of a cycle (whether it be a 1H or a higher harmonic unfoldment) would be accompanied by the rebirth of all of the sub-cycles that unfold within it.

In addition, taking the first point of Aries to be the point of renewal of the zodiacal cycle is congruous with the traditional system of associating each zodiacal sign with a particular area of the body – i.e. Aries with the head, Taurus with the neck....Aquarius with the calves and Pisces with the feet. We can see that in this system, the first point of Aries is crossed as one passage through the body ends at the feet and another begins at the head.

Thus, throughout this book, the quarters of the cycle of being are labelled as in Figure 2.3. The hemicycle during which the principle of multiplicity is dominant is referred to as the *first hemicycle*, and the hemicycle during which the principle of unity is dominant is referred to as the *second hemicycle*.

Rudhyar[†] suggests that as the point of multiplicity becomes dominant, a "ball of potentiality" is released which, to a greater or lesser extent, comes to fruition during the unfoldment of the cycle. The essential nature of the potentiality is defined partly by the general meaning of the cycle concerned, and partly by the unique quality of that particular unfoldment.

Given the various types of correspondence noted in the above section *Macrocosm and Microcosm*, we can see that such potentiality will come to fruition on many different levels over many different timescales. For example, the potentiality released as two transiting factors perfect a conjunction comes to fruition as the transiting cycle unfolds; and any whole born during this unfoldment will be predisposed – throughout its existence – to enact the point of the unfoldment at which it is born, and to enact the continuing unfoldment of the cycle from that point at various progressed and directed speeds. Furthermore, other celestial cycles that begin anew during the unfoldment of this transiting cycle will carry forward its unique

---

[*] Sub-harmonics are defined on page 107.

[†] *Cycles of Life: The Structure and Unfoldment of Cyclic Processes in Astrology* (1975) RudhyarAudioArchives.com

quality on some level.

For practical reasons, the astrologer must limit the number of cycles that are interpreted as unique unfoldments. In psychological astrology, this type of consideration is generally applied in only two ways (with many psychological astrologers avoiding this type of consideration altogether). A minority of psychological astrologers interpret the transiting pattern of the new moon prior to birth to gain added insight into the relationship between the Sun and Moon in a whole's natal pattern. A larger number of psychological astrologers refer to solar return charts. Mundane astrologers routinely interpret transiting patterns for the perfection of significant aspects between transiting factors, the perfection of significant aspects between transiting and natal factors, and the passage of transiting factors from one zodiacal sign to another.

According to the proposed model, as a factor moves from one distinct stage of a cycle to another, the cycle of being begins anew at certain harmonic frequencies. Chapter 5 discusses the significance of this for the interpretation of the moment at which a factor enters a new stage of a zodiacal cycle. Chapter 7 discusses the significance of this for the similar treatment of the synodic cycle.

The Cycle of Being and the Individual Psyche

In a number of written works and recorded lectures on psychological astrology, Rudhyar* interprets various types of celestial cycles as cycles of being, but does not refer to sub-cycles such as the element cycle in the same way. The account of the cycle of being offered below draws heavily from Rudhyar's work, but also incorporates my own viewpoint. It attempts to describe the core themes that arise whenever a cycle of being unfolds in the individual psyche – whether in synchrony with a celestial cycle (at the same frequency of unfoldment or a higher harmonic frequency), or independently of any celestial cycle.

In this chapter, we will look at the meaning of each hemicycle and quarter of the cycle of being, because dividing the cycle using its pivotal points gives the clearest picture of the cycle's basic structure. In later chapters, we will see that when using the proposed model, it is often necessary to divide the

* References are given in later chapters. Many of the terms attributed to Rudhyar in the following account of the cycle of being are used by Rudhyar in his talk, *Cycles of Life: The Structure and Unfoldment of Cyclic Processes in Astrology* (1975) RudhyarAudioArchives.com

cycle into portions that are not defined by its pivotal points, such as thirds or fifths.

The account includes comment on how each theme is experienced by consciousness in each of two states: the *egoic* state and the *unconditioned* state. Inherent in both states is the experience of selfhood; but in each state, the Self is experienced to be something different.

Consciousness in the egoic state says, "I am this particular being, with these particular needs", and can be thought of as conditioned self-consciousness. In an attempt to keep anxiety at bay, egoic consciousness constantly strives to fulfil these needs. However, true and lasting peace is unattainable for egoic consciousness, because the extent to which an egoic need can be fulfilled is always limited to a greater or lesser extent by the realities of life – not least of which is the fact that the individual's various egoic needs conflict with one another.

Consciousness in the unconditioned state says, "I am aliveness – or awareness – itself", and exists in a state of ongoing contentment that is unaffected by phenomenal conditions. Unconditioned consciousness responds spontaneously – thus, creatively – to the potential inherent in each moment.

Each phenomenon can be viewed as a contraction occurring within the unity, and egoic consciousness – which is immersed in the phenomenal world, and which identifies certain phenomena as aspects of 'me' or 'my life' – can be viewed as a contraction occurring within a universal field of consciousness. Fear of the demise of 'me' manifests as the ongoing exaggeration of the contracted state, both physiologically (as body armour*) and psychologically (as complexes). Thus, the transition of consciousness from the egoic state to the unconditioned state is essentially a process of relaxation.

Astrological techniques can be used to show the types of egoic needs and fears to which an individual is particularly prone. Alerted to these tendencies, the individual is better able to observe their habitual egoic responses and see the futility and destructiveness of egoic striving. As the individual relinquishes this striving and relaxes into a state of contentment and spontaneity, the expression of the unique character reflected in the natal pattern becomes increasingly clear, creative and effortless.

The difficulty in trying to use astrology as a tool for psychological healing is

---

* See the work of Wilhelm Reich.

that egoic consciousness can only view life in terms of striving. For egoic consciousness, astrological significators are indicators of what 'I' (or a client) must do or become in order to find fulfilment, or even why 'I' (or a client) will never be able to find true fulfilment. Thus, care is needed to ensure that the use of astrology leads to the relaxation of consciousness rather than the spawning of new goals for egoic consciousness to pursue.

The First Hemicycle

As noted above, the point at which the principle of multiplicity becomes dominant can be thought of as the point of release of a 'ball of potentiality'. At first, there is little or no objective awareness of the nature of the potentiality – only an instinctive urge or compulsion to act it out. Through this activity, the individual gives form to the potentiality and thus becomes increasingly conscious of it, and at the same time becomes increasingly conscious of their unique individuality. This process continues throughout the first hemicycle, which Rudhyar refers to as the *form-building* or *consciousness-building hemicycle*. The potentiality may acquire form by influencing the formation of any phenomenon, for example: a type of behaviour or character trait; an attitude or viewpoint; a skill or capacity; a work of art; a tangible object; a group or business; or a relationship or family.

Egoic consciousness approaches the form/consciousness-building activity with the agenda of trying to prove that the individual is a self-sufficient, self-contained, autonomous and unique whole in their own right, and views each result as 'my success' or 'my failure'. As consciousness relaxes, there is a lessening of the sense of personal ownership of the power behind the process of manifestation and the forms manifested, and the form/consciousness-building activity becomes more spontaneous, creative and effortless.

The unfoldment of the cycle of being can be observed in the life cycle of a typical annual plant. The principle of multiplicity becomes dominant as the seed shell is split by the emerging shoot. The first hemicycle unfolds during spring and summer, as the potentiality contained within the seed takes shape as a full-grown, seed-laden plant. Just as this growth is driven by forces operating within the plant, so the building of form/consciousness is driven by the potentiality's own momentum, which is experienced by the individual as the power of self-propulsion and self-determination. Rudhyar refers to this as *root power*.

The Second Hemicycle

At the end of the first hemicycle, dominance shifts from the principle of multiplicity to the principle of unity, giving rise to a more encompassing viewpoint. To the extent that the form/consciousness-building activity of the first hemicycle has been fruitful, the emerging quality can now be held in consciousness as an object of reflection; and the individual is able to comprehend the value and meaning of the quality for encompassing wholes and share this understanding with others. Thus, Rudhyar refers to the halfway point as the *point of illumination*, and to the second hemicycle as the *consciousness-developing and spreading hemicycle.* During the second hemicycle, neither the consciousness/form built during the first hemicycle nor the individual's unique character are valued for their own sake, but only for any capacity they have to facilitate the development and spreading of consciousness – i.e. to help realise the potential of some greater whole.

Egoic consciousness approaches the development and spreading of consciousness with the agenda of trying to prove that the individual can function as a cell in the body of an encompassing whole in a spirit of cooperation, mutuality and common purpose, and views each result as 'my success' or 'my failure'. As consciousness relaxes, the individual's contribution to the development and spreading of consciousness becomes more spontaneous, creative and effortless, and the sense of personal investment in the results decreases.

In the life cycle of a typical annual plant, the second hemicycle unfolds during autumn and winter, as the seeds find places within the encompassing ecosystem and prepare for germination, and the biomass of the plant – having served its purpose – is returned to the soil. At the beginning of the first hemicycle, there is only the seed; at the beginning of the second hemicycle, the full-grown plant <u>holds</u> seeds in readiness for their dispersal. Just as the dispersal of the seeds is dependent upon forces operating in the plant's environment, so the development and spreading of consciousness during the second hemicycle is dependent upon socio-cultural dynamics. Rudhyar refers to the power inherent in such dynamics as *seed power.*

The First Quarter

Throughout the first quarter, the principle of multiplicity is dominant and becoming stronger – less compromised by the principle of unity than during any other part of the cycle.

This is the most subjective quarter of the cycle, during which situations are experienced primarily as opportunities or invitations to act out the impulses and emotions arising within. Thus, conditions are right for the potentiality seeking expression through the individual to acquire vivid, original and distinctive form and make its mark on the phenomenal realm, and there is a sense of an abundance of possibilities. There is a tendency to try to ignore or rebel against anything that threatens to compromise freedom of expression (such as practical and cultural constraints, and unresolved issues from the past). The experience of acting as a channel for some vital, creative force infuses the activity with a sense of meaningfulness that is simply self-evident rather than the product of a train of thought.

During the first quarter, egoic consciousness continually seeks reassurance that the individual is sufficiently potent and unique to be a form/consciousness-builder of some significance. Fear of inadequacy in this regard may result in, for example: impatience with obstacles; self-aggrandisement; excessive competitiveness; retreat into an imaginary world where anything is possible; the glamorisation of those who are seen to create or initiate something new and inspiring; and/or preoccupation with other symbols of potency. Egoic consciousness may also recoil from situations that may lead to the individual feeling or appearing impotent and insignificant.

As consciousness relaxes, the process of giving form to emerging potentiality becomes more spontaneous, creative and effortless. The sense of pride in the individual's uniqueness decreases, as does the sense of ownership of the vital force behind the release of potentiality. The compulsion to try to impress and compete with others falls away, and others are encouraged and inspired to celebrate their own uniqueness and act on their own initiative.

In the life cycle of a typical annual plant, the first quarter is the spring phase, during which the emerging shoot grows into a plant and comes into bloom.

The Second Quarter

At the beginning of the second quarter, the dominance of the principle of multiplicity peaks and the polar tide turns in favour of the principle of unity. Throughout this quarter, the principle of multiplicity is dominant but becoming weaker.

During the second quarter, the individual realises that all phenomena coexist as constituent parts of an orderly matrix, which has, for example, a physical, biological, psychological and cultural dimension. The individual realises that the unfoldment of change in the phenomenal realm is subject to various laws, and that each phenomenon is the product of a chain of past events. The individual also realises that to bring the potentiality to fruition, they must take stock of which existing form/consciousness must be discarded, and what new form/consciousness must take shape (both within the individual and in the world around them). Thus, Rudhyar suggests that the turning of the polar tide at the beginning of the second quarter brings about a *crisis in action*. The reorientation that occurs at the beginning of the second quarter has the effect of consolidating the sense of individual wholeness, allowing individual power to be harnessed and focused more effectively.

During the second quarter, egoic consciousness continually seeks reassurance that the individual is able to create and maintain a state of orderly synthesis between those phenomena that are considered important. Fear of inadequacy in this regard may result in, for example: compulsive acquisition of, and attachment to, those resources and skills that seem to enhance one's control over the orderly matrix; resisting the manifestation of forms that are unfamiliar or that threaten to disrupt the status quo; striving to be needed and appreciated by others; trying to coerce others into conformity with a particular system of order; blindly following others' approaches to working with the matrix (especially approaches that have become established traditions); focusing disproportionately on particular features of the matrix; and/or trying to exist within a circumscribed compartment of the matrix within which order seems easier to maintain.

As consciousness relaxes, the individual is better able to build, utilise and discard forms in accordance with the needs of the moment, and to support others in a way that encourages them to explore their own potential for self-sufficiency, productivity, and internal and external integration.

In the life cycle of a typical annual plant, the second quarter is the summer phase, during which the plant fulfils its individual potential by engaging in cross-fertilisation with other plants, then releasing its petals and producing fruit and seeds.

The Third Quarter

Throughout the third quarter, the principle of unity is dominant and becoming stronger – less compromised by the principle of multiplicity than during any other part of the cycle.

As emphasis shifts from multiplicity to unity, awareness of the orderly coexistence of seemingly separate phenomena gives way to awareness of the essential unity of all phenomena. The forms built during the first hemicycle are now seen to be particular expressions of universal (i.e. archetypal) principles, and an understanding of these principles can be shared with others and applied to a variety of subject areas. With the focus on abstract, universal principles, empathy may be lacking, but meeting the needs of individuals may be deemed appropriate as a matter of principle.

For those astrologers who take the peak in emphasis on unity to be the beginning of the cycle of being, this is the final quarter. Indeed, the realisation that all – or a particular group of – phenomena are simply different expressions of common underlying principles can give rise to a sense of completion or return.

During the third quarter, egoic consciousness continually seeks reassurance that the individual is able to comprehend underlying principles, achieve shared understanding with others, and contribute something of value to the ongoing development of their community. Fear of inadequacy in this regard may result in, for example: clinging to the belief that one's current understanding is already complete; embracing the thoughts of others too readily; affecting a pretence of shared understanding and willingness to cooperate; and/or relying too heavily on rigid notions of what constitutes a reasonable (i.e. ethical and/or logical) standpoint or course of action.

As consciousness relaxes, it is seen that shared understanding is an ever-present possibility by virtue of the essential unity – and thus unanimity – of all beings. The individual becomes more open to new understanding but does not crave it, and is better able to strike a balance between guiding others towards clearer understanding, and encouraging them to think for themselves.

In the life cycle of a typical annual plant, the third quarter is the autumn phase, during which seeds are disseminated and the biomass of the plant is returned to the soil. At this time, the benefits of collaboration are seen in the bountiful harvest. Food is prepared according to the values and traditions of the culture in which it is consumed, whether the culture is based on familial, regional, racial and/or ideological commonality. Similarly, the consciousness that has taken shape during the first hemicycle is now developed and shared according to the values and traditions of the collective concerned.

The Fourth Quarter

At the beginning of the fourth quarter, the strength of the principle of unity peaks and the polar tide turns in favour of the principle of multiplicity. Throughout this quarter, the principle of unity is dominant but becoming weaker.

As the polar tide turns, the personal viewpoint of the individual acquires renewed significance. They ask: "Is this experience of connectedness truly meaningful to me? Is it real for me?", and some or all of their current values and allegiances may begin to feel futile. Thus, Rudhyar suggests that the turning of the polar tide at the beginning of the fourth quarter brings about a *crisis in consciousness*. This reorientation enables the individual to act as a more effective focus for the power inherent in encompassing wholes. On the one hand, this heightens powers of seduction and influence; on the other hand, it renders the individual more susceptible to taking on the unfinished business of their family, community, nation, race, etc. – i.e. more susceptible to being cast in the role of redeemer, martyr or scapegoat. While the sense of connectedness that arises in the third quarter is relatively impersonal, that which arises in the fourth quarter is more empathic.

Of the two schools of thought discussed above, one takes this to be the final quarter of the cycle of being, while the other takes it to be the first quarter. Indeed, the relinquishing of outmoded values and allegiances is experienced as a time of both closure and renewal.

During the first and third quarters of the cycle of being, there is strong emphasis on the expression of the dominant principle, but during the second and fourth quarters, the two principles operate in a more integrated manner. During the second quarter, there is sense of being a distinct entity (multiplicity) bound in a state of coexistence with other entities (unity). During the fourth quarter, the oneness of all (unity) is experienced from a unique, personal standpoint (multiplicity).

During the fourth quarter, egoic consciousness continually seeks reassurance that the individual will not become alienated from the larger life. Fear of alienation is likely to result in, for example: craving and idealising that which provides a sense of belonging; trying to instil a sense of dependency in others; and/or retreating into a fantasy world in search of a less precarious experience of connectedness. Egoic consciousness may also believe that alienation is inevitable due to alleged flaws in the individual and/or the prejudices of others.

The susceptibility of egoic consciousness to the experience of guilt – and its propensity to try to induce guilt in others – seems to increase throughout the cycle of being. During the first quarter, this is minimal, for the individual simply wishes to get on with expressing their own uniqueness. During the second quarter, awareness of the orderly matrix gives rise to the notion of responsibility and the need to impose order. During the third quarter, awareness of ideals and the potential for unity gives rise to the need to uphold principles and create harmony. During the fourth quarter, the individual psyche is porous to the needs of others and the needs of encompassing wholes, and fears alienation.

As consciousness relaxes, it is seen that true peace and fulfilment arise through the relinquishing of outmoded values and allegiances, and through identification with larger, more inclusive wholes. The individual becomes a more effective ambassador for the universal whole, able to see what an individual or collective must relinquish in order to open to a more intimate and fruitful connection with source. They are able to offer reassurance to others that such a path, while it may seem daunting, brings an increasing sense of fulfilment and the lessening of unnecessary suffering.

In the life cycle of a typical annual plant, the fourth quarter is the winter phase, during which seeds swell, seed-shells soften, and various chemical processes occur prior to germination. It is interesting to note that just as the seeds of some species of plant will not germinate unless they have been exposed to cold, so in order to continue to grow, we may sometimes have to relinquish the feeling of warmth provided by identification with a relationship or group.

If outmoded values and allegiances are not relinquished during the fourth quarter, then 'unfinished business' is carried into the next unfoldment of the cycle. Any issues and attachments that are not laid to rest during the fourth quarter can at least be acknowledged and accepted so that they can be worked with in a more conscious and creative manner in the future.

The Polar Hemicycles

This section discusses the hemicycles that begin and end at a pole. Throughout a *polar hemicycle*, one principle becomes stronger, while its polar-opposite becomes weaker.

Throughout the hemicycle that consists of the fourth and first quarters, emphasis on multiplicity increases, emphasising the individual's unique viewpoint and encouraging diversification. During the fourth quarter – throughout which the principle of unity is dominant – diversification is facilitated by the tendency to question one's existing values and allegiances. During the first quarter – throughout which the principle of multiplicity is dominant – diversification is facilitated by obliviousness to, or a tendency to rebel against, limits and constraints.

In the life cycle of a typical annual plant, this hemicycle unfolds during winter and spring. At the beginning of this hemicycle, the seed has been dispersed and is lying dormant; and at the end, the plant is in full bloom.

Throughout the hemicycle that consists of the second and third quarters, emphasis on unity increases, encouraging the *organ*-isation of a whole's constituent parts, and heightening awareness of consensus reality. During the second quarter – throughout which the principle of multiplicity is dominant – organisation is facilitated by pragmatic understanding of how seemingly distinct phenomena coexist. During the third quarter – throughout which the principle of unity is dominant – organisation is facilitated by abstract understanding of universal principles.

In the life cycle of a typical annual plant, this hemicycle unfolds during summer and autumn. During this hemicycle, the flowers and then the rest of the plant are returned to the earth, and the genetic coding (i.e. the set of organising principles) that will direct the development of future plants is encapsulated within seeds and dispersed.

****

It should be noted that Rudhyar sometimes correlates the cycle of being with the life cycle of a typical annual plant in an alternative manner, correlating the halfway point of the cycle of being with the plant coming into bloom, and correlating the second hemicycle not only with the dispersal of seeds but also with their formation.

The approach adopted in this book is congruous with the fact that a typical annual plant flowers around the end of spring and beginning of summer, with the seeds ready for dispersal around the end of summer and beginning of autumn. Thus, the transition from germinating seed to blossoming flower is correlated with the initial realisation of individual uniqueness (first quarter). The initiation of cross-fertilisation is correlated with the realisation that this uniqueness can be meaningfully expressed only in relation to a greater whole (beginning of the second quarter). The production of seeds – which occurs <u>within the plant</u> – is correlated with the final part of the form/consciousness-building hemicycle (second quarter). And the point at which the seeds and fruit are fully formed and ready for dispersal is correlated with the point of illumination – the conscious realisation of the nature and purpose of the potentiality (end of the first hemicycle).

Experiencing the Cycle of Being

In the psyche of each individual, countless cycles of being are continuously unfolding. Each astrologically significant celestial cycle, and each of its progressed and directed reiterations, corresponds to a cycle of being unfolding not only at the fundamental frequency, but also at each higher harmonic frequency. Each of these cycles enters into awareness only intermittently – if at all – and even then, always entwined with many others. However, cycles of being also arise in the individual psyche independently of any celestial cycle, and some of these can remain at the forefront of awareness throughout a complete unfoldment.

In the breathing cycle, for example, emphasis on multiplicity increases during the inhalation of air into the body, and emphasis on unity increases during the exhalation of air into the surrounding environment. Thus, a pole is reached as inhalation gives way to exhalation, and vice versa, and a point of equilibrium is reached midway through inhalation and exhalation.

Inhalation (the fourth and first quarters of the cycle of being) engenders a sense of being the locus of a unique viewpoint, while exhalation (second and third quarters) engenders a sense of operating within a consensus reality. Relative fullness (first hemicycle) engenders a sense of independence from one's environment, while relative emptiness (second hemicycle) engenders a sense of dependence upon, and connection with, one's environment.

The last half of inhalation (the first quarter of the cycle of being) engenders a sense of self-assurance and entitlement. The first half of exhalation (second quarter) engenders awareness that, as a distinct organism, one is still part of an encompassing matrix. The last half of exhalation (third quarter) engenders willingness to surrender to unity and unanimity. The first half of inhalation (fourth quarter) engenders awareness that the continuation of 'me and my viewpoint' is dependent upon sustainment by the environment.

The assimilation of a new idea into one's consciousness may also unfold as a perceptible cycle of being. During the first quarter, the possibility of new understanding becomes apparent, and the mind seizes upon this with enthusiasm. During the second quarter, the new idea and one's existing understanding are subjected to pragmatic scrutiny, and anything that does not seem to make sense is discarded. During the third quarter, the new idea is understood in terms of abstract principles, and parallels with other pieces of understanding may become apparent, perhaps leading to a sense of completeness of understanding. However, the potential clarity and objectivity of the third quarter may be undermined by enthusiasm for building new concepts. During the fourth quarter, it is realised that one's understanding is still incomplete, perhaps giving rise to disappointment and a sense of being in limbo. There is heightened awareness of which ideas need to be discarded or looked at more deeply; and if such issues are not dealt with, a gnawing sense of doubt lingers on into the future. However, the fourth quarter also brings greater openness to inspiration from beyond the realm of conscious thought – the emergence of such inspiration marking the beginning of a new cycle.

The Cycle of Being and the Relaxation of Consciousness

In an attempt to minimise anxiety, egoic consciousness tries to reconcile the need to experience autonomy and specialness with the polar-opposite need to experience a sense of belonging and relatedness. Thus, the individual may try to be a special member – perhaps a leader – of one or more collectives, or may fixate on the alleged specialness of collectives that they identify with. However, true peace and fulfilment can only arise to the extent that both individualistic and collectivistic egoic striving fall away.

As a cycle of being unfolds in a particular context, emphasis on multiplicity highlights and exposes individualistic striving, and at the same time provides distance from – and thus leverage against – collectivistic striving. Similarly, emphasis on unity highlights and exposes collectivistic striving, and at the same time provides distance from – and thus leverage against – individualistic striving. Thus, each unfoldment of a cycle of being within the individual psyche facilitates the observation and relinquishment of individualistic and collectivistic egoic striving.

By simply focusing awareness on the body, we can allow each unfoldment of the breathing cycle to act as a vehicle for the relaxation of consciousness. During activities such as yoga, general stretching, guided relaxation or simply witnessing the breathing cycle, we are better able to notice tension in the body-mind during inhalation, and better able to release this tension during exhalation.

The Relaxation of Consciousness and the Path of Human Development

Rudhyar* describes the broad developmental path of a human being as a process of being centred in each of four levels of functioning in turn, in the following order: At the *biological level*, a human being functions instinctively according to their biological programming. At the *social level*, a human being functions as a person and seeks a sense of meaning, purpose and identity in the stories,† symbols and rituals of the collectives to which they belong. At the *individual level*, the sense of identity, meaning and purpose becomes free of cultural conditioning. At the *transpersonal level*, there is awareness of the unity of all, and thus freedom from identification with the human form; and there is a willingness to serve as a (still unique) vehicle for bringing the potential inherent in encompassing wholes to fruition.

As this process unfolds, both the way the individual expresses their unique nature, and the way the individual collaborates with others, become more spontaneous and creative, and the sense that self-expression and collaboration are polar-opposites falls away.

Egoic consciousness emerges during the transition from the biological to the social level of functioning, much of which occurs during childhood. With this transition comes increased capacity to blossom as a unique individual and to collaborate creatively with others. However, at the social level of functioning, the individual compulsively employs rebellion and conformity as survival strategies, and exists in a state of tension between the two.

During the transition from social to individual functioning, the individual's self-expression and collective participation become still more spontaneous and creative. Now that neither biological anxiety nor social anxiety have centre stage, the individual experiences a sense of liberation, but the consciousness arising in the individual is still contracted around a sense of identification with a particular body-mind. Thus, true peace and fulfilment cannot be experienced.

Relaxation into a state of true peace and fulfilment comes only with the consecration of the self to the larger life – the shift to the transpersonal level of functioning.

---

* See, for example, *Beyond Individualism* (1979) Khaldea.com/rudhyar/

† Myths, religious teachings, social discourses, scientific theories, etc. are all examples of such stories.

CHAPTER THREE

HARMONICS IN ASTROLOGY

This chapter looks at the ways in which harmonic theory is currently used in astrology: the interpretation of aspects and zodiacal position, and the analysis of research data.

Harmonics and Sub-harmonics

As noted in Chapter 2, harmonics is concerned with the way that a cycle can unfold at different frequencies simultaneously. At each of these frequencies, the cycle unfolds a whole number of times over a given period: once at the 1H (or fundamental) frequency, twice at the 2H frequency, and so on. Consequently, the wavelength of the 2H is one-half that of the 1H, the wavelength of the 3H is one-third that of the 1H, and so on.

Since the frequency of the 4H is double that of the 2H, the 4H may be referred to as the *2nd sub-harmonic* of the 2H (2 x 2 = 4). As another example, the 6H is the 2nd sub-harmonic of the 3H (3 x 2 = 6) and the 3rd sub-harmonic of the 2H (2 x 3 = 6). From this point, *2nd sub-harmonic* is abbreviated to *2SH*, *3rd sub-harmonic* is abbreviated to *3SH*, and so on.

Aspects and Harmonics

As noted in Chapter 1, two factors form a perfect aspect when their celestial longitudes differ by a factor* of 360° or by a multiple of a factor of 360°. Consequently, some astrologers have suggested that the significance of these angular relationships may be founded upon the existence of harmonic waves. Whether or not this is the case, harmonic theory provides an invaluable framework for working with aspects.

---

* In this book, the word *factor* is underlined when used as a mathematical term; e.g. 2 is a factor of 4.

Since a perfect sextile spans 60° of celestial longitude ($^{1}/_{6}$ of 360°), it may be referred to as a *6H aspect*, and a sextile between two factors shows that the relationship between the corresponding functions is imbued with the qualities of the number six. Because 60° is equal to $^{2}/_{12}$ of 360°, the sextile is also a 12H aspect; and because 60° is equal to $^{3}/_{18}$ of 360°, the sextile is also an 18H aspect, and so on. (Note that the 12H and 18H are sub-harmonics of the 6H.)

An *aspect configuration* is formed when three or more factors are all linked to one another by aspects that have a particular harmonic in common. In each case, the configuration is named after the lowest-numbered harmonic that is common to all of the aspects involved. For example, a 6H configuration is comprised solely of 6H aspects – the conjunction ($^{6}/_{6}$), opposition ($^{3}/_{6}$), trine ($^{2}/_{6}$) and sextile ($^{1}/_{6}$) – including at least one sextile.

When noting aspect configurations, the conventional approach is to include only celestial bodies. However, the involvement of a nodal axis with an aspect configuration is significant, especially when the nodal axis concerned is the horizon axis or the meridian axis.

Aspect configurations are also formed across two or more patterns. For example, if two factors that form an opposition aspect in one pattern are each in square aspect to a factor in another pattern, then a 4H configuration is formed across the two patterns.

On the chart shown on pages 265 and 266, Mercury, Venus, Mars and Uranus form a 12H configuration; Mercury, Venus and Saturn form another 12H configuration; and Mercury, Mars and Saturn form another. These five planets may be considered to form a single 12H configuration if orbs of just over 3° are allowed for the Venus-Mars semi-sextile and the Saturn-Uranus quincunx. Even if an astrologer does not usually allow such orbs for these aspects, they may do so in this case because Venus and Mars each make more exact 12H aspects to the other three planets; and the same may be said of Saturn and Uranus. In the same chart, the Sun, Venus and Uranus form an 8H configuration.

The interpretation of aspect configurations can be daunting. Students are often taught to focus first on the personal planets and those aspects that are closest to exact. In some cases, the astrologer may find it easier to note the number on which each type of aspect is based, and look at each type in numerical order, thus beginning with the most fundamental type of relationship.

Aspects and the Twelve-sign Zodiac

The division of the chart wheel into twelve zodiacal signs highlights the presence of 12H aspects: the conjunction ($^{12}/_{12}$), opposition ($^{6}/_{12}$), trine ($^{4}/_{12}$), square ($^{3}/_{12}$), sextile ($^{2}/_{12}$), semi-sextile ($^{1}/_{12}$) and quincunx ($^{5}/_{12}$). Since the semi-sextile aspect spans one sign-length, the sextile aspect spans two sign-lengths, etc., it is easy to see whether two factors are forming a 12H aspect by noting the sign and degree of each factor (see Figure 3.1).

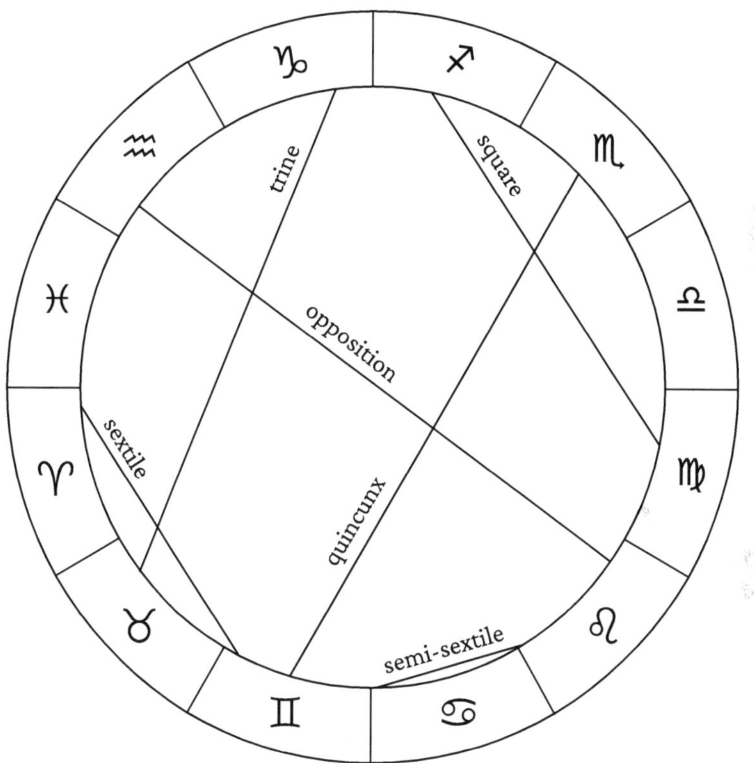

Figure 3.1 An example of each 12H aspect (other than the conjunction) on a twelve-sign zodiacal wheel

A factor near the end of a sign may form a 12H aspect with a factor near the beginning of the same or a different sign. For example, a semi-sextile may be formed between two factors positioned at the beginning and end of the same sign; and a sextile may be formed between a factor at the end of Aries and a factor at the beginning of Capricorn. In such cases, the aspect type does not match the geometric relationship between the signs involved, and the aspect is referred to as an *out of sign aspect* or a *dissociate aspect.*

Other commonly used aspects – such as the quintile and biquintile (5H aspects), aspects from the septile series (7H aspects), the semisquare and sesquiquadrate (8H aspects), and aspects from the novile series (9H aspects) – are more difficult to spot because their root numbers are not factors of twelve. Some or all of these aspects, along with the 12H aspects, are typically shown by lines drawn from one factor to another in the central area of a chart. These lines are often colour-coded to distinguish between aspect types, with closer and wider aspects represented, respectively, by thicker and thinner lines. As long as the maximum orbs allowed are not too great, and as long as aspect lines are not drawn to too many factors, all of these aspect types can usually be shown on a chart without the central area becoming too crowded.

However, as the number of aspect types increases, these aspect lines become increasingly difficult to read, with each pair of factors eventually seen to form aspects of different types simultaneously. To solve this problem, a chart can be redrawn using a number of *higher harmonic zodiacs.* The result is a series of *higher harmonic charts,* each of which highlights a different group of aspect types.

Higher Harmonic Charts

To see how a higher harmonic chart is created and used, we will use the 5H chart as an example. Figure 3.2 shows the 1H of a zodiac against the five occurrences of the zodiac's 5H, each of which is divided into the twelve zodiacal signs. One of the factors shown has a 1H zodiacal position of 9°00 ♒ and a 5H zodiacal position of 15°00 ♋, while the other factor has a 1H zodiacal position of 27°00 ♉ and a 5H zodiacal position of 15°00 ♑.

Figure 3.3 shows the 5H chart wheel, which is formed by superimposing the 5H zodiacs onto one another and stretching them to form a circle. Thus, the 5H chart wheel represents all five 5H zodiacs simultaneously, and each point on this wheel simultaneously represents five equally spaced lines of celestial longitude. For example, the first point of Aries on the 5H chart wheel represents the lines of absolute celestial longitude 0°, 72°, 144°, 216° and 288°.

On the 5H chart wheel, the two factors are shown as forming a perfect opposition aspect. Since the opposition is based on the division of the circle by two, an opposition aspect on a 5H chart wheel signifies a 10H aspect (because the 10H is the 5SH of the 2H). In fact, the difference between the celestial longitude of the factors is 108° and the factors are forming a perfect tridecile aspect ($^{3}/_{10}$).

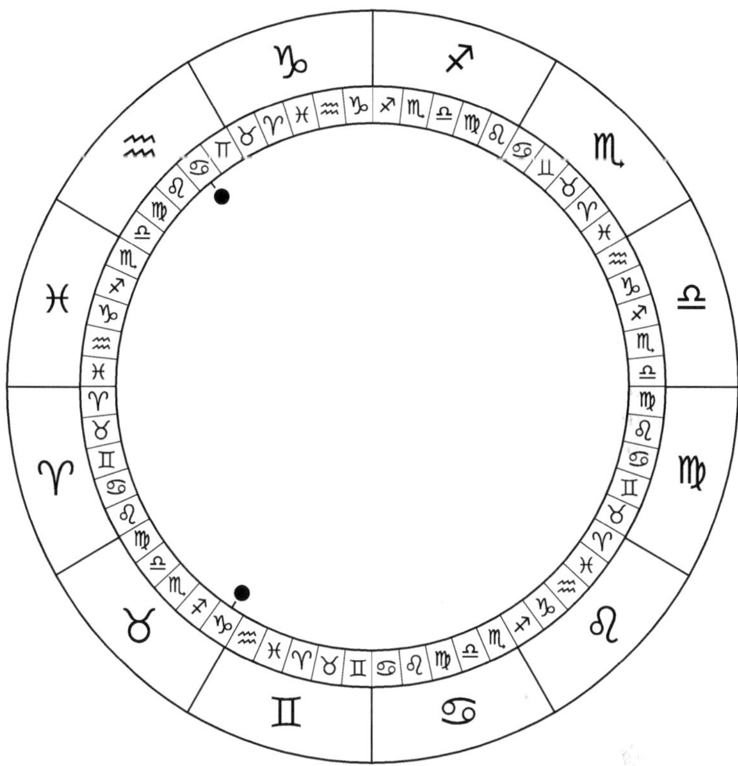

Figure 3.2 The 1H and 5H of a twelve-sign zodiac

Decile ($^{1}/_{10}$), tridecile ($^{3}/_{10}$) and opposition ($^{5}/_{10}$) aspects all appear on the 5H chart as oppositions. The other 10H aspects – the conjunction, quintile and biquintile – are also 5H aspects and therefore appear on the 5H chart as conjunctions.

A 1H zodiacal sign position can be converted to a higher harmonic zodiacal position in the following way: First, the position of the factor is expressed as the arc-length measured anticlockwise along the chart wheel from the first point of Aries to the factor. Figure 1.5 (page 9) can be used to determine this arc-length, regardless of which zodiac is being used. Second, this value is multiplied by the number of the harmonic for which the zodiacal position is sought. Third, 360° is repeatedly subtracted from this value (if necessary) until a value between 0° and 360° is obtained. Fourth, this value is expressed as a value between 0° and 30° of a particular sign. (Again, Figure 1.5 can be used for this conversion.)

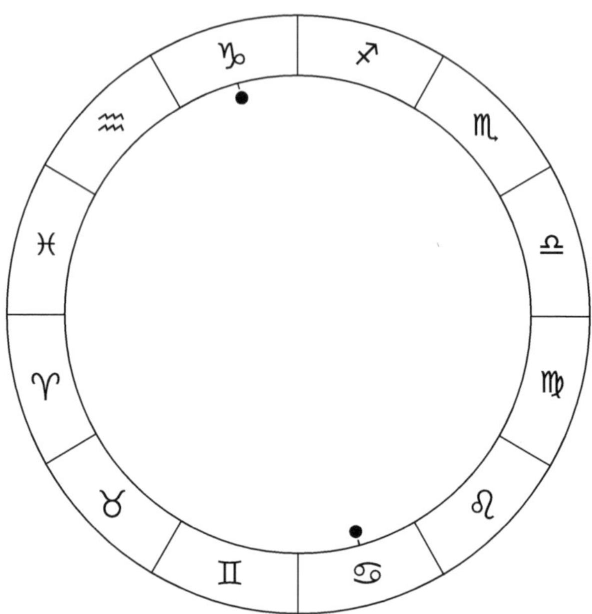

Figure 3.3 The placements shown in Figure 3.2 as they appear on the 5H chart wheel

We can illustrate this using the above example of a factor with 1H zodiacal position 9° ♒. Since there are ten signs prior to Aquarius, the first point of Aquarius is 300° (10 x 30°) east of the first point of Aries, and so 9° ♒ is 309° from the first point of Aries. 309° x 5 = 1545°, and 1545° - (4 x 360°) = 105°, so the factor is 105° east of the first point of Aries on the 5H chart wheel. The first point of Cancer is 90° from the first point of Aries; thus, the 5H zodiacal sign position of the factor is 15°00 ♋ (105° - 90° = 15°).

The higher harmonic positions of the ascendant and midheaven are usually indicated on a higher harmonic chart due to the significance of aspects formed between these points and other factors. On any odd-numbered harmonic chart, the ascendant and descendant remain opposite one another, as do the midheaven and lower heaven. On any even-numbered harmonic chart, the ascendant and descendant occupy the same point on the chart wheel, as do the midheaven and lower heaven (because an opposition aspect appears as a conjunction on any even-numbered harmonic chart).

The higher harmonic positions of the house cusps do not proceed in numerical order around a higher harmonic chart wheel, and so it is not possible to reconstruct the diurnal wheel on a higher harmonic chart. Some astrologers draw Equal House or Whole Sign cusps on the higher harmonic chart wheel, using the higher harmonic zodiacal position of the ascendant to define the positions of the house cusps.

On a 5H chart, expressions of pure five-ness are shown by conjunctions, quintiles and biquintiles. (A 5H aspect appears on a 5H chart as a conjunction, while a 25H aspect that is not also a 5H aspect appears as a quintile or biquintile.) Similarly, on a 7H chart, expressions of pure seven-ness are shown by conjunctions, septiles, bi-septiles and tri-septiles. (A 7H aspect appears on 7H chart as a conjunction, while a 49H aspect that is not also a 7H aspect appears as a septile, bi-septile or tri-septile.)

Because 9 is a power of 3 ($9 = 3^2$), nine-ness is an expression of a certain order of pure three-ness, as are twenty seven-ness ($27 = 3^3$) and eighty one-ness ($81 = 3^4$). On a 9H chart, a 9H aspect appears as a conjunction, while a 27H aspect that is not also a 9H aspect appears as a trine, and an 81H aspect that is not also a 27H aspect appears as a novile, bi-novile or quadri-novile (a tri-novile being a trine.)

In order to avoid being overwhelmed or distracted by the large numbers of aspects that a series of higher harmonic charts reveals, the astrologer must be selective about which higher harmonic charts are used. If the goal of interpretation is such that a particular harmonic seems especially pertinent, the astrologer may wish to interpret the chart for that harmonic in some detail. However, where a series of higher harmonic charts are to be considered alongside the 1H chart, it is advisable to focus solely on any strong aspect configurations found within any of the charts.

Aspect Orbs

The majority of astrologers sort aspects into groups, giving the same orb allowance to all aspects in a particular group. In some cases, the sole criterion for belonging to a group may be that the number on which the aspect is based falls within a certain range, as when the same orb is used for the conjunction, opposition, trine and square (based on numbers 1, 2, 3 and 4, respectively). However, because two-ness lends itself to obvious manifestation, aspects based on an even number are often allowed larger orbs. Thus, the conjunction, opposition and square may be grouped together and allowed a larger orb than the trine; the sextile (6) is usually allowed a larger orb than the quintile (5); and the semi-sextile and quincunx (12) are often allowed larger orbs than aspects from the quintile (5), septile (7) and/or novile (9) series.

John Addey,* pioneer in the field of harmonic astrology, suggested that the appropriate maximum orb for each type of aspect is inversely proportional to the number on which it is based. For example, if a 10° orb is allowed for a conjunction aspect (1), then 5° would be the maximum orb for an opposition ($^1/_2$), 3°20' would be the maximum orb for a trine ($^1/_3$), and so on. However, the grouping approach outlined in the previous paragraph remains by far the most commonly used.

It should be noted that the orb allowed for a given aspect type varies according to the technique being used. For example, the orb allowed for a given aspect type in synastry (e.g. inter-chart aspects and aspects in composite and Davidson charts) is smaller than that allowed for aspects between factors in a natal chart.

Aspect Orbs and Higher Harmonic Charts

Once the maximum orb for an aspect has been decided, the astrologer uses this limit every time the aspect appears in any harmonic chart. On the 5H chart, the opposition represents the decile, tridecile and quindecile – aspects based on too high a harmonic to be allowed an 8° orb. However, because the 5H zodiac spans only 72° of celestial longitude and has been stretched to five times this arc to form a 360° circle, the orb of the opposition shown on the 5H chart is five times larger than the actual orb of the decile, tridecile or quindecile. Thus, an opposition with an orb of 8° on a 5H chart represents a decile, tridecile or quindecile with an orb of $^8/_5$° (i.e. 1.6° or 1° 36').

If two factors form a conjunction with an orb of 5° on the 1H chart, they are separated by 25° on the 5H chart wheel. The fact that the factors form a conjunction on the 1H chart shows that they are attuned to one another at the level of one-ness. However, although the conjunction is also a 5H aspect, the fact that the factors do not form a conjunction on the 5H chart shows that the conjunction is not exact enough for them to also be attuned to one another at the level of five-ness.

---

* *Harmonics in Astrology* (2009) p. 131. (1st ed. 1976)

Modulus

The *modulus* of a harmonic is equal to 360° divided by the number of the harmonic. For example, the modulus of the 5H is 72° because this is $^1/_5$ of 360°. A *modulus strip* is a straight line that represents all occurrences of the harmonic concerned simultaneously. A modulus strip is marked from 0° to the modulus value (rather than to 360°); thus, when two factors are separated by 1° on a modulus strip, they are forming an aspect of the harmonic concerned with an actual orb of 1°.

Figure 3.4 shows the 30° and 45° degree modulus strips for the chart shown on pages 265 and 266. The modulus of the 12H is 30°, and we can see that the 12H configuration in this chart shows up on the 30° modulus strip as the clustering together of Mercury, Venus, Mars, Saturn and Uranus. The modulus of the 8H is 45°, and we can see that the 8H configuration in the chart shows up on the 45° modulus strip as the clustering together of Venus, Uranus and the Sun.

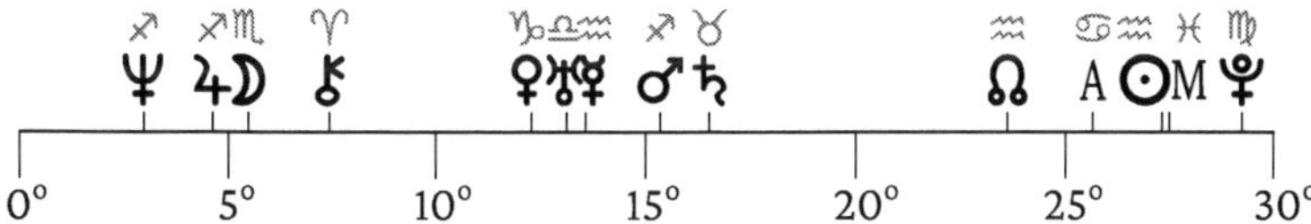

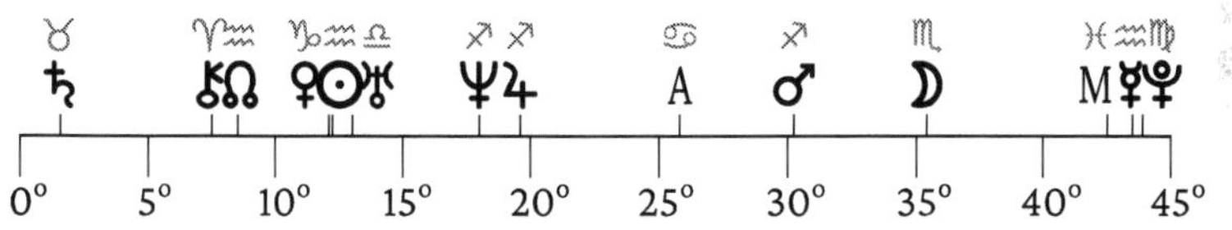

Figure 3.4 The 30° and 45° modulus strips for the chart shown on pages 265 and 266

On the 30° modulus strip, Mercury and Uranus are each a similar distance from Saturn. However, because the square is allowed a larger orb than the quincunx, the Mercury Saturn square is reasonably close, whereas the Saturn Uranus quincunx is wide. By including the 1H zodiacal sign of each factor, the aspect made between any two factors can be seen (unless a modulus of less than 30° is used). For example, if the 1H zodiacal sign placements were not given, the 45° modulus strip would show only that Mercury and Pluto are forming an 8H aspect, but because we can see that

Pluto is in Virgo and Mercury is in Aquarius, we know that this aspect is a waxing sesquiquadrate.

Note that the Mercury-Saturn square shows up on both strips because the square is both an 8H aspect and a 12H aspect. (Mercury is near the end of the 45° modulus strip while Saturn is at the beginning, but the first and last points on the strip each represent the same eight lines of celestial longitude.)

The equivalent modulus strips of two or more charts can be displayed alongside one another; or factors from all of the charts can be placed on one strip, with glyphs from each chart shown in a different colour, or glyphs from one chart placed above the strip and glyphs from a second chart placed below it. This can help the astrologer to see aspects and aspect configurations that involve factors in more than one chart.

On a graphic ephemeris (see Figure 1.16 and Figure 1.21 on pages 31 and 36), the degrees of a modulus strip are marked on the vertical axis, and time is marked along the horizontal axis. Each non-moving factor shown – such as a natal factor – appears on the graph as a horizontal line. Each moving factor shown – such as a transiting, progressed or directed factor – is shown by a line that slopes upwards and/or downwards, periodically leaving the graph at the top or bottom and immediately re-entering at the bottom or top, respectively.

The perfection of an aspect is shown by the intersection of two lines, with the glyph for the type of aspect usually shown at the point of intersection. In this way, each graphic ephemeris shows all – and only – those aspects that are multiples of the modulus used (i.e. aspects of the corresponding harmonic). For example, a graphic ephemeris that uses a 30° modulus shows all – and only – 12H aspects.

On a graphic ephemeris drawn to the appropriate modulus, a natal configuration shows as a cluster of horizontal lines. The intersection of a sloping line with this cluster shows that a moving factor has temporarily joined with the configuration. For example, an 8H configuration in a natal chart appears as a cluster of horizontal lines on a 45° graphic ephemeris, and this cluster is crossed by the sloping line of a moving factor each time the factor temporarily joins the natal configuration. A 22.5° graphic ephemeris would show when a moving factor forms a 16H configuration with the factors in the natal 8H configuration. As another example, a strong 4H configuration in the 7H chart discloses the presence of a significant 28H configuration (7 x 4 = 28). A 12°51'25" (360° ÷ 28) graphic ephemeris would show when moving factors join with this configuration.

Because midpoints seem much more responsive to aspects based on powers of two (1, 2, 4, 8, etc.), it may be useful to add the most important natal midpoints to graphic ephemerides, using a modulus equal to 360° divided by a power of 2 (360°, 180°, 90°, 45°, etc.).

Tracking the General Strength of a Harmonic

Rather than limiting their attention to higher harmonic charts and graphic ephemerides, some astrologers consult graphs that show fluctuations in the general strength of a harmonic. Each graph shows changes in the number of aspects being formed between the factors selected by the astrologer. For example, a graph that shows fluctuations in the number of 49H aspects formed between the factors gives an indication of changes in the strength of pure seven-ness. The capacity to produce such graphs is a feature of some astrological software programs (for example, Sirius).

Zodiacal Placement in Higher Harmonic Charts

While some astrologers believe that a factor's zodiacal position in a higher harmonic chart is a meaningful significator in its own right, others do not. According to the harmonic model of segmentation introduced in the previous chapter, higher harmonic zodiacal position *is* meaningful (see Chapter 4). This being the case, just as the meaning of a square aspect in a 5H chart combines the meaning of the number 5 with the meaning of the square aspect, so the meaning of Sun in Capricorn in a 5H chart combines the meaning of the number 5 with the meaning of Sun in Capricorn.

As with the interpretation of aspects, it is easy to become overwhelmed or distracted when looking at zodiacal positions in a number of higher harmonic charts. Thus, where a series of higher harmonic charts are to be considered, it is advisable to focus solely on instances of a strong emphasis by sign, element, mode, etc. found within any of the charts.

Harmonics and Astrological Research

Some astrologers (and some non-astrologers) have become involved in statistical research in an effort to improve understanding of astrology or to test its validity. Much of this research involves gathering the birth data of a group of people who have something in common (such as a character trait, vocation, physical or psychological condition, or type of achievement). A celestial cycle is divided into stages, and the proportion of the sample group born during each stage is compared to the proportion of a control group born during that stage. This gives an idea of how the likelihood of having the trait, etc. varies according to which stage of the celestial cycle was unfolding at birth.

Let us suppose, for example, that a researcher has collected the birth data of 3,600 people, all of whom have in common a particular trait, and the birth data of a control group. Let us also suppose that the researcher has chosen to divide the lunation cycle into 72 stages, each covering 5° of celestial longitude. If 1.5% of births in the control group occurred at stage 37 of the cycle, we would expect to find that 54 (1.5% of 3,600) of the sample group were born at this stage. If 61 members of the sample group were born at this stage, then the deviation from expected results is approximately +13% (61 is approximately 113% of 54).

In many research studies of this type, when the results for each stage are plotted on a line graph, the line is seen to rise and fall a number of times in a seemingly irregular manner. By subjecting results to harmonic analysis, John Addey discovered that such irregular waveforms are typically a composite of a number of regular waves, and that each of these regular waves has a wavelength that is a factor of 360°.

Now let us suppose that we are analysing the results of the hypothetical research mentioned above and wish to look for a 6H fluctuation in the deviation from expected results. To do this we must re-organise and re-plot the data so that any 6H fluctuation is highlighted. The 6H undergoes six complete oscillations during the unfoldment of the cycle, with each unfoldment occurring over a span of 60° of celestial longitude. If there is a 6H oscillation in the deviation from expected results, then the peak of this oscillation will recur at intervals of twelve stages (5° per stage x 12 stages = 60°), as will the trough, the ascending node and the descending node. Thus, to look for a 6H fluctuation, the stages would be divided into twelve groups, each consisting of six equally spaced stages (the first group consisting of stages 1, 13, 25, 37, 49 and 61; the second group consisting of stages 2, 14, 26, 38, 50 and 62, and so on). For each group of stages, the total number of people from the sample group can be compared to the total number of people from the control group to find the deviation from expected results.

If the deviation for each group were to be plotted on a new graph, a 6H fluctuation would be appear as a waveform that unfolds once across the graph. A 12H fluctuation would be shown as a twofold cycle of rising and falling across the graph because the 12H has a wavelength of 30° of celestial longitude, and so unfolds twice in each 60° span of celestial longitude. Similarly, an 18H oscillation would be shown on this graph as a triple wave. Any fluctuation other than the 6H or a sub-harmonic of the 6H would be cancelled out by grouping the stages in this way.

In order to exclude any 6H fluctuation and show more clearly any 12H fluctuation, the stages could be reorganised so that the stages of each group begin at intervals of 30° of celestial longitude (the first group consisting of stages 1, 7, 13, 19..., the second group consisting of stages 2, 8, 14, 20...., and so on). This graph would also exclude any 18H oscillation, for the 18H is not a sub-harmonic of the 12H; but the graph would reveal any 24H oscillation as a double wave, and any 36H oscillation as a triple wave.

The number of stages into which a cycle is divided determines which harmonics can be discerned without the aid of a computer. Dividing the cycle into 72 stages, for example, allows the 2H, 3H, 4H, 6H, 8H, 9H, 12H, 18H, 24H and 36H be highlighted using the method outlined here, because the numbers 2, 3, 4, 6, 8, 9, 12, 18, 24 and 36 are all factors of 72. To highlight any 36H oscillation, the stages would be grouped into just two groups – one group consisting of the odd-numbered stages and the other consisting of the even-numbered stages. To highlight any 2H oscillation, the stages would be grouped into 36 groups, the first group consisting of stages 1 and 37; the second group consisting of stages 2 and 38, and so on.

Having isolated a harmonic, the researcher is interested primarily in two things. One is the amplitude of the waveform (recorded as a percentage deviation from expected results), which shows the statistical significance of the deviation. The other is the position of the waveform relative to the some reference point on the celestial sphere. This is often recorded as the waveform's *peak phase angle.*

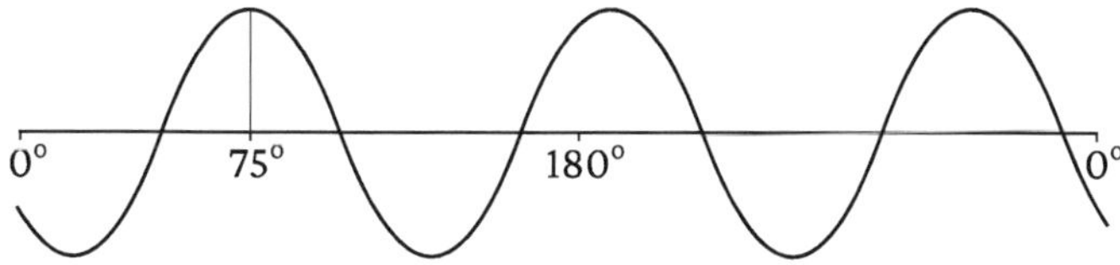

Figure 3.5 A 3H waveform with a peak phase angle of 225°

Figure 3.5 shows a 3H waveform unfolding three times during a single unfoldment of a celestial cycle. Each point marked 0° could also be marked 360° and would refer, for example, to the perfection of the conjunction in a synodic cycle or the first point of Aries in a zodiacal cycle. We can see that the first peak occurs 75° after the beginning of the cycle, which is $^{5}/_{8}$ of its wavelength (120° ÷ 75° = $^{5}/_{8}$). The peak phase angle of the waveform is this fraction expressed as a portion of 360°, which in this case is 225° (360° x $^{5}/_{8}$ = 225°).

Some of the implications of Addey's findings for our understanding of astrology are discussed in Chapter 4.

CHAPTER FOUR

A HARMONIC MODEL OF SEGMENTATION

This chapter discusses the harmonic model of segmentation introduced in Chapter 2, and considers how it might contribute to the development of a more unified understanding of astrology.

Defining the Model

The harmonic model of segmentation discussed in this book is founded upon the following assumptions: First, just as a celestial cycle can be interpreted as a cycle of being, so any pattern of change that unfolds a whole number of times within that cycle can be interpreted as a higher harmonic unfoldment of the cycle of being. Second, each way of dividing a cycle into distinct stages brings certain harmonics into focus while excluding others from consideration. Third, during the unfoldment of a celestial cycle, as the principle of multiplicity becomes dominant in the 1H, it does so simultaneously in all higher harmonics.

In order to apply the model, we must make a further assumption – about the relationship between a harmonic's waveform on a given section of the model, and the contribution that the harmonic makes to the meaning of the corresponding stage of the celestial cycle. Here we have (at least) two options.

On the one hand, we could assume that the relevant characteristic is the general orientation of the harmonic throughout the stage. For example, we could assume that the first, fifth and ninth stages of a twelve-fold division are fiery in nature because throughout each of these stages, the principle of multiplicity is dominant and becoming stronger in the 3H; that the second, sixth and tenth stages are earthy in nature because throughout each of these stages the principle of multiplicity is dominant but becoming weaker in the 3H, and so on (see Figure 2.5 on page 88).

A problem with this approach is that in many cases, a harmonic is observed to give rise to a distinct change of theme at each stage boundary, even though most of the stage boundaries do not coincide with a pivotal point of the harmonic. In the twelve-sign zodiac, for example, Aries, Cancer, Libra and Capricorn are observed to share the theme of *cardinality*; Taurus, Leo, Scorpio and Aquarius the theme of *fixity*; and Gemini, Virgo, Sagittarius and Pisces the theme of *mutability*. This is illustrated in Figure 4.1, in which C, F and M indicate the cardinal, fixed and mutable signs respectively. We can see that the mode cycle of *cardinal sign > fixed sign > mutable sign* unfolds four times during each unfoldment of the zodiacal cycle and is thus a 4H phenomenon. In other words, it is by virtue of the 4H that modality changes at the beginning of each sign. However, because the 4H is divided into thirds by the sign cusps, the points of the 4H contained within a given mode do not share a distinct theme that is unique to those points. Yet, as is shown in Chapter 5, the general orientation of the 4H during each cardinal sign does reflect the theme that those signs – and only those signs – have in common; and the same may be said of the fixed signs and the mutable signs.

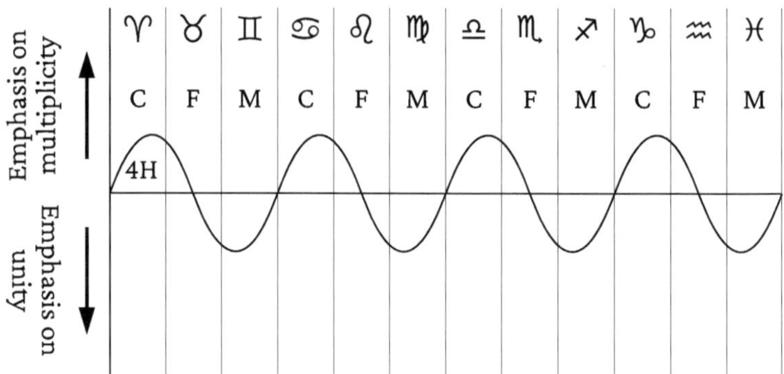

Figure 4.1 The 4H and the cardinal, fixed and mutable signs

On the other hand, we could assume that the relevant characteristic is the state of the harmonic at the beginning of the stage. For example, we could assume that the first, fifth and ninth stages of a twelve-fold division are fiery in nature because at the beginning of each of these stages, the principle of multiplicity is just becoming dominant in the 3H, with the momentum of the polar tide peaking; that the second, sixth and tenth stages are earthy in nature because at the beginning of each of these stages, the principle of multiplicity is peaking in strength in the 3H as the polar tide turns in favour of the principle of unity, and so on (see Figure 2.5). This approach is congruous with the idea that each unfoldment of a cycle is coloured by whatever is happening as that cycle begins anew (as discussed in Chapter 2 – *The Rebirth of a Cycle*). In a twelve-fold division, for example, the 12H begins anew at each stage boundary.

In my view, despite the drawback discussed above, the former approach accounts for the meanings of stages at least as effectively as the latter approach and is generally more straightforward in its application. Thus, throughout the remainder of this book, the contribution that a harmonic makes to the meaning of a given stage of a celestial cycle is correlated with the general orientation of the harmonic during the corresponding section of the model. As an example of how to apply this approach in cases where a cycle of being is divided into parts other than hemicycles or quarters, let us consider the thirds.

The Thirds of the Cycle of Being

Throughout the first third of the cycle of being, the principle of multiplicity is dominant. By the end of this third, the polar tide has turned in favour of the principle of unity, but has not gathered momentum. The meaning of the first third falls somewhere between the meaning of the first quarter and that of the first hemicycle. This third is concerned with establishing a sense of individual selfhood by engaging in form/consciousness-building activity in a relatively subjective and autonomous manner, and awareness of the wider implications of this activity tends to be lacking. There is a tendency to focus purposefully on one goal at a time, but to lose interest relatively quickly and move on to the next thing. Egoic consciousness is prone to wilfulness, impulsiveness and riding roughshod over others.

Throughout the second third, the principle of unity is becoming stronger more quickly than at any point of the other two thirds. The second third has a similar meaning to that of the polar hemicycle during which the principle of unity is becoming stronger, but with greater emphasis on the sense of being polarised with respect to that which is other. The relationship between the individual and their socio-cultural environment is emphasised, and there is heightened awareness of consensus reality, socio-cultural values, and issues of morality and justice. In order to optimise the value of phenomena, the phenomena are arranged and utilised in line with ideals or principles of organisation. With the polar tide moving strongly in opposition to diversification, there is increased ability to focus on long-term goals. The challenge of integration (second third) prepares the previously naïve and 'self-centred' individual (first third) for exposure to some greater power (final third), and so the second third is associated with transformative experiences and rites of passage. Egoic consciousness experiences a sense of inertia, intensity and ongoing struggle, and tries to achieve and maintain control, often through stubbornness.

Throughout the final third, the principle of unity is dominant. The polar tide moves weakly in favour of the principle of unity at the beginning of this third, but soon turns in favour of the principle of multiplicity and gathers momentum. The meaning of the final third falls somewhere between the meaning of the fourth quarter and that of the second hemicycle. After prioritising social integration and trying to optimise the functionality and value of phenomena in the second third, the individual now looks beyond established systems of organisation in order to connect with source. This requires a more transcendent, holistic, devotional and compassionate perspective, and openness to new understanding. Powers of persuasion and seduction are heightened, for others sense that the individual can act as a bridge to something greater. Egoic consciousness is prone to becoming caught up in superficial experiences of connectedness and tends to be inconsistent and easily swayed.

Let us now consider some examples of how each way of dividing a cycle into distinct stages focuses exclusively on certain harmonics.

The Two-fold Division

There are two ways to divide a cycle into distinct hemicycles, and in each case, the meaning evident throughout each hemicycle is derived solely from the state of the 1H (see Figure 2.3 on page 82). Using one option, each hemicycle begins and ends at a 1H point of equilibrium (with a different principle dominant throughout each hemicycle). Using the other option, each hemicycle begins and ends at a 1H pole (with a different principle increasing in strength throughout each hemicycle).

The Four-fold Division

The harmonics that play a part in distinguishing the stages of a four-fold division from one another are the 1H and 2H. Looking at Figure 4.2, we can see that the quarters are defined by the pivotal points of the 1H, and that in the 2H, multiplicity and unity are emphasised, respectively, in the odd and even-numbered stages.

Thus, when the strength of the dominant principle is increasing in the 1H (during its first and third quarters), the principle of multiplicity is dominant in the 2H; and when the strength of the dominant principle is decreasing in the 1H (during its second and fourth quarters), the principle of unity is dominant in the 2H. According to the proposed model, this relationship exists between any given harmonic and its 2SH.

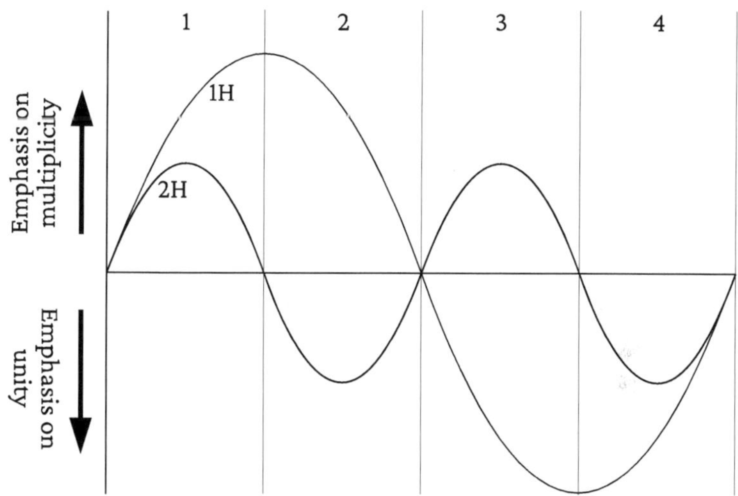

Figure 4.2 The harmonic basis of the four-fold division

The Eight-fold Division

The harmonics that play a part in distinguishing the stages of an eight-fold division from one another are the 1H, 2H and 4H (see Figure 4.3). In this division, each stage boundary coincides with a 2H pivotal point, and each stage coincides with a 2H quarter. In the 4H (the 2SH of the 2H), multiplicity and unity are emphasised, respectively, in the odd and even-numbered stages.

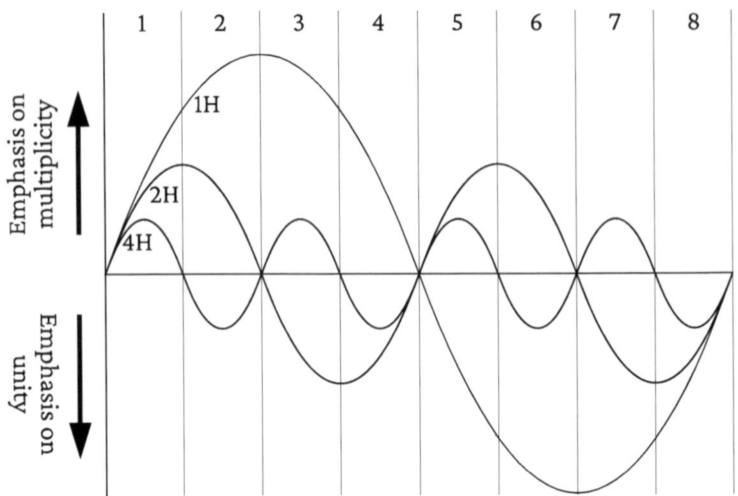

Figure 4.3 The harmonic basis of the eight-fold division

The Twelve-fold Division

The harmonics that play a part in distinguishing the stages of a twelve-fold division from one another are the 1H, 2H, 3H, 4H, and 6H (see Figure 4.4 and Figure 4.5). In this division, each stage boundary coincides with a pivotal point of the 3H, and each stage coincides with a 3H quarter. In the 6H (the 2SH of the 3H), multiplicity and unity are emphasised, respectively, in the odd and even-numbered stages. The 4H is divided into thirds by the twelve stage boundaries, and the 1H is divided into thirds by the stage boundaries that begin stages 1, 5 and 9.

Assuming that there is a point at which the principle of multiplicity becomes dominant in all harmonics simultaneously, the relationship between a given harmonic and one of its odd-numbered sub-harmonics adheres to the following pattern: As a point of equilibrium is reached in the harmonic, the harmonic and the sub-harmonic are in sync; and as a pole is reached in the harmonic, the opposite pole is reached in the sub-harmonic. (See, for example, the 1H and 3H in Figure 4.4 and Figure 4.5.)

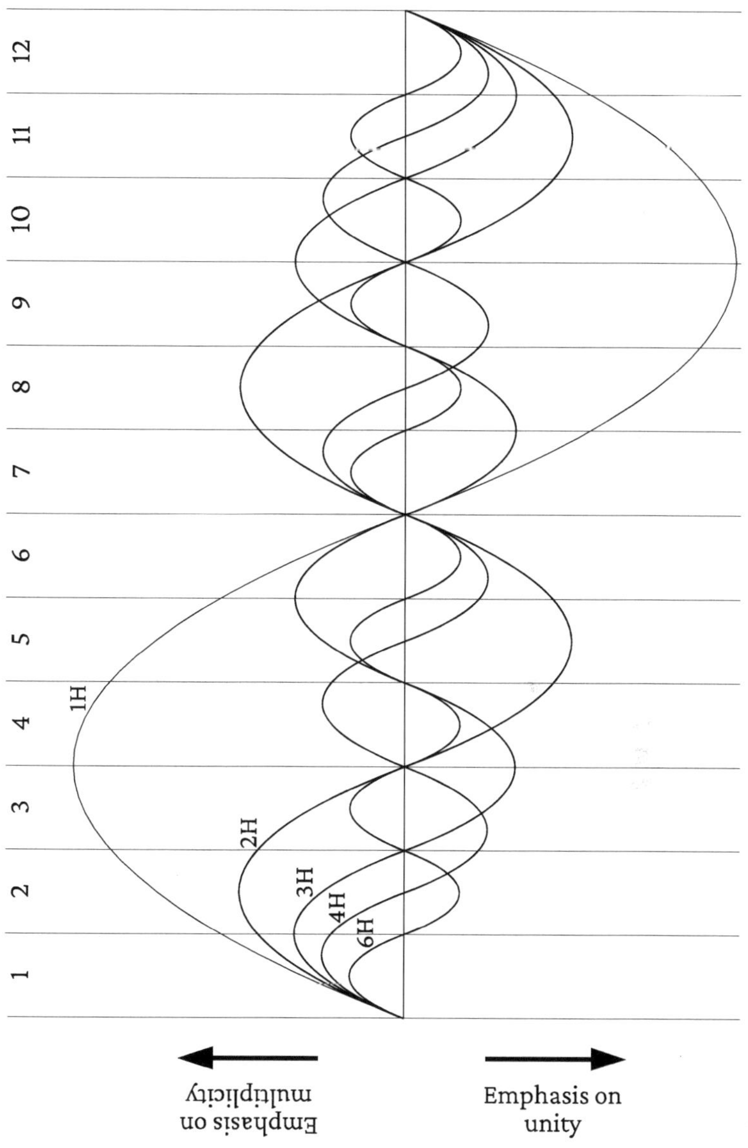

Figure 4.4 The harmonic basis of the twelve-fold division

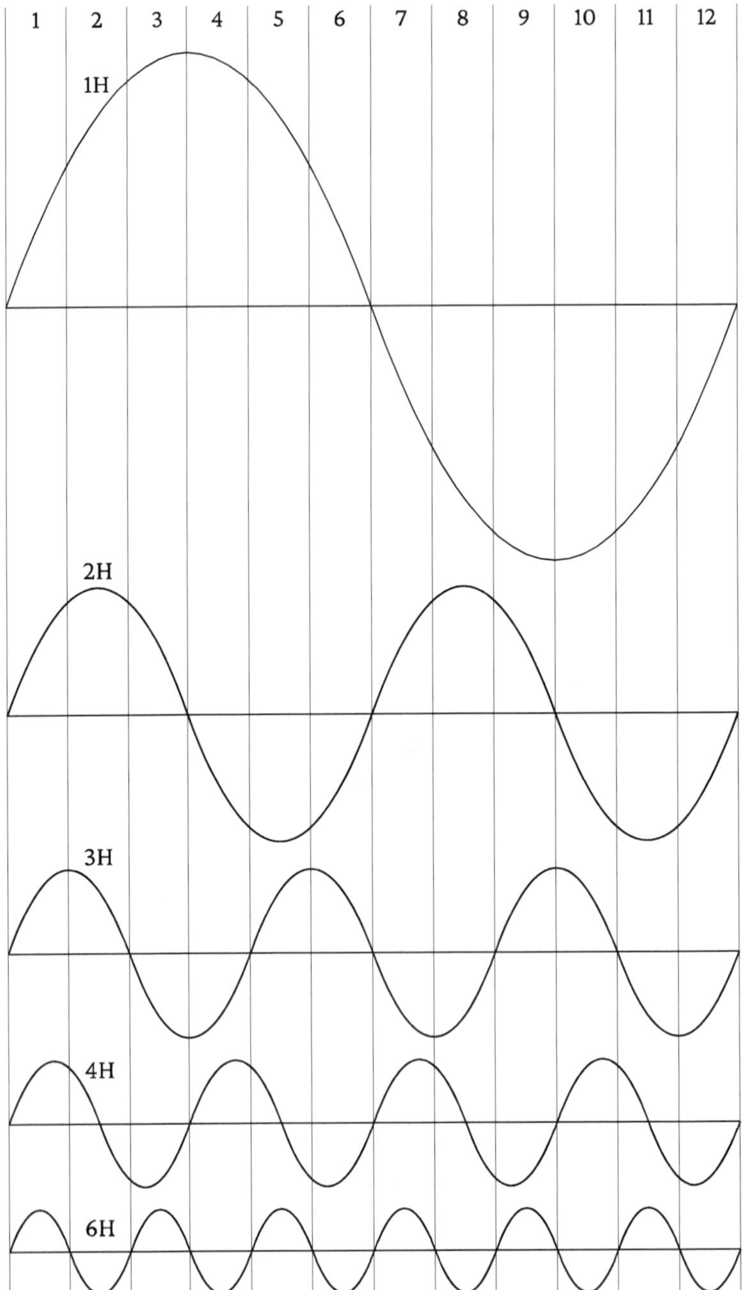

Figure 4.5 The harmonic basis of the twelve-fold division with waves shown separately

Consequently, in any division in which each stage coincides with one quarter of an odd-numbered higher harmonic, we see the following: During a stage that occurs immediately before or after a 1H point of equilibrium, the same quarter is unfolding in the 1H and the higher harmonic; and during a stage that occurs immediately before or after a 1H pole, opposite quarters are unfolding in the 1H and the higher harmonic. (The first and third quarters are opposites, as are the second and fourth quarters.)

Applying this to the twelve-fold division, we see that during stages 1, 6, 7 and 12, the quarter unfolding in the 1H is also unfolding in the 3H; and during stages 3, 4, 9 and 10, the quarter unfolding in the 1H is the opposite quarter to the one that is unfolding in the 3H. During stages 2, 5, 8 and 11, the same principle is dominant in both harmonics, but the direction of the polar tide in one harmonic is opposite to that in the other. The significance of these groupings is discussed in Chapter 5.

It is often said that many celestial cycles divide naturally into twelve distinct stages because the cycle is divided into distinct quarters by its pivotal points, and each quarter divides naturally into three parts due to the influence of a trinitarian principle of some kind. This view has perhaps arisen largely because in a twelve-fold division, the same three-stage pattern of change unfolds during each 1H quarter (as in the case of the mode cycle). However, it may be that the significance of the twelve-fold division is largely due to the significance of the 3H, whose pivotal points divide the cycle into twelve.

Using the Model to Understand Higher Harmonic Charts

As noted in Chapter 3, there is disagreement amongst astrologers concerning whether or not zodiacal position on a higher harmonic chart is significant. If it is not significant, then a higher harmonic chart wheel serves only as a device for measuring differences in celestial longitude, and the way in which higher harmonic zodiacs are positioned along the ecliptic is arbitrary. If it *is* significant, then we must ensure that higher harmonic zodiacs are positioned correctly so that the correct higher harmonic zodiacal positions are obtained.

The proposed model is congruous with the notion that higher harmonic zodiacal positions *are* significant, and with the established practice of aligning the first point of 1H Aries with one occurrence of the first point of Aries in each higher harmonic zodiac (and thus of using the first point of Aries as the zero point for converting IH zodiacal position to a higher harmonic zodiacal position).

According to the proposed model, the harmonics that are relevant to the twelve-fold division of a cycle are the 1H, 2H, 3H, 4H and 6H. Thus, the harmonics that are relevant to the twelve-fold division of the 5H of a cycle are the 5H, 10H, 15H, 20H, and 30H (the 5SH of each of the 1H, 2H, 3H, 4H and 6H). When only the 5H, 10H, 15H, 20H and 30H are taken into account, the same pattern repeats during each unfoldment of the 5H; and the five occurrences of this pattern can be superimposed onto one another and stretched to create the 5H chart wheel (see Chapter 3). We can see that according to the proposed model, the 5H twelve-sign zodiac is the 1H twelve-sign zodiac replicated at the level of five-ness, and so the meanings of the 5H zodiacal signs are the same as those of the 1H zodiacal signs, except that the former are overlaid with the qualities of five-ness. Thus, the proposed model is congruous with the notion that higher harmonic zodiacal position is significant.

Given that the principle of multiplicity becomes dominant in all relevant harmonics simultaneously at the first point of Aries in any given zodiac (1H or higher harmonic), one occurrence of the first point of Aries in any given higher harmonic zodiac must coincide with the first point of Aries in the 1H zodiac. Thus, the proposed model is congruous with the established practise of aligning the 1H and higher harmonic zodiacs in this way.

Different Approaches to Dividing the Signs

Where a zodiac is divided into stages that number a multiple of twelve (i.e. where each zodiacal sign contains a whole number of stages), the resulting chart may be referred to as a *divisional chart, D chart, sub chart* or *varga chart.* The interpretation of the stages of such divisions is approached in a variety of ways, and while some approaches are congruous with harmonic principles, others are not. Of those that are not, some associate each stage with a luminary (the Sun or Moon) or a visible planet (these being the only planets known when these associations were introduced), while others associate each stage with a zodiacal sign. In some approaches in which each stage is associated with a celestial body, the stages are of unequal size, but each sign is still divided into the same number of stages.

To explore this further, let us take the example of the *D-2 chart,* in which each sign is divided into two stages. In Vedic astrology, the D-2 chart is also referred to as the *hora varga* and the stages of the chart are referred to as *horas* (because each stage takes one hour to rise, on average). This section uses material from a series of articles by Rok Koritnik.*

In Figure 4.6, each of the rows numbered 1 to 6 shows a different method of associating each hora with a luminary or sign. Each of these methods is arguably proposed by at least one traditional Vedic text (see Koritnik's articles for details).

In row 1, each yang sign is divided into a solar hora followed by a lunar hora, while each yin sign is divided into a lunar hora followed by a solar hora. The approach shown in row 2 is the sign version of that shown in row 1, with the Sun and Moon replaced by the signs that they rule: Leo and Cancer, respectively. The only connection that can be made with these approaches and the proposed model is that the emphasis on multiplicity is increasing in the 6H during each solar/Leo hora, while emphasis on unity is increasing in the 6H during each lunar/Cancer hora.

In row 3, the first hora of each sign is associated with the sign itself, while the second hora is associated with the opposite sign. The D-3, D-4 and D-12 charts are often interpreted using the same principle:

Approaching the D-3 chart in this manner, the first third of each sign is associated with the sign itself (or alternatively, the luminary or visible planet that rules that sign), and the second and final thirds are associated with the remaining signs of the same element (in zodiacal order); thus, the three signs associated with the thirds of a given sign form an equilateral triangle. For example, the first, second and final thirds of Virgo are associated, respectively, with Virgo, Capricorn and Taurus.

Approaching the D-4 chart in this manner, the first quarter of a sign is associated with the sign itself, and the remaining quarters are associated with the remaining signs of the same mode (in zodiacal order); thus the four signs associated with the quarters of a given sign form a perfect cross. For example, the first, second, third and fourth quarters of Virgo are associated, respectively, with Virgo, Sagittarius, Pisces and Gemini.

Approaching the D-12 chart in this manner, the first twelfth of each sign is associated with the sign itself, and the remaining twelfths are associated with the other signs (in zodiacal order); thus, the twelve parts of Aries run from Aries to Pisces, the twelve parts of Taurus run from Taurus to Aries, and so on.

---

* *The secret meeting of East and West – Understanding divisional and/or harmonic charts* – Parts 1 to 7 (2019) RokKoritnikAstrologer.com

	♈		♉		♊		♋		♌		♍		♎		♏		♐		♑		♒		♓	
1	☉	☽	☽	☉	☉	☽	☽	☉	☉	☽	☽	☉	☉	☽	☽	☉	☉	☽	☽	☉	☉	☽	☽	☉
2	♌	♋	♋	♌	♌	♋	♋	♌	♌	♋	♋	♌	♌	♋	♋	♌	♌	♋	♋	♌	♌	♋	♋	♌
3	♈	♎	♉	♏	♊	♐	♋	♑	♌	♒	♍	♓	♎	♈	♏	♉	♐	♊	♑	♋	♒	♌	♓	♍
4	♈	♒	♉	♓	♊	♈	♋	♉	♌	♊	♍	♋	♎	♌	♏	♍	♐	♎	♑	♏	♒	♐	♓	♑
5	♈	♉	♊	♋	♌	♍	♎	♏	♐	♑	♒	♓	♈	♉	♊	♋	♌	♍	♎	♏	♐	♑	♒	♓
6	♈	♉	♋	♊	♌	♍	♏	♎	♐	♑	♓	♒	♈	♉	♋	♊	♌	♍	♏	♎	♐	♑	♓	♒

Figure 4.6 Proposed methods of associating each stage of the D2 chart with a celestial body or zodiacal sign

While a more complex version of the proposed model could no doubt be developed to account for this approach, there is no intention here to argue that the model and this approach are congruent.

In row 4, the first hora of each sign is associated with the sign itself, and the second hora is associated with the eleventh sign from that sign. As Koritnik notes, the use of the eleventh sign seems somewhat arbitrary.

In the approach shown in row 5, the horas run from Aries to Pisces twice around the zodiac, forming two 2H twelve-sign zodiacs. Thus, in this case, the first twelve horas could be superimposed onto the last twelve and stretched to form the 2H chart wheel. According to the proposed model, the 2H twelve-sign zodiac is based on the 2H, 4H, 6H, 8H and 12H (the 2SH of each of the 1H, 2H, 3H, 4H and 6H). Thus, a unique meaning can be attributed to each hora by combining the meanings of the 1H and 2H zodiacal signs. According to the proposed model, meanings derived in this way are based on the 1H, 2H, 3H, 4H, 6H, 8H and 12H.

The D-9 chart, or *navamsha varga*, is the only divisional chart that is always interpreted as a sequence of higher harmonic twelve-sign zodiacs. The navamsha varga is discussed further in Chapter 5.

The approach shown in row 6 seems to combine the harmonic approach shown in row 5 with the approaches shown in rows 1 and 2 (in which the horas are reversed in the even-numbered signs).

An alternative harmonic approach is to interpret the first and second halves of each sign as emphasising multiplicity and unity; in other words, to simply add consideration of the 12H to those that are brought into focus by the twelve-fold division. Thus, this approach has the same harmonic basis as the approach shown in row 5, less the 8H. In Chapter 5, it is suggested that this approach may underpin the way that Rudhyar* divides each sign into two distinct stages in *An Astrological Mandala*.

With regard to the interpretation of divisional charts, it seems reasonable to assume that a number of viewpoints may be valid simultaneously – with each coming into its own in a particular context. However, we should not automatically assume that the authors of ancient texts were infallible. Some of these texts may convey ideas that had not been properly tested at the time of writing and/or may be based on misunderstandings of earlier texts.

---

* *An Astrological Mandala* (1974). (1st ed. 1973)

Using the Model to Interpret Research Data

As noted in Chapter 3, statistical research suggests that as a celestial cycle unfolds, the likelihood of a trait or event occurring does not tend to change suddenly at each stage boundary, but as a composite of a number of smooth harmonic fluctuations. The purpose of this section is to consider whether the proposed harmonic model of segmentation goes some way towards reconciling the traditional segment-based approach to astrology with the revelation of harmonic fluctuations, by showing that the cycle of being underpins the latter as well as the former.

The waveform drawn in grey in Figure 4.7 represents the 3H fluctuation in the deviation from expected results of the diurnal position of Jupiter in the birth charts of a group of scientists.* The grey text on the vertical axis shows that this waveform is "negatively phased" at the ascendant. Addey assumes that in general, the 3H fluctuation of the diurnal strength of Jupiter must be positively phased at the ascendant, and so he interprets the results as showing that the greater the 3H diurnal strength of Jupiter at the time of birth, the less likely the native is to become a scientist. Addey accounts for this with the claim that science tends to attract individuals of a more serious disposition, whereas a strongly placed Jupiter tends to coincide with a more jovial disposition.

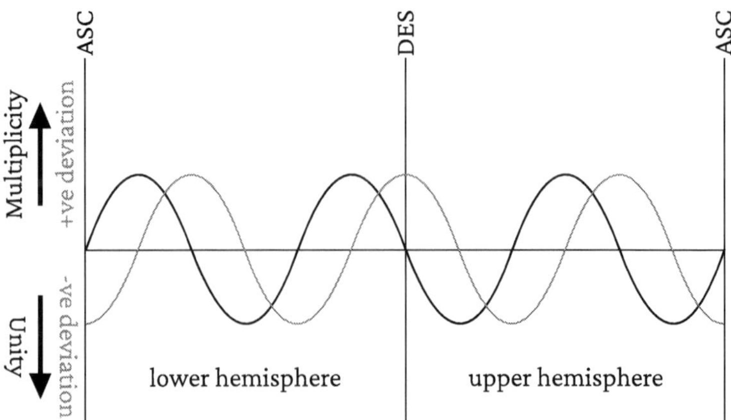

Figure 4.7 The 3H fluctuation in the diurnal position of Jupiter in the birth charts of a group of scientists, and the 3H of the diurnal cycle

* *Harmonics in Astrology* (2009) p. 190. (1st ed. 1976)

But suppose we view this data not as an indication of a 3H fluctuation in the strength of some kind of astrological force, but rather as an indication of the presence of a 3H unfoldment of a cycle of being. As discussed in Chapter 6, according to the proposed model, the ascendant is the point of the diurnal cycle at which the principle of multiplicity becomes dominant in all harmonics simultaneously. On this basis, the waveform drawn in black in Figure 4.7 shows the movement of emphasis back and forth between multiplicity and unity at the 3H frequency during the unfoldment of the diurnal cycle. Looking at the relationship between the two waveforms, we can see that the deviation from expected results in the research data is positive while the strength of the principle of unity is increasing, and that positive deviation peaks at those points where emphasis on unity is increasing most quickly. Thus, the data could be interpreted as showing that the likelihood of an individual becoming a scientist increases with the rate at which the strength of the principle of unity increases in the 3H of Jupiter's diurnal cycle at the moment of birth. The movement of the polar tide in favour of the principle of unity emphasises the need for organisation and heightens awareness of consensus reality. Jupiter is associated with discovery, and the 3H is associated with enjoyment, insight and natural ability. Thus, the data may reflect that science tends to attract those who have the ability to discover the universal laws according to which existence is organised, and who feel inspired to do so.

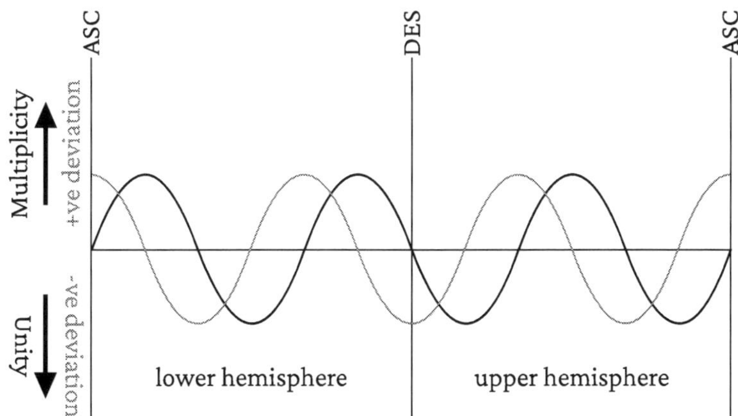

Figure 4.8 The 3H fluctuation in the diurnal position of Mars in the birth charts of a group of sportspeople, and the 3H of the diurnal cycle

To take another example, the waveform drawn in grey in Figure 4.8 shows the 3H fluctuation in the deviation from expected results of the diurnal position of Mars in the birth charts of a group of successful sportspeople.* Addey interprets the data as showing that the greater the 3H diurnal strength of Mars at the time of birth, the more likely the individual is to become a successful sportsperson. However, the data could be interpreted as showing that the likelihood of an individual playing sport as a vocation increases with the rate at which the strength of the principle of multiplicity increases in the 3H of Mars' diurnal cycle at the moment of birth. The movement of the polar tide in favour of the principle of multiplicity emphasises the need to trust one's own potential to find a way forward. Since Mars is associated with initiative and competitive spirit, the data may reflect that sporting vocations tend to attract those who enjoy testing their individual strength and initiative.

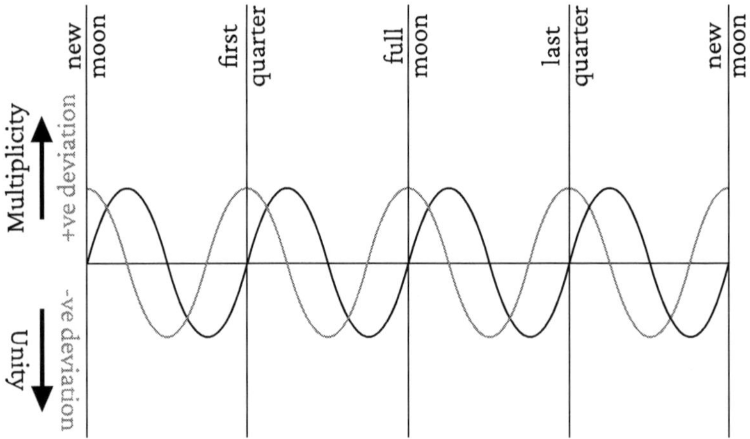

Figure 4.9 Variation in the rate of water absorption by dried beans during the lunation cycle, and the 4H of the lunation cycle

The waveform drawn in grey in Figure 4.9 approximates the results of an experiment in which the absorption of water by dried beans was measured at different points of the lunation cycle.† The waveform drawn in black shows the movement of emphasis between multiplicity and unity at the 4H frequency during the unfoldment of the lunation cycle according to the proposed model (see Chapter 7). Water absorption peaks around the new

* *Harmonics in Astrology* (2009) p. 190. (1st ed. 1976)

† *A New Study of Astrology* (1996, 1st ed.), p. 82. Addey wrote this material in 1982, but sadly died before he was able to complete it. Others have since prepared for publication the material that Addey had produced.

moon, first quarter, full moon and last quarter – the points at which emphasis on multiplicity is increasing most quickly in the 4H. This is not surprising, since the cyclical absorption and release of a substance by a biological organism is an example of a cycle of being in which emphasis on multiplicity increases during absorption and emphasis on unity increases during release (as in the breathing cycle, discussed on page 103).

These few, simple examples do not prove that the harmonic fluctuations discovered by Addey are expressions of higher harmonic unfoldments of the cycle of being. This section merely proposes that this is a possibility worth keeping in mind as we try to develop of a more unified and consistent understanding of astrology.

A final point worth mentioning is that Addey* expresses concern that the twelve-fold division is highly prominent in astrological interpretation, and yet harmonic analysis of astrological research data reveals the number twelve to be one of "extreme poverty". However, as we have seen, the 12H does not play a part in distinguishing the stages of a twelve-fold division from one another. Those harmonics that *are* relevant to the twelve-fold division – the 1H, 2H, 3H, 4H and 6H harmonics – feature strongly in Addey's findings.

Using the Model to Understand Aspects

Following his discovery of harmonic fluctuations in astrological research data, Addey† suggested a connection between harmonic waveforms and aspects. Addey speculates that each factor is accompanied by its own set of harmonics, and that one of the peaks of each harmonic coincides with the position of the factor. This being the case, as two factors perfect a 4H aspect – a conjunction (4/4), opposition (2/4) or square (1/4) – each factor would be at a peak of the 4H of the other factor.

Figure 4.10 shows the 4H waveform associated with Factor A, as envisaged by Addey. The points marked 0° represent all points on the line of celestial longitude of Factor A. According to Addey, as the faster-moving Factor B moves around the celestial sphere relative to Factor A – thus moving through A's 4H wave – the 4H connection between A and B rises and falls in the same manner as the waveform. (Note that A would arrive at a peak of B's 4H as B arrives at a peak of A's 4H, and so with the troughs.) Addey suggests that the 4H connection between the factors is operative for one-half of the

* *Harmonics in Astrology* (2009) p. 36. (1st ed. 1976)

† *Harmonics in Astrology* (2009) p. 69. (1st ed. 1976)

time (waveform above the horizontal line) and inoperative for the other half of the time (waveform below the horizontal line). Thus, the 4H connection is suggested to be operative while any 4H aspect is being formed with an orb of 22.5° or less.

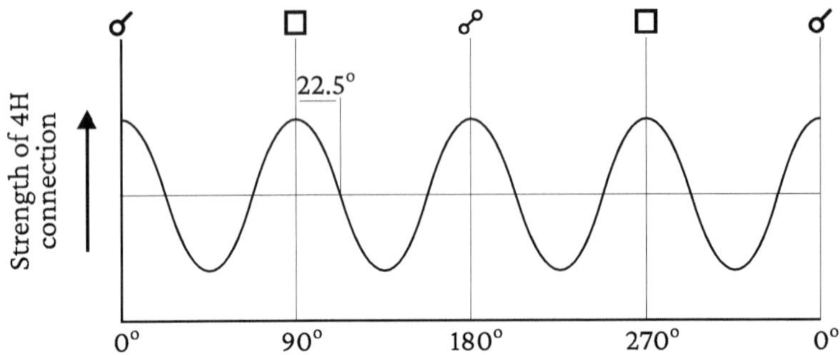

Distance between Factor A and Factor B, measured eastwards from Factor A in celestial longitude

Figure 4.10 The fluctuation in the 4H connection between two factors during the unfoldment of their synodic cycle, as envisaged by Addey

Addey argues that the appropriate orb for any given aspect is equal to one quarter of the wavelength of the lowest-numbered harmonic from which the aspect can be derived (for example, the 4H in the case of the square, or the 12H in the case of the semi-sextile or quincunx). Addey acknowledges that aspects have a noticeable effect only within much smaller orbs, and suggests that this could be because the closer the aspect is to perfection, the more sub-harmonics are also within orb. For example, while two factors are forming a square aspect with an orb of 5 $^{5}/_{8}$° or less, the 8H and 16H connections of the factors would also be operative. (5 $^{5}/_{8}$° is one quarter of the wavelength of the 16H.)

However, it could be that a 4H connection between two factors is simply a product of the alignment – and thus resonance – of their 4H waves. (This would account for the observation that aspects based on higher-numbered harmonics require smaller maximum orbs, for we would expect the range over which alignment has a noticeable effect to be proportionate to the wavelength of the harmonic concerned.) This being the case, the harmonics of a factor could be phased such that the principle of multiplicity becomes dominant in all harmonics simultaneously at the position of the factor, rather than as shown in Figure 4.10. Thus, the same harmonic waves could underpin the significance of both segments and aspects (or at least the same model could be used to account for both).

CHAPTER FIVE

INTERPRETING ZODIACAL POSITION

This chapter discusses the meaning of the tropical and sidereal zodiacal cycles in psychological astrology, and shows how the proposed model can help to make clear the core meanings of the stages of some commonly used divisions of these cycles.

The Ecliptic

The meaning of a celestial cycle incorporates the meaning of each plane and body involved in the unfoldment of the cycle. A zodiacal cycle is a cycle of changing celestial longitude, and a line of celestial longitude is a projection of a point on the ecliptic. Thus, the meaning of a zodiacal cycle – and any other cycle of changing celestial longitude – incorporates the meaning of the ecliptic plane. The ecliptic plane is the plane that Earth shares with the Sun, representing the coming together of the animating energy of the Sun and the fertile blend of elements on Earth, and thus the potential for increasingly complex terrestrial wholes to evolve and thrive. Thus, a zodiacal cycle – and any other cycle of changing celestial longitude – corresponds to a cycle of change in the way terrestrial wholes are motivated or predisposed to utilise the energy available to them.

The Meaning of the Tropical Zodiacal Cycle

Each type of zodiacal cycle is founded upon the relationship between the ecliptic plane and another factor. The tropical zodiacal cycle exists by virtue of the inclination of the equatorial plane to the ecliptic plane. Because of this inclination, as a factor moves eastwards or westwards around the celestial sphere, the point at which its line of celestial longitude meets the ecliptic undergoes a cycle of changing declination. The points of equilibrium of the tropical zodiacal cycle (the first points of tropical Aries and Libra) are the lines of celestial longitude that meet the ecliptic where it crosses the celestial equator and thus has zero declination. The poles of this cycle (the first points of tropical Cancer and Capricorn) are the lines of celestial longitude that meet the ecliptic at its points of maximum northerly and southerly declination (see Figure 1.6 on page 10).

The equatorial plane is defined by Earth's rotation around its own axis rather than Earth's relationship to another celestial body. Thus, the tropical zodiacal cycle differs from other zodiacal cycles in that its meaning emphasises particularly strongly the meaning of Earth. As do each of the other major celestial bodies* of our solar system, Earth corresponds to a vital psychological function. Just as Earth is the standpoint from which we observe the celestial sphere, so the Earth-function in the individual human psyche gives rise to a focal point from which the needs and drives associated with the other celestial bodies are experienced as 'my' needs and drives.† Thus, the tropical zodiacal cycle of a celestial body corresponds to a cycle of change in the way the individual is motivated to use the corresponding function to express 'my' unique identity and will. Other zodiacal cycles refer to motivation that is more removed from the sense of autonomy and separate identity.

The Tropical Zodiacal Cycle and the Seasonal Cycle

As the Sun moves through a tropical zodiacal sign, the behaviour of the natural world in temperate northern hemisphere regions broadly reflects the meaning of that sign. For example, the Sun passes through tropical Aries during the first part of northern hemisphere spring, as new life bursts forth in temperate northern hemisphere regions; and Aries is associated with the initial emergence of potentiality into the phenomenal realm. Broadly speaking, as the Sun passes through tropical Taurus, large amounts of foliage are generated; as the Sun passes through tropical Gemini, cross-pollination is underway; as the Sun passes through tropical Cancer, new seeds begin to gestate, and so on.

In temperate southern hemisphere regions, however, the seasonal cycle is out of sync with the Sun's tropical zodiacal cycle by one-half of a year. Consequently, some astrologers have suggested that for southern hemisphere locations, it is appropriate to use an alternative tropical zodiac –

---

* From the geocentric viewpoint, the Moon is one such major celestial body.

† In *The Astrology of Personality* (1991) p.148 (1st ed. 1936), Rudhyar suggests that "[Earth's] polar axis symbolizes the power to be an individual self, an 'I' ", and that "the cyclic motion of the Earth's globe around [its rotation] axis must refer to the cyclic development of individual selfhood. In *heliocentric* – or *Sun-centred* – astrology, Earth is often associated with 'the ego'.

one in which the first point of Aries is the anti-vernal point (the position of the Sun at the southern hemisphere spring equinox). However, empirical observation consistently shows that the tropical zodiac in which Aries begins at the vernal point is valid for all locations on Earth.

Rudhyar* suggests the following reason for this:

> As races [inhabiting temperate northern hemisphere regions] have been, during the last millennia, the *active* factor in the evolution of human consciousness, their experience has come to acquire a universal validity in the determination of cosmic meaning and purpose. Civilization, as we know it today, is therefore centred in a northern hemisphere and temperate-climate kind of consciousness. It may not conceivably remain so in the future, but for the time being it is; and our present astrology interprets thus accurately its cyclic evolution.

Rudhyar seems to be suggesting that if developments in human consciousness during the last millennia had been spear-headed by races inhabiting temperate southern hemisphere regions, human civilisation as a whole would be centred in a southern hemisphere and temperate-climate kind of consciousness, and a tropical zodiac in which the first point of tropical Aries coincides with the anti-vernal point would be valid for human civilisation as a whole. It is not possible to prove or disprove the truth of Rudhyar's suggestion, but it seems more likely to me that the tropical zodiac in use today would be valid for all regions on Earth, no matter where advances in human civilisation had arisen. (Some justification for this is offered in Chapter 9.)

It could be argued, however, that such advances were always more likely to occur in northern temperate regions, where people's experiences of – and instinctive responses to – the natural world (determined by the stage reached in the seasonal cycle) continuously reflect those values seeking individualised expression (determined by the stage reached in the tropical zodiacal cycle of the Sun). This may have stimulated the development of individualised self-expression, which naturally occurs in tandem with the development of increasingly complex social systems.

(The primary reason why northern hemisphere civilisations advanced more quickly may be that the large Eurasian landmass allowed northern-

---

* *The Pulse of Life* (1970), p. 14; Khaldea.com/rudhyar/ Pt. 1, p. 7. (1st ed. 1943). Rudhyar's italics.

hemisphere cultures to prosper and stimulate one another's development. However, there will come a time when the majority of land is in the southern hemisphere, and a synchronistic relationship may exist between the timing of the accumulation of landmass in the northern hemisphere and the emergence and ongoing development of human civilisation.)

The Meaning of the Sidereal Zodiacal Cycle

While the tropical zodiac is founded upon the relationship between the ecliptic and equatorial planes, the sidereal zodiac is founded upon the relationship between the ecliptic plane and the wider galaxy. Thus, while tropical zodiacal positions show how energy is used to build a personality and to contribute to collectives through the expression of that personality, sidereal zodiacal positions show how energy is utilised at a less personalised level to make collective contributions that the individual identifies less closely with.

As discussed in Chapter 1, there is disagreement amongst sidereal astrologers concerning which of the proposed sidereal zodiacs is valid, and whether sidereal zodiacal stages should be equal or unequal in size. What unites the majority of sidereal astrologers is the belief that each astrologically significant star has a unique meaning, and that the meaning evident throughout a given zodiacal stage is determined by the meaning(s) of the star(s) within that stage. However, the way meaning changes around a sidereal (or any) zodiac is subject to cyclic patterns, suggesting that the meaning of a given point or stage of the zodiac is geometrically predetermined and therefore resides in lines of celestial longitude rather than stars. Some sidereal astrologers believe that a seemingly fixed zodiac may exist that is founded upon an undiscovered and extremely slow-moving Aries node.

Tropical vs Sidereal Astrology

The vast majority of astrologers work exclusively with either the tropical zodiac or a sidereal zodiac. Many of these astrologers are open to the possibility that the tropical and sidereal approaches are both valid, but some only accept the validity of their adopted approach. Those who adopt the latter approach often look to alleged historical precedents to support their viewpoint; however, historical evidence may be unreliable and open to multiple interpretations, and it is not necessarily the case that the older an astrological technique, the more profound or valid it is.

On the tropical side, it is argued that when Babylonian astrologers divided the ecliptic into twelve constellations and then signs, they thought of these frames of reference as being tropical, or seasonal, in nature. It is argued that the Babylonians deliberately positioned their zodiac so that the vernal point would occupy the constellation (and later the sign) Aries, and that because they were unaware of the precession of the equinoxes, they believed that the stars would remain in the same positions relative to the vernal point. It is suggested that early astronomers needed to use stars as celestial markers until advances in astronomy and mathematics made it possible to divide the celestial sphere using geometry alone, and that in the relatively animistic cultures of the first millennium BCE, people needed to project archetypes onto tangible phenomena in order to relate to them.

Some Vedic astrologers argue that tropical astrology predates sidereal astrology in India, and that at one time, Vedic astrologers used stars as markers on a tropical zodiac. It is claimed that these astrologers understood that the tropical zodiacal positions of the stars were gradually changing due to precession, but that a number of generations of Vedic astrologers failed to update the tropical zodiacal positions of the stars, and that consequently, the Vedic zodiacal frame of reference became sidereal by default.

On the sidereal side, it is argued that stars were always the fundamental basis for creating zodiacal frames of reference in ancient civilisations, and that tropical divisions of the ecliptic were introduced only as a calendar for tracking the annual seasonal cycle. It is argued that the tropical zodiac only took hold in the West due to confusion caused by Ptolemy.

In the second century CE, Ptolemy wrote *Tetrabiblos*, in which he defines the first point of Aries as the vernal point. (The vernal point was around the middle of the sign Aries when the Babylonians first defined their twelve-stage zodiac, but was only 1° of arc (approximately) from the first point of Aries at the time of Ptolemy.) *Tetrabiblos* was translated into Arabic around the middle of the first millennium CE, as the Ottoman Empire spread across parts of the Mediterranean region; and around the same time, astrology virtually disappeared from those parts of Western Europe that did not become part of the Ottoman Empire. Arabic astrologers used Ptolemy's definition of the first point of Aries, and when their astrological texts were translated into Latin during the twelfth-century Renaissance, the twelve-sign tropical zodiac was taken up by Western European astrologers.

The Timing of Transits to Natal factors

Although relationships between natal factors (aspects, midpoints, etc.) are not affected by the astrologer's choice of zodiac, the timing of transits to natal factors *is*. Each point on the tropical zodiac moves westwards around the celestial sphere at a rate of approximately 1° of celestial longitude every 72 years due to the precession of the equinoxes (see page 14). This means, for example, that the solar return of a 72-year-old individual occurs 24 hours earlier if the tropical zodiac is used than if a sidereal zodiac is used. Whether one approach gives better interpretations of zodiacal position (in general or in certain circumstances), and whether one approach is better for the timing of transits to natal and progressed factors (again, in general or in certain circumstances), may be two distinct questions.

The Rise of Tropical Astrology in the West

In the West – where individualism is valued relatively highly – most astrologers practise tropical astrology, while in the East – where collectivism is valued relatively highly – most astrologers practise sidereal astrology. Thus, the approach that is now prevalent in each region is that which best reflects the region's dominant cultural bias. With this in mind, it is worth briefly discussing how the rise to prominence of tropical astrology in the West occurred in tandem – and perhaps in synchrony – with certain cultural changes that made the tropical approach more relevant there.

The emergence of the tropical zodiac as a distinct frame of reference coincided with the birth and growth of Christianity, which many see as marking the beginning of a shift of consciousness in the West. Rudhyar[*] suggests that Christ is a symbol of the power in each human being to find fulfilment as a complete and unique individual, while Rudolph Steiner[†] suggests that "[Christ's] mission consisted in bringing to mankind the full force of the ego, an inner independence in the soul".

As noted above, the translation of Arabic astrological texts into Latin occurred as part of the twelfth-century Renaissance. In the build-up to this period, a number of Western European monarchs had begun to play a stronger integrating role in their respective nation states. Consequently, these states became more stable and powerful, and acquired a clearer sense

---

[*] *The Pulse of Life* (1970), p. 93; Khaldea.com/rudhyar/ Pt. 2, Capricorn, p. 1. (1st ed. 1943)

[†] *The Gospel of St. John* (1962), p. 82. (1st ed. 1908)

of identity. Many European states adopted Roman style legal systems, which emphasised individual liberty; and in order to keep pace with a growing awareness of the significance of individual psychology, the Christian Church began to teach the value of introspection (having previously discouraged it). The first autonomous* universities in Western Europe were established at this time, encouraging independent thought.

The Astrological Ages

As noted in Chapter 1, the retrograde transit of the vernal point through a sidereal sign or constellation is referred to as an *Astrological Age*. Much has been said about the significance of this, despite a lack of consensus concerning where the true sidereal zodiac begins and whether it divides naturally into unequal constellations or equal signs. Very little has been said about the other consequence of the motion of the vernal point: the motions of seemingly fixed factors through the tropical zodiac.

The galactic centre is an example of a seemingly fixed factor whose tropical zodiacal position appears to be astrologically significant. Between 1867 and 1938, for example, the galactic centre was in the 26th degree of tropical Sagittarius. Thus, this significator appears in the birth charts of almost all those who fought or participated in the First and Second World Wars. The Sabian Symbol for Sagittarius 26 is "a flag bearer in battle", which Rudhyar† interprets as a symbol of "the nobly accepted subservience of the individual to collective values and goals".

Between 1938 and 2009, the galactic centre was in the 27th degree of tropical Sagittarius, which Rudhyar associates with "the individual creatively expressing his own individuality". This seems very apt given the cultural changes that have occurred since the Second World War (including the liberation of many colonies previously controlled by European nations) and the opportunities for self-expression afforded by the World Wide Web.

At the time of writing (2020), the first of those born with the galactic centre in the 28th degree of tropical Sagittarius are about to enter their teenage years. Rudhyar associates this degree with "the mastery over material factors of a few imaginative and trained individuals, [enabling] their community to remain well integrated and able to function easily in the best possible environment". On the one hand, over the coming decades, technological advances may make it possible to begin to heal the biosphere

---

* Autonomous as in independent of the church.

† *An Astrological Mandala* (1974), p. 225. (1st ed. 1973)

and create good living conditions for all; and artificially intelligent software may be developed that can discern the best way to guide a given individual towards greater understanding of a particular subject, or towards inner peace, in any given moment. On the other hand, technological advances could allow increasing numbers of people to live in comfort while ignoring the ongoing deterioration of the biosphere; and artificially intelligent software may be developed that allows personal neuroses and social dysfunction to be 'swept under the carpet', by providing each individual with their own virtual reality.

Assuming that either the Lahiri or Fagan/Bradley zodiac is valid, the galactic centre will be in tropical Sagittarius for approximately 90% of the Age of Pisces; and since the planet Jupiter is said to rule both Sagittarius and Pisces, perhaps we should refer to the last two millennia as the *Age of Jupiter*. Much has been written about the Piscean nature of the last two millennia, but there is much to suggest that a Sagittarian zeitgeist has also been underway. This period has been riddled with warfare and colonisation, motivated by religious/ideological fanaticism and the urge for ever-expanding wealth, power and influence; and due to advances in transport and communication, a world of segregated cultures has been replaced by the 'global village' of today.

Thinking along these lines, the Age of Jupiter will be followed by a double-length Age of Saturn, during which the vernal point will move retrograde through sidereal Aquarius then Capricorn, and the galactic centre will move through tropical Capricorn then Aquarius. This will be followed by another Age of Jupiter, followed by an Age of Mars, an Age of Venus, an Age of Mercury, two 'Luminary Ages', another Age of Mercury, and so on. This pattern extends indefinitely into the past and future.

Dividing Zodiacal Cycles

The remainder of this chapter looks at some of the divisions that astrologers use to interpret zodiacal position. For some of these divisions, I have been unable to find both tropical and sidereal sources; however, I believe that just as each zodiacal sign has a core meaning that can be applied to the tropical or a sidereal zodiac, so the same may be said of each stage of any valid division.

The first part of the discussion looks at divisions in which each stage consists of a whole number of signs: the two, three, four, six and twelve-fold divisions. This is followed by discussion of divisions in which the number of stages is a multiple of twelve. The last part of the discussion looks at the twenty-seven and twenty-eight-fold divisions, focusing on the former.

From this point on, *first third*, *second third* and *final third*, respectively, are abbreviated to *1T*, *2T* and *3T*; and *first hemicycle* and *second hemicycle*, respectively, are abbreviated to *1Hem* and *2Hem*. As noted in previous chapters, *1st harmonic* is abbreviated to *1H*, and so on; and *2nd sub-harmonic* is abbreviated *2SH*, and so on.

As discussed in Chapter 4, the two and three-fold divisions are based solely on the 1H, the four-fold division is based on the 1H and 2H, and the twelve-fold division is based on the 1H, 2H, 3H, 4H and 6H. These harmonics are shown with the twelve zodiacal signs in Figure 5.1 and Figure 5.2.

The 1st Harmonic

Each positive integer (1, 2, 3, 4, etc.) is associated with a particular quality, which is the quality generated when a cycle unfolds at the corresponding harmonic frequency. The 1H unfoldment is imbued with the quality of one-ness, the 2H unfoldment with the quality of two-ness, and so on.

The quality of one-ness is that of *wholeness* itself. Thus, when a cycle of being unfolds at the 1H frequency, the movement of emphasis back and forth between a sense of individual wholeness and a sense of collective wholeness is experienced in its purest form. Each higher harmonic is a sub-harmonic of the 1H; thus, when the cycle of being unfolds at a higher harmonic frequency, the same movement of emphasis between individual and collective wholeness arises, but overlaid with the quality of the number concerned.

The 1H of a zodiacal cycle corresponds simply to a shift of emphasis back and forth between a sense of the importance of functioning as an individual whole and a sense of the importance of functioning as a constituent part of encompassing wholes.

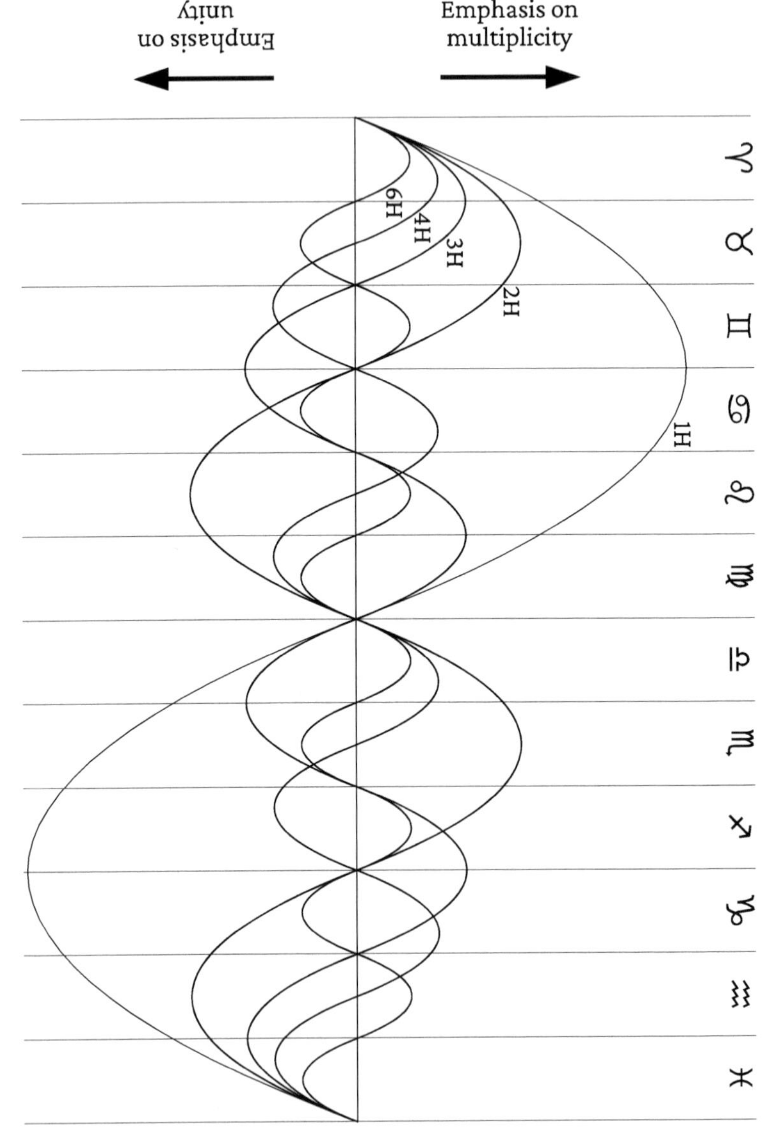

Figure 5.1 The harmonic basis of the twelve-fold division

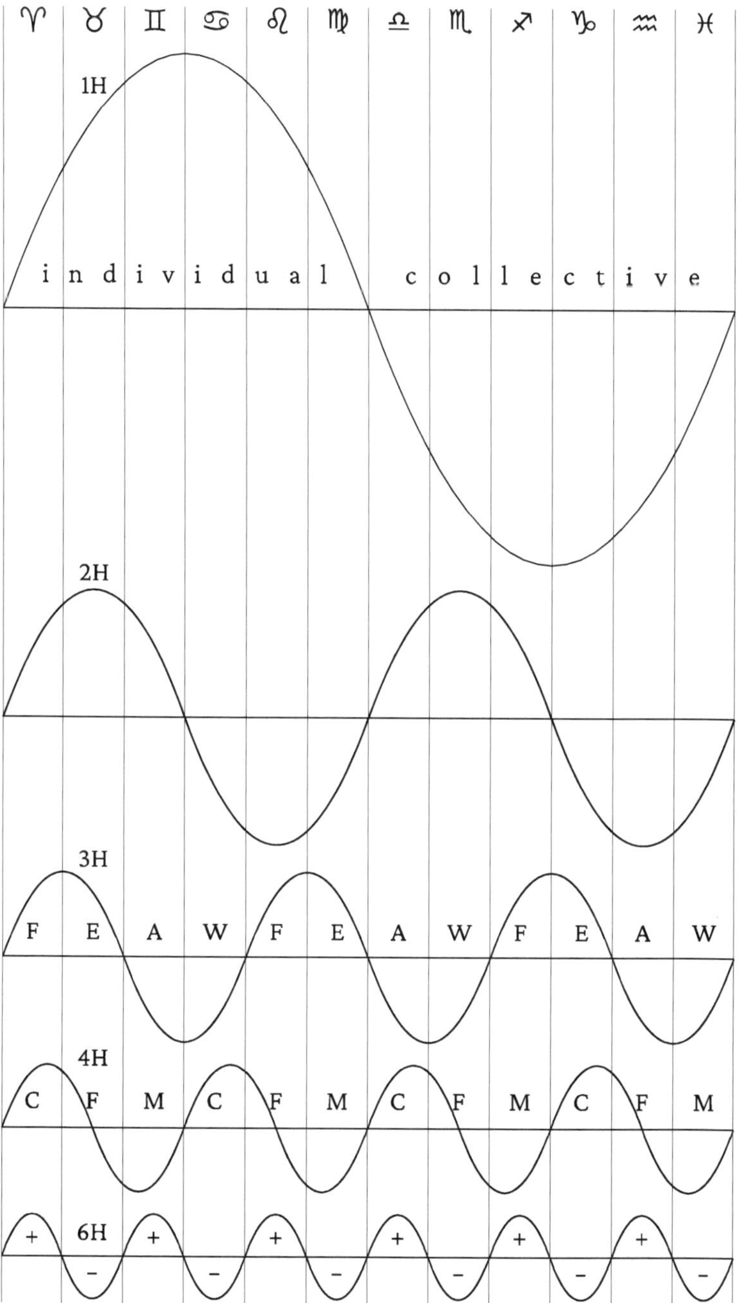

Figure 5.2 The harmonic basis of the twelve-sign zodiac with waves shown separately

The Two-fold Division

The 1H 1Hem – throughout which the principle of multiplicity is dominant – is comprised of the signs Aries through Virgo, which are often referred to as the *personal* or *individual signs*. During this hemicycle, the individual is motivated to function as a relatively self-sufficient, self-contained, autonomous and unique whole in their own right, which is necessary for the success of the form/consciousness-building process. Egoic consciousness strives to prove that the individual can function in this way.

The 1H 2Hem – throughout which the principle of unity is dominant – is comprised of the signs Libra through Pisces, which are often referred to as the *social* or *collective signs*. During this hemicycle, the individual is motivated to function as a cell in the body of an encompassing whole, focused on cooperation, mutuality, shared understanding and common purpose – all of which are necessary for the successful development and spreading of consciousness. Egoic consciousness strives to prove that the individual can function in this way.

In *The Pulse of Life*, Rudhyar* describes the tropical zodiacal cycle as the shift of dominance back and forth between the *Day-force* (an expression of the principle of multiplicity) and the *Night-force* (an expression of the principle of unity). Rudhyar describes the Day-force as a "personalising energy", stating that:

> The natural result of the action of the Day-force is the stressing of that individual uniqueness of human being which is known today as 'personality'.

Rudhyar describes the Night-force as an "ingathering energy", stating that:

> The natural result of the action of the Night-force is to emphasize all values related to 'society'.

The Polar Hemicycles of the 1st Harmonic

During the polar hemicycle that consists of the fourth and first quarters (the signs Capricorn through Gemini), the individual is motivated (at the level of one-ness) to break away from systems of organisation in the name of autonomy and diversity. During the polar hemicycle that consists of the second and third quarters (the signs Cancer through Sagittarius), the individual is motivated (at the level of one-ness) to develop and adhere to

---

* *The Pulse of Life* (1970), p. 27; Khaldea.com/rudhyar/ Pt. 1, p. 11. (1st ed. 1943)

systems of organisation in the name of cooperation and integration.

The Three-fold Division

In *The Magic Thread*, Richard Idemon* suggests that the signs within a given third of the tropical zodiac have in common a particular orientation. Idemon refers to the first four signs as the *personal signs*, describing them as essentially "primitive and primeval" in their expression and oriented towards a concern with 'me'. He refers to the next four signs as the *social signs*, describing them as being oriented towards a sense of 'me and you' and concerned with "interconnections, social relationships [and] validation from other people". He also notes that these signs are aware of the importance of morals and taboos in binding people together within a community. Idemon describes the last four signs as the *collective* or *transpersonal signs*, oriented towards a sense of 'me with the universe' and concerned with "causes, theories, ideas [and] great concepts".

In *Saturn – A New Look at an Old Devil*, Liz Greene† has this to say about how the signs of a given element differ according to the third of the zodiac in which they occur:

> The first sign or house belonging to [an] element is generally the clearest and most direct in meaning and relates to the development of the individual personality and its integration. The second sign of [an] element denotes a point of crisis for here the individual must take his own experience and integrate it into the group of which he is a part. This is rarely done without struggle, for this is an expansion of consciousness from the personal to the universal. The third and last sign or house refers to the larger unit of the group and infers the final purpose of the particular level of consciousness symbolised by that element.

The 2nd Harmonic

The quality of two-ness is that of *division*. At the level of two-ness, existence is endlessly divisible into *this* and *that*, and experiences of being in relationship to that which is other highlight any partiality in the subjective experience of wholeness that arises at the level of one-ness.

---

* *The Magic Thread* (2010) p. 20. (1st ed. 1996)

† *Saturn – A New Look at an Old Devil* (1987) p. 23. (1st ed. 1976)

The 2H of the cycle of being corresponds to a shift of emphasis back and forth between multiplicity and unity that affects the individual's experience of the relationship between the spheres of individual and collective wholeness. This effect of the 2H reiterates something that is already present at the level of one-ness. As noted in Chapter 2, during the 1Q and 3Q of a cycle of being, the dominant principle is increasing in strength, its expression relatively uncompromised by the weaker principle. During the 1H 1Q and 1H 3Q, the principle of multiplicity is dominant in the 2H, which reiterates the need for the uncompromising expression of the principle that is dominant in the 1H. During the 2Q and 4Q of a cycle of being, the dominant principle is becoming weaker, and there is a need to recognise the growing significance of the weaker principle by expressing the principles in a more integrated manner. During the 1H 2Q and 1H 4Q, the principle of unity is dominant in the 2H, which reiterates the need for such integration.

The Four-fold Division

As noted in Chapter 2, the first hemicycle of any cycle of being is its form/consciousness-building hemicycle, and the second hemicycle is its consciousness-developing and spreading hemicycle (during which the forms built during the first hemicycle are only valued insofar as they perform a useful role in the development and spreading of consciousness). Keeping this in mind when considering the 2H, we gain added insight into the meaning of each 1H quarter. During the 1H 1Q (coinciding with the 2H 1Hem), the individual builds form/consciousness simply for the joy of being a builder. During the 1H 2Q (coinciding with the 2H 2Hem), the individual is motivated to build form/consciousness that has value within a consensus (i.e. interpersonal) reality and is inclined to discard form/consciousness that is no longer viewed as having such value. During the 1H 3Q (coinciding with the 2H 1Hem), the individual is motivated to develop and spread consciousness by focusing on the building of unifying structures (communities, conceptual frameworks, symbols, etc.) within the sphere of collective wholeness. And during the 1H 4Q (coinciding with the 2H 2Hem), the individual is motivated to develop and spread consciousness by seeking – and encouraging others to seek – a personal connection to source; and those communities, conceptual frameworks, symbols, etc. that do not support this are no longer valued.

The tropical astrologers Charles Carter*, Alexander von Schlieffen† and Dane

---

* *The Zodiac and the Soul* (1968) pp 14 to 24. (1st ed. 1928)

† *When Chimpanzees Dream Astrology* (2004, 1st ed.) pp. 1, 12, 30 and 49.

Rudhyar* have all commented on the unique meaning of each quarter of the zodiacal cycle.

Carter refers to the signs Aries, Taurus and Gemini as the *fontal triad,* capturing the sense of new beginnings and abundant potential that arises during the first quarter of a cycle of being, and notes the subjective and instinctive nature of these signs. Schlieffen describes the first quarter of the tropical zodiac as that of the *lone wolf* – where we "feel ourselves as ourselves" and value autonomy and the capacity to thrive as an individual. Rudhyar refers to this quarter as the stage of *differentiation.*

Carter refers to Cancer, Leo and Virgo as the *natural triad,* capturing the heightened awareness of the natural order that arises during the second quarter of a cycle of being. Schlieffen describes the second quarter as that of the *eternal child* – where we experience ourselves as the offspring of a particular culture, which we must navigate and utilise in order to express ourselves. Rudhyar refers to this quarter as the stage of *stabilisation.*

Carter refers to the signs Libra, Scorpio and Sagittarius as the *human triad,* capturing the focus on abstraction, conceptualisation and civilisation that arises during the third quarter of a cycle of being. Schlieffen notes that in this quarter, the individual asks others to "mirror me". Here, we view ourselves as an object in the subjective experience of others – as first and foremost a member of various collectives. Rudhyar refers to this quarter as the stage of *group-integration.*

Carter refers to the signs Capricorn, Aquarius and Pisces as the *superhuman triad,* capturing the increased capacity during the fourth quarter of a cycle of being to harness and express the power inherent in encompassing wholes. Schlieffen uses the title *Astronauts in the Desert,* noting that in the fourth quarter, the individual may act as "a symbol for the bigger stream" (i.e. for collective movements), though the individual is not the bigger stream itself. This image is also evocative of the sense of isolation that may arise during this quarter. Rudhyar refers to the fourth quarter as the stage of *capitalisation* – here the individual can better understand how to use the resources of an encompassing whole to best effect.

Correlating the Zodiacal Quarters with the Elements

It is sometimes suggested that a given quarter of the zodiac, and the corresponding season, have an affinity with the element of the zodiacal sign

---

* *An Astrological Mandala* (1974) p 31. (1st ed. 1973)

that begins that quarter. Thus, spring and the first quarter are associated with the element fire, because this quarter begins with the fire sign Aries; summer and the second quarter are associated with water, because this quarter begins with the water sign Cancer; autumn and the third quarter are associated with air, because this quarter begins with the air sign Libra; and winter and the fourth quarter are associated with earth, because this quarter begins with the earth sign Capricorn.

However, as is shown in this chapter: the same themes that arise at the level of one-ness during the first quarter of the zodiac also arise at the level of three-ness during each fire sign; the same themes that arise at the level of one-ness during the second quarter of the zodiac also arise at the level of three-ness during each earth sign, and so on. This being the case, the first, second, third and fourth quarters of a zodiacal cycle – and spring, summer, autumn and winter – have affinity with the elements fire, earth, air and water, respectively. Interestingly, a water theme runs through the figures associated with the last three signs of the zodiac. Capricorn is represented by a creature whose front half is that of a goat and whose rear half is that of a fish; the Truth with which Aquarius seeks to replenish humankind is symbolised by water; and Pisces is the only zodiacal sign represented by a type of animal that is found only in water. (The other water signs are each represented by a type of animal that is found both on land and in water.)

The 3rd Harmonic (and its 2nd Sub-harmonic, the 6th)

The quality of three-ness is that of *enjoyment* and *insight*. At the level of three-ness, the tension inherent in two-ness is transcended and we have a standpoint from which to reflect upon, play with and find satisfying ways of adapting to the world around us. Thus, the 3H of a zodiacal cycle corresponds to shift of emphasis between multiplicity and unity in the way the individual is motivated to understand, enjoy and adapt to life.

The Quarters of the 3rd Harmonic

Each quarter of the 3H corresponds to one of the four elements (see Figure 5.2, in which the letters F, E, A and W refer to the elements fire, earth, air and water, respectively). The elements may also be referred to as the *triplicities*, since there are three zodiacal signs of each element. Because the elements are so familiar to most people, we will discuss the 3H quarters before the 3H hemicycles.

In Ancient Greece, the elements were viewed as the building blocks of reality; and as noted in Chapter 2, for Rudhyar, reality is the cyclic interplay between the principles of multiplicity and unity. The proposed model suggests that both of these ideas point to the same truth, for it portrays the elements as stages of a cycle of being. It may be more accurate, however, to say that the quarters of the cycle of being *in general* are the building blocks of reality, and that these building blocks are simply more apparent at the level of three-ness.

Carl Jung refers to four *functions of consciousness* that individuals use to adapt to life, correlating each function with one of the four elements (see Figure 5.3). In *Barriers and Boundaries*, Greene notes that inherent in a particular way of adapting to life are particular values, and thus particular defences designed to preserve those values. Greene then discusses the type of defence that corresponds to each element and function of consciousness. Three of these defences are those that Sigmund Freud refers to as *oral*, *anal* and *oedipal defence*; and the fourth is referred to by Greene as *dissociation*.

3rd Harmonic quarter	Element	Function of consciousness	Defence
First	Fire	Intuition	Oedipal
Second	Earth	Sensation	Anal
Third	Air	Thinking	Dissociation
Fourth	Water	Feeling	Oral

Figure 5.3 The element, function of consciousness, and type of defence that corresponds to each 3H quarter

Fire: First Quarter of the 3rd Harmonic

The element fire corresponds to the *intuitive function*, which is used to perceive and act upon the potential for creative change, and to attribute meaning and significance to creative processes. Those who are strongly attuned to this element value the individual potency and uniqueness needed to use the intuitive function effectively, using what Freud refers to as *Oedipal defence* to guard against impotence and ordinariness. Rudhyar[*] associates fire with *rhythm* (as the "animating principle").

Egoic consciousness uses oedipal defence in a compulsive and fearful

[*] *A New Approach to the Zodiac*, Khaldea.com/rudhyar/ Pt.2. (1st ed. 1962)

manner, reverting to the first quarter strategies outlined in Chapter 2. Compulsive Oedipal defensiveness is especially likely to take hold during the *phallic stage* of childhood development (age 3 to 6 years approximately), as the child typically tries to affirm their potency and specialness by competing with one parental figure for the admiration and affection of another.

Unconditioned consciousness uses oedipal defence in a relaxed and healthy manner, bolstering the individual's self-belief in a way that inspires them to celebrate the specialness of everyone.

Earth: Second Quarter of the 3rd Harmonic

The element earth corresponds to the *sensation function*, which is used to perceive the nature of concrete form and to work with the concrete realm. Those who are strongly attuned to this element value the pragmatism, self-discipline, autonomy and orderliness needed to use the sensation function effectively, using what Freud refers to as *anal defence* to guard against chaos and lack of control. Rudhyar* associates earth with *consolidation*.

Egoic consciousness uses anal defence in a compulsive and fearful manner, reverting to the second quarter strategies outlined in Chapter 2. Compulsive anal defensiveness is especially likely to take hold during the *anal stage* of development (age 1 to 3 years, approximately), as the child discovers their capacity to exercise independent will through, for example, control of the sphincter muscles.

Unconditioned consciousness uses anal defence in a relaxed and healthy manner, engaging with the concrete realm appreciatively, productively and flexibly, and striking a balance between supporting others, and helping them to become more self-sufficient.

Air: Third Quarter of the 3rd Harmonic

The element air corresponds to the *thinking function*, which is used to acquire, develop and disseminate conceptual understanding, to evaluate the most reasonable (i.e. logical and/or ethical) way to adapt to a given situation, and to achieve mutual understanding with others. Those who are strongly attuned to air value the impartiality and mental clarity needed to use the thinking function effectively, using *dissociation* to guard against oversensitivity to personal concerns. Rudhyar* associates air with *essentialisation*.

---

* *A New Approach to the Zodiac*, Khaldea.com/rudhyar/ Pt.2. (1st ed. 1962)

Egoic consciousness uses dissociation in a compulsive and fearful manner, reverting to the third quarter strategies outlined in Chapter 2.

Unconditioned consciousness uses dissociation in a relaxed and healthy manner, able to reach rational conclusions without becoming excessively detached, and able to strike a balance between guiding others towards clearer understanding, and encouraging them to think for themselves.

Water: Fourth Quarter of the 3rd Harmonic

The element water corresponds to the *feeling* function, which is used to judge the pleasantness or unpleasantness of an experience. A feeling can be thought of as an instinctive response experienced through the lens of selfhood; where instinctive responses arise irrespective of selfhood, feelings are always 'my' feelings. Every animal is guided by instinct to relate to its environment in ways that enhance the wellbeing of itself or its kind, and to the extent that an animal has a sense of selfhood, this guidance arises partly as feelings. Rudhyar[*] associates water with *assimilation*.

Ideally, feelings guide the individual toward truly satisfying and meaningful experiences of connectedness – i.e. toward recognition of their inclusion within increasingly universal wholes. This occurs in tandem with an internal process whereby the person consciously embraces more of their true self by allowing limiting structures of consciousness within the psyche to dissolve. Thus, the element water is concerned with the assimilation of the entire psyche around the 'I-centre' and with the individual's assimilation into encompassing wholes.

Oral defence is described by Greene[†] as "the defence against loneliness and extinction", and can be thought of as the protection of assimilation (both internal and external). Egoic consciousness uses oral defence in a compulsive and fearful manner, reverting to the fourth quarter strategies outlined in Chapter 2. The key issue for watery egoic consciousness is that separation anxiety makes it difficult to shift identification to increasingly universal wholes and thus to achieve a more fulfilling – and less precarious – experience of connectedness.[‡] Compulsive oral defensiveness is especially likely to take hold during the *oral* stage of development (0 to 1 year,

---

[*] *A New Approach to the Zodiac*, Khaldea.com/rudhyar/ Pt.2. (1st ed. 1962)

[†] *Barriers and Boundaries* (2002) p 6. (1st ed. 1996)

[‡] Over recent decades, it has become apparent that addiction is fuelled by a sense of alienation, and that cultivating a sense of connectedness to life is paramount when trying to move beyond an addiction.

approximately), as the child tries to bond with the mother and/or other caregivers to help ensure the provision of food and protection.

Unconditioned consciousness uses oral defence in a relaxed and healthy manner, flowing with the process of internal and external assimilation and helping others to do the same, perhaps using inspiration from the imaginal and spiritual realms to facilitate this.

****

In everyday experience, the functions of consciousness seem to operate in the order of the corresponding 3H quarters. A sense impression (earth) is made intelligible by the nervous system and conceptual mind (air) and then assessed as favourable or unfavourable (water), thus, triggering an emotional response (fire) that results in a change to the sensory landscape (earth), and so on.

Pairing the Elements

There are three ways to group the quarters of the cycle of being into two pairs. In each case, the theme common to the quarters of one pair and the theme common to the quarters of the other pair are polar-opposites. During the 1Q and 2Q, the principle of multiplicity is dominant, while during the 3Q and 4Q, the principle of unity is dominant. During the 1Q and 3Q, the dominant principle is becoming stronger, while during the 2Q and 4Q, the dominant principle is becoming weaker. During the 4Q and 1Q, the principle of multiplicity is becoming stronger, while during the 2Q and 3Q, the principle of unity is becoming stronger.

Fire and Earth – Air and Water

Fire and earth make up the 3H 1Hem and correspond to intuition and sensation, respectively, which Jung refers to as the *perceiving functions*. Thus, during the form/consciousness-building hemicycle of the 3H, the individual understands, enjoys and adapts to life by generating perceptions. Individuals who are strongly attuned to both fire and earth value self-sufficiency and autonomy, and tend to be headstrong and 'hands-on' rather than reflective.

Air and water make up the 3H 2Hem and correspond to thinking and feeling, respectively, which Jung refers to as the *evaluating functions*. Thus, during the consciousness-developing and spreading hemicycle of the 3H, the individual understands, enjoys and adapts to life by making evaluations (both alone and together with others). Individuals who are strongly attuned to both air and water value cooperation and mutuality, and tend to reflect upon their environment rather than trying to make an immediate impression upon it.

This way of pairing the elements is relevant to the six-fold division, for the odd and even-numbered stages of the six-fold division coincide, respectively, with the 3H 1Hem and 3H 2Hem. The hemicycles and thirds of the 1H also play a part in distinguishing the stages of the six-fold division from one another: The 1H 1Hem and 1H 2Hem coincide, respectively, with stages 1 through 3 and stages 4 through 6; and the 1H 1T, 1H 2T and 1H 3T coincide, respectively, with stages 1 and 2, stages 3 and 4, and stages 5 and 6. The six-fold division is rarely used by astrologers – perhaps because the contrast between fire and earth, and the contrast between air and water, are so stark that the mind naturally skips to the twelve-fold division. The six-fold division is also obscured by the prominence of the four-fold division, which is emphasised by the mode cycle. The meanings of the stages of the six-fold division can be discerned from the harmonics listed in this paragraph, and are described by Rudhyar* in *An Astrological Mandala.*

Fire and Air – Earth and Water

The fire and air signs are referred to as the *positive, active, masculine, yang* or *Apollonian signs,* while the earth and water signs are referred to as the *negative, passive, feminine, yin* or *Dionysian signs.* The positive and negative signs are shown, respectively, by + and – in Figure 5.2.

Fire and air correspond, respectively, to the 3H 1Q and 3H 3Q, during which the dominant principle is becoming stronger. Thus, at the level of three-ness, the principle of multiplicity operates with relative freedom in fire, and the principle of unity operates with relative freedom in air. Fire and air also correspond to the 6H 1Hem, during which the principle of multiplicity is dominant. Thus, at the level of six-ness, these elements are concerned with consciousness/form-building. Fiery consciousness is free to perceive special significance in any given phenomenon and to build unique and diverse forms. Airy consciousness is free to evaluate and communicate, and to build conceptual frameworks, without being caught up in particulars and personal concerns. Individuals who are strongly attuned to both fire and air tend to be optimistic, restless and dynamic (outwardly and/or inwardly) and tend to enjoy the process of discovery. Fear of becoming bogged down by practical considerations or feelings may cause these individuals to shy away from nourishing and restorative experiences, and so they may become

---

* *An Astrological Mandala* (1974) pp. 303 to 310. (1st ed. 1973)

'burnt out'.

Earth and water correspond, respectively, to the 3H 2Q and 3H 4Q, during which the dominant principle is becoming weaker. Thus, at the level of three-ness, these elements are concerned with the integration of the principles of multiplicity and unity. Earth and water also correspond to the 6H 2Hem, during which the principle of unity is dominant. Thus, at the level of six-ness, both earth and water are concerned with the development and spreading of consciousness and with relinquishing those forms that do not facilitate this. Earthy consciousness perceives the interrelatedness of seemingly separate phenomena and connects with others through its work with form, ideally relinquishing those forms that do not enhance this connection. Watery consciousness evaluates with a sense of the importance of the personal viewpoint of oneself and others, ideally relinquishing values and allegiances that blinker this viewpoint. Individuals who are strongly attuned to both earth and water try to preserve and improve the quality of the connection between constituent part and encompassing whole. Fear of compromising this connection may cause these individuals to resist change, stifle aspiration and initiative, and accept burdens too readily.

Another point of interest concerning these pairings is that attunement to earth or water heightens awareness of our apparent containment within space-time, while attunement to fire or air does the opposite. Attunement to earth heightens awareness of the relationship between phenomena in three-dimensional space, with time experienced as a fourth dimension – the dimension in which spatial relationships change. Attunement to water exaggerates the apparent quickening and slowing of time, with changes in spatial relationships experienced as markers of the passage of time. (The passage of time tends to feel slower during unpleasant experiences – i.e. when we feel unsupported by the larger life or when we feel a lack of internal assimilation. The passage of time also tends to feel slower during the formation of new memories – i.e. when we are trying to become more familiar with something in order to adapt more effectively to similar circumstances in the future.)

In fact, in any given harmonic, awareness of space-time is stronger during the second and fourth quarters of the cycle of being, when the principles of multiplicity and unity operate in a more integrated manner. This is not surprising given that spatial awareness combines awareness of the distinctiveness of at least two phenomena (multiplicity) with a sense of the continuity of the space between them (unity); and awareness of time combines awareness of the distinctiveness of each moment with a sense of continuity from one moment to the next.

This phenomenon is perhaps most clearly illustrated by the way signs of a given element experience the passage of time: one sign of each element is noticeably more or less aware of the passage of time than the other two, and in each case this can be attributed to the 1H quarter in which the sign occurs.

Of the three earth signs, Taurus has the greatest tendency to become lost in subjective, timeless enjoyment of the material realm, oblivious to rhythms and routines. Taurus occurs in the 1H 1Q while the other earth signs, Virgo and Capricorn, occur in the 1H 2Q and 1H 4Q, respectively.

Scorpio occurs in the 1H 3Q, while the other water signs, Cancer and Pisces, occur in the 1H 2Q and 1H 4Q, respectively. While Cancer and Pisces have an innate sense of the rhythmic and tidal nature of connectedness, and a propensity for nostalgia, "fusion for Scorpio is an immobile and eternal union, impervious to time and change" (Greene*); it must be experienced as the expression of an unchanging and timeless universal truth.

Of the three fire signs, Leo is most aware of the fact of mortality and heritage, and most inclined to try to create a legacy of some kind for future generations. Leo occurs in the 1H 2Q, while the other fire signs, Aries and Sagittarius, occur in the 1H 1Q and 1H 3Q, respectively.

Of the three air signs, Aquarius has the strongest sense of the potential to use the abstract mind to create a future that improves upon the past. Aquarius occurs in the 1H 4Q, while Gemini and Libra occur in the 1H 1Q and 1H 3Q, respectively.

Water and Fire – Earth and Air

Water and fire correspond, respectively, to the 3H 4Q and 3H 1Q, throughout which the principle of multiplicity is becoming stronger. Carter† and others have referred to these as the *emotional elements*, for they give rise to personal – i.e. emotive – responses. They are also often referred to as the *intuitive elements*, for watery evaluations and fiery perceptions arise relatively independently of facts or conscious deliberation. Eric Meyers‡ refers to water and fire as the *charged elements*, capturing the sense of instability and possibility that accompanies increasing emphasis on multiplicity. Individuals who are strongly attuned to both these elements tend to be

---

* *Barriers and Boundaries* (2002) p. 49. (1st ed. 1996)

† *The Foundations of Astrology* (1978) p. 78. (1st ed. 1947)

‡ *Elements and Evolution* (2010, 1st ed.) Ch. 2

quick to follow their own impulses (doing this through fantasy if necessary) and open to inspiration, and tend to find it difficult to attune to the requirements of consensus reality.

Earth and air correspond, respectively, to the second and third quarters of the 3H, throughout which the principle of unity is becoming stronger. Earth and air are associated, respectively, with the pragmatic and conceptual mind, and are referred to by Carter* as the *mental elements*. Meyers† refers to earth and air as the *neutral elements*, capturing the tendency toward impartiality and objectivity that accompanies increasing emphasis on unity. Individuals who are strongly attuned to both these elements try to understand and honour the organising principles at work in their environment (and within their own being), and are more attuned to consensus reality – perhaps to the extent of being impervious to inspiration from the imaginal or spiritual realms.

The Four Basic Qualities

Aristotle taught that fundamental to existence are four *basic qualities*. *Hot* is a yang quality that corresponds to *activity*, while its polar-opposite – *cold* – is a yin quality that corresponds to *passivity*. *Dry* is a yang quality that corresponds to *separateness*, while its polar-opposite – *wet* – is a yin quality that corresponds to *cohesion*.

Each element is assigned one quality from the hot/cold polarity and one quality from the dry/wet polarity (see Figure 5.4). As noted in Chapter 2, the principle of multiplicity is a yang principle and the principle of unity is a yin principle. Thus, the yang quality *hot* corresponds to the yang hemicycle of the 6H (fire and air), while the yin quality *cold* corresponds to the yin hemicycle of the 6H (earth and water). The yang quality *dry* corresponds to the yang hemicycle of the 3H (fire and earth), while the yin quality *wet* corresponds to the yin hemicycle of the 3H (air and water).

We can see that fire is reaching towards an extreme yang condition, because heat causes further drying; and water is reaching towards an extreme yin condition, because coldness attracts further moisture. In contrast, earth and air each combine a yang quality with a yin quality. Thus, the instability of fire and water may be due not only to the increasing emphasis on multiplicity in the 3H, but also to the way the 3H and 6H reinforce one another in these elements; and the stability of earth and air may be due not

---

* *The Foundations of Astrology* (1978) p. 78. (1st ed. 1947)

† *Elements and Evolution* (2010, 1st ed.) Ch. 2

only to the increasing emphasis on unity in the 3H, but also to the way the 3H and 6H complement one another in these elements. (According to the proposed model, this principle may be applied to any given harmonic and its 2SH.)

Element	Hot/cold polarity (6th harmonic)	Dry/wet polarity (3rd harmonic)
Fire	Hot (active, yang)	Dry (separating, yang)
Earth	Cold (passive, yin)	Dry (separating, yang)
Air	Hot (active, yang)	Wet (cohesive, yin)
Water	Cold (passive, yin)	Wet (cohesive, yin)

Figure 5.4 The qualities of the elements

Correlating the Elements, Qualities and Seasons

As noted above, the 1H 2Q and 1H 4Q have traditionally been associated with water and earth, respectively, because the 1H 2Q begins with the water sign Cancer, while the 1H 4Q begins with the earth sign Capricorn. Thus earth (a separating element) is traditionally correlated with the 1H 4Q (during which unity is emphasised in the 1H), and water (a cohesive element) is traditionally correlated with the 1H 2Q (during which multiplicity is emphasised in the 1H). According to the proposed model, fire and earth (the separating elements) have affinity, respectively, with the 1H 1Q and 1H 2Q (emphasis on multiplicity); and air and water (the cohesive elements) have affinity, respectively, with the 1H 3Q and 1H 4Q (emphasis on unity).

Both the traditional approach and the approach suggested by the proposed model correlate the hot elements – fire and air – with spring and autumn, respectively. This may seem strange given that summer is the hottest month, but makes sense when we consider that heat is essentially a form of energy transfer, and that the quality *hot* relates to activity. Spring and autumn are seasons of tremendous activity, with foliage being generated at great speed during spring, and much of it being returned to the earth during autumn. During summer and winter, the natural world is not subject to such rapid change.

The 4th Harmonic

Four-ness has the quality of *substantiality*. It is as though the two polarities inherent in four-ness (2 X 2 = 4) combine as the weft and weave of the fabric of reality.

It is noted above that any partiality in the subjective sense of wholeness (arising at the level of one-ness) is highlighted by experiences of being in relationship to that which is other (arising at the level of two-ness). Similarly, any polarisation between self and other at the level of two-ness is highlighted by the power struggles that arise when both parties try to affect tangible change at the level of four-ness (the 4H being the 2SH of the 2H). In fact, any number that is a multiple of two (2, 4, 6, 8, etc.) contains some degree of friction or tension, which is eased only by the expansion of the subjective sense of self to include the apparent cause of the friction or tension. This is especially so where the number is also a power of two (2, 4, 8, 16, etc.) and thus an expression of pure two-ness.

The 4H of a zodiacal cycle corresponds to a shift of emphasis back and forth between multiplicity and unity in the way the individual is motivated to use power to effect tangible change.

As noted in Chapter 4, the stage boundaries of the twelve-fold division divide the 4H into thirds; and in the twelve-sign zodiac, this gives rise to the mode cycle of *cardinal sign* (4H 1T) > *fixed sign* (4H 2T) > *mutable sign* (4H 3T), which unfolds once during each 1H quarter (see Figure 5.2). Since there are four zodiacal signs of each mode, the modes may be referred to as the *quadruplicities*. (Discussion of the core themes of each third of the cycle of being can be found starting on page 123.)

Cardinality: First Third of the 4th Harmonic

The cardinal mode is self-motivated, pro-active, impulsive, opportunistic, goal-oriented, dynamic, intolerant of restriction, and more suited to the instigation of new projects than sustained commitment to established ones. Erin Sullivan* speaks of the "instinctive, creative thrust" of the cardinal signs. Michael R. Meyer† notes that a preponderance of cardinality in the birth chart "denotes an individual who may be constantly attempting to project himself into experience, possibly without regard or consideration for others" and who is "not particularly concerned with values or ideals".

---

* *The Signs* (You Tube).

† *A Handbook for the Humanistic Astrologer* (2000) p. 154. (1st ed. 1974)

Rudhyar* associates cardinality with motion in a straight line, capturing the subjective, goal-oriented nature of this mode.

Fixity: Second Third of the 4th Harmonic

The fixed mode is usually associated with stability, reliability, stubbornness, endurance, determination and possibly a 'might makes right' approach to making things happens. Meyer† notes that a preponderance of fixity in the birth chart suggests a person who is concerned with "the definition and perfection of function in its purest form" and "the karmic consequences surrounding any action or situation", and for whom "values and ideals are placed above individuals and situations". All of these characteristics can be seen as arising from a heightened awareness of – and an inclination towards alignment with – organising principles.

Fixity is also associated with intense experiences and challenges that may lead to transformation and to initiation into a new way of being (the transition from cardinal subjectivity to mutable breadth of understanding). Rudhyar* associates fixity with motion in a circle, capturing the circumscribing and focalising effect that organising principles have on the expression of power.

Mutability: Final Third of the 4th Harmonic

With the polar tide moving in favour of the principle of multiplicity (once the polar tide turns), diversification is now prioritised over organisation; but with the principle of unity still dominant, the need for harmony is prioritised over the need for autonomy. Thus, mutability is the most adaptable mode, being more open to change than fixity and less inclined to take the driving seat than cardinality. Robert Hand‡ notes that the mutable signs have the "flexibility needed to allow structures to survive amid changing realities" (and, we might add, to relinquish those structures that are no longer viable). Hand also notes that the mutable signs "are able to take whatever has been created and sustained by the other two quadruplicities and transmute it so it can operate at a higher level" (i.e. in response to the needs of an encompassing whole). Meyer† notes that a preponderance of mutability in the birth chart suggests "a possibility of much personal freedom, though the person may be incapable of self-willed action". Meyer also notes that a person with a mutable emphasis may be

---

* *A New Approach to the Zodiac*, Khaldea.com/rudhyar/ Pt.2. (1st ed. 1962)

† *A Handbook for the Humanistic Astrologer* (2000) p. 154. (1st ed. 1974)

‡ *Horoscope Symbols* (1981, 1st ed.) page 199

"devotional", "sentimental" and "concerned with people and relationships rather than ideals and personal ambitions". This concern with people and relationships stems from a desire for fluid assimilation with a greater whole. (Fixity is also concerned with relationships, but this stems from a desire for structured interpersonal integration.)

Mutability is also associated with knowledge, understanding and consciousness. The mutable signs sweep the environment in a radar-like manner, acquiring understanding that promotes the ongoing process of internal and external assimilation. These signs are prone to restlessness and nervous agitation – a sign that the intensity and frequency of the sweep has become excessive due to fear of internal and/or external fragmentation. Rudhyar[*] associates mutability with motion in a spiral, which combines the motions of cardinality and fixity. Mutability works towards ever-greater synthesis and inclusiveness by combining a capacity to embrace change with a capacity for integration.

The Twelve-fold Division

The twelve-fold division would have originally been adopted because the Sun transits approximately one twelfth of the ecliptic between successive new moons. That a particularly significant change of meaning occurs at each stage boundary of a twelve-fold division is one of the many examples of synchronicity that the study of astrology reveals.

We have seen that the twelve-fold division emphasises the 3H and thus the quality of three-ness, which transcends the polarisation inherent in two-ness and brings the potential for understanding and insight. Thus, it is interesting to note that the first known use of the twelve-fold division is thought to have begun during the sixth century BCE. The Buddha, Loa Tzu and Confucius all lived in this century, which was, in the words of Rudhyar,[†] "a most significant turning point in human civilization". Towards the end of this century, the Roman Republic was established, from which arose a new type of legal system and a new understanding of what it means to be an individual human being – both of which are clearly visible in the democracies of today.

The following account of the zodiacal signs focuses on the roles played by the 1H, 3H and 4H. Although the 2H and 6H are also relevant to any twelve-

---

[*] *A New Approach to the Zodiac*, Khaldea.com/rudhyar/ Pt.2. (1st ed. 1962)

[†] *Astrological Timing – The Transition to the New Age* (1972, 1st ed.) p. 109; Khaldea.com/rudhyar/ Ch. 5, p. 3.

fold division, the contributions of these harmonics are largely implicit in those of the 1H and 3H, respectively, due to the relationship which exists between a harmonic and its 2SH. We simply need to keep in mind that as the dominant principle grows stronger in a given harmonic (during the 1Q and 3Q), there is scope for prolific building within the emphasised sphere of wholeness; and as the dominant principle grows weaker (during the 2Q and 4Q), there is a need for adjustment and refinement in recognition of the growing significance of the opposite sphere of wholeness.

Before looking at each zodiacal sign in turn, it is worth considering how the relationships between the 1H, 3H and 4H harmonics change around a twelve-sign zodiac (and any other twelve-fold division). This aids understanding not only of the meanings of the individual signs, but also of the themes that are brought into focus by each sign pairing. (The sign pairings are to be discussed in the next book in this series).

Awareness of three such patterns of change dates back to the Ancient Greeks: there is one sign of each mode within each quarter of the zodiac (due to the relationship between the 1H quarters and 4H thirds); there is one sign of each element within each third of the zodiac (due to the relationship between the 1H thirds and 3H quarters); and each element-mode combination is represented by one sign (due to the relationship between the 3H quarters and 4H thirds).

Another pattern involves the relationship between the 1H thirds and the 4H thirds. When each mode is viewed as a particular 4H third, we see that there is an emphasis on a particular third during the first and last sign of each 1H third: the 1H 1T begins and ends with a cardinal sign (4H 1T); the 1H 2T begins and ends with a fixed sign (4H 2T); and the 1H 3T begins and ends with a mutable sign (4H 3T).

A final pattern to consider involves the relationship between the 1H quarters and 3H quarters:

In a sign that begins or ends at a 1H point of equilibrium (Aries, Virgo, Libra and Pisces), the same quarter is unfolding in both the 1H and 3H. Thus, the form/consciousness-building that occurs throughout the 1H 1Q gets off to a flying start in Aries; and the concept/community-building that occurs at the level of one-ness throughout the 1H 3Q gets off to a flying start in Libra. (Because these signs begin their respective 1H quarters, this is further enhanced by the impulsiveness and initiative of cardinality.) The processes of adjustment and refinement that occur throughout the 1H 2Q and 1H 4Q are brought to a strong conclusion in Virgo and Pisces, respectively.

(Because these signs come at the end their respective 1H quarters, these processes are further enhanced by the adaptability and assimilating power of mutability.)

In a sign that occurs in the middle of its respective 1H quarter (Taurus, Leo, Scorpio and Aquarius), the same principle – i.e. the same sphere of wholeness – is emphasised in the 1H and 3H, but the direction of the polar tide in one harmonic is opposite to that in the other. On the one hand, this gives rise to tension between the need to build freely within the sphere concerned and the need for adjustment and refinement. On the other hand, looking at that sphere from both directions, so to speak, results in great depth of understanding; and because these are the fixed signs, the question of whether anything of real value is being generated in that sphere comes to the fore. Thus, Taurus and Leo are concerned with self-worth and the generation of form that has real value, while Scorpio and Aquarius are concerned with the worth of the group and with developing and spreading consciousness that has real value.

In a sign that begins or ends at a 1H pole (Gemini, Cancer, Sagittarius and Capricorn), the quarter that is unfolding in the 1H is the opposite quarter to that which is unfolding in the 3H. Thus, in each of these signs, the principle that is dominant in the 1H is the opposite of the principle that is dominant in the 3H, with both harmonics in agreement on whether discovery (1Q and 3Q) or sustainment/containment (2Q and 4Q) is more important. In Gemini and Sagittarius – the mutable signs that end the 1H 1Q and 1H 3Q, respectively – the 3H helps to objectify the process of discovery in preparation for the turning of the 1H polar tide. In Cancer and Capricorn – the cardinal signs that begin the 1H 2Q and 1H 4Q, respectively – the 3H helps to initiate the integration of the two spheres.

The emphasis on opposite principles at the levels of one-ness and three-ness may explain why each of these signs is generally better at seeing the potential for humour than the other two signs of the same element. (Note that three-ness is associated with both enjoyment and insight.) Peter McGraw's *benign violation theory* states that we see humour in that which challenges – in a non-threatening way – our expectations of how things should be.* Benign violation can perhaps be understood as the realisation

---

* Experiences of spiritual awakening involve the benign violation of one's limited sense of selfhood, and such experiences tend to feel humorous, often causing the individual to laugh aloud. Whether or not the object of benign violation is one's sense of selfhood, all humour brings a sense of release; and given the close

that a particular view of something (principle of multiplicity) is one of a number of views that coexist within a wider perspective (principle of unity). The types of humour associated with 'positive' signs Gemini and Sagittarius are playful and upbeat, with a light and agile quality that is partly attributable to mutability. The types of humour associated with 'negative' signs Cancer and Capricorn are dry and downbeat, with a forthright quality that is largely attributable to cardinality.

Aries

In Aries, a sense of the importance of being free to blossom as a unique individual and to spontaneously express that uniqueness (1H 1Q) combines with a natural ability to act as an agent for creative change and imbue life with meaning (fire), and an impulsive, self-motivated and goal-oriented approach to effecting tangible change (cardinal).

With the 1H, 3H and 4H all in the 1Q and/or 1T, Aries is predisposed to act out impulses and emotions in a subjective and impetuous manner, and is thus able to give vivid and distinctive form to emerging potentiality. As Rudhyar* notes, in Aries, the dominance of the Day Force over the Night Force is marginal. Thus, there is a sense that action must be taken without hesitation in order to make full use of the strength of the polar tide and break free of that which has gone before.

In an attempt to lessen anxiety, egoic consciousness continually tries to affirm that the individual is an effective agent or channel for – or perhaps even the source of – some vital, creative force. This is attempted with first quarter strategies such as those outlined in the Chapter 2 (page 97).

Taurus

In Taurus, a sense of the importance of being free to blossom as a unique individual and to spontaneously express that uniqueness (1H 1Q) combines with a natural ability to work with and enjoy the physical world (earth), and a determined, organisational and idealistic approach to effecting tangible change (fixed).

---

connection between humour and spiritual awakening, it is not surprising that humour has such power to heal people and bring people together.

* *The Pulse of Life* (1970) p. 32; Khaldea.com/rudhyar/ Pt. 2, Aries, p. 1. (1st ed. 1943). In this incredibly insightful account of the zodiacal signs, Rudhyar comments on the significance of the relationship between the Day Force and the Night Force (i.e. the state of the 1H) during each sign.

The principle of multiplicity is still dominant in the 3H, and Taurus, like Aries, is very wilful; however, the 3H polar tide has turned, and Taurian wilfulness is pragmatic, persistent and focused on turning available resources into something of enduring worth. The combination of 1Q and 2Q themes endows Taurus with great ability as a builder of form/consciousness. The sense of value of fixity combines with the sensory awareness of earth, giving rise to a refined aesthetic sense.

Egoic consciousness tries to alleviate anxiety by, for example: striving to enhance one's strength, productivity and worth through the acquisition and retention of assets and skills; insisting on acting according to one's own subjective sense of order and timing (resulting in stubbornness or proceeding 'like a bull in a china shop'); seeking external validation of one's worth and vitality by conforming to the values of others; and/or over-indulging the senses in an attempt to feel more fully alive. In these strategies we can see the juxtaposition of the need to spontaneously express one's specialness and potency (1H 1Q) and the need to engage with the world of cause and effect (3H 2Q and 4H 2T).

Gemini

In Gemini, a sense of the importance of being free to blossom as a unique individual and to spontaneously express that uniqueness (1H 1Q) combines with a natural ability to see the underlying principles that unite phenomena (air) and a holistic, adaptable and insightful approach to effecting tangible change (mutable).

Combining the particularising tendency of the 1H 1Q with the synthesising tendencies of air and mutability, Gemini dissects reality into a multitude of distinct phenomena in order to explore the principles and relationships that unite them. Although less overtly wilful than the previous two signs, Gemini insists on having sufficient freedom to play with ideas and follow any trail of connections that arouses its curiosity. This agile, inquisitive and often eccentric sign has an affinity with the archetype of the *eternal youth*.

Egoic consciousness tries to alleviate anxiety by, for example: striving to acquire as much knowledge as possible; trying to impress others with knowledge, wit and gossip; trying to achieve a sense of one-upmanship through pranks and trickery; using communication with others to express one's own ideas and recollections in an attempt to feel more fully alive; filtering information subjectively rather than allowing one's current understanding to be challenged; and using distorted logic and reason to push a personal agenda. A tendency towards subjective identification with each phenomenon encountered (1H 1Q), combined with a need for a wide variety of experiences (air) and a tendency to sweep for data (mutable), may result in nervous agitation, restlessness and a sense of being scattered and fragmented.

Cancer

In Cancer, a sense of the importance of blossoming as a unique individual by working effectively with the limits and possibilities inherent in one's situation (1H 2Q) combines with a natural ability to orient oneself and others toward more fulfilling experiences of connectedness (water) and an impulsive, self-motivated and goal-oriented approach to effecting tangible change (cardinal).

Cancer is concerned with the process of gestation, wherein potentiality is nurtured within a compartment of the orderly matrix (1H 2Q) until it is ready to exist independently of that compartment and assimilate into a larger compartment (watery assimilation into every-greater wholes). Gestation is an expression of the 1H 1T and 4H 1T in that it begins with the emergence of new potentiality and moves purposefully toward the goal of bringing that potentiality to fruition. Parenting and counselling are examples of how an individual can act as a womb for the gestation of new consciousness in others. Artistry and being present with one's own feelings are examples of how new consciousness can be nurtured within one's own psyche.

Throughout the 1H 2Q, the sense of individual selfhood is being stabilised and refined; and in watery Cancer this process is facilitated by the permeability of the I-centre to the encompassing individual psyche. As the subjective sense of self expands to include more of the psyche, the individual feels more at home within their own being, and the sphere of the external world within which they experience a sense of belonging expands. In accordance with the subjective self-image carried in any given moment, Cancer responds to changes occurring in the orderly matrix in ways that seem likely to enhance internal and external assimilation.

Cardinality instinctively pushes forward, but there is awareness of the role of past events in shaping the present (1H 2Q), and awareness of the need for continuity in the relationship between constituent part and encompassing whole (1H 2Q, 3H 4Q). Thus, there is a tendency to preserve traditions and artefacts, and to try to empathise (water) with those who lived in previous eras.

Egoic consciousness tries to alleviate anxiety by, for example: hoarding things that may help sustain the individual in the future; engaging in clannish protectionism; clinging to a nurturing role or to one's inclusion within a supportive collective; hiding within some kind of shell; eating compulsively or indulging in other types of habitual behaviour; and compulsively organising one's own or others' lives. The extent to which something is necessary to sustain, stabilise and protect the individual's corporeal existence (1H 2Q) is assessed using the feeling function (3H 4Q), which projects onto the thing the power to redeem the gnawing sense of isolation and vulnerability that plagues watery egoic consciousness. The 1T emphasis manifests as a compulsive need to take action to acquire and retain those things that are felt to be necessary.

Leo

In Leo, a sense of the importance of blossoming as a unique individual by working effectively with the limits and potentials inherent in one's situation (1H 2Q) combines with a natural ability to act as an agent for creative change and imbue life with meaning (fire), and a determined, organisational and idealistic approach to effecting tangible change (fixed).

The second fire sign occurs in the 1H 2Q, the 1H 2T and the 4H 2T; thus, the spontaneity and creativity of fire are expressed with a strong sense of social and moral obligation,* an appreciation of order, and an ability to utilise internal and external resources (including the effective management and leadership of people). Combining 1Q themes with 2Q and 2T themes, Leo is adept at generating form/consciousness, and places importance on producing something of real value.

Egoic consciousness tries to alleviate anxiety by, for example: pursuing or clinging to power and authority; insisting that others live according to one's vision; compromising one's creative integrity to secure the attention and admiration of others; recoiling from self-expression due to excessive self-consciousness and fear of criticism; and entertaining a sense of specialness and entitlement (perhaps tending to take chances on shortcuts to success through, for example, gambling and risky entrepreneurial activity). A need to celebrate one's uniqueness (1H 1Q) combines with a need to engage effectively and productively with that which is other (3H 2Q, 4H 2T),

---

* In *The Luminaries* (1992, 1st ed.) p. 99, Greene associates the Sun (the celestial body that 'rules' Leo) with a sense of being indebted to life for having usurped a piece of the life-force, and a need to contribute something of worth to life in order to repay this debt.

bringing the issue of self-worth to the fore. The need to be appreciated and admired by others may give rise to fantasies about being special in a way that others are not. The collapse of the fantasy can trigger enquiry into the true nature of selfhood, which may lead to a more peaceful and fulfilling experience of being 'me', and a more spontaneous and creative approach to using internal and external resources.

Virgo

In Virgo, a sense of the importance of blossoming as a unique individual by working effectively with the limits and potentials inherent in one's situation (1H 2Q) combines with a natural ability to work with and enjoy the physical world (earth), and a holistic, adaptable and insightful approach to effecting tangible change (mutable).

With the 2Q unfolding in both the 1H and 3H, attention is focused on the refinement of the form/consciousness-building process, fundamental to which is the purification and fine-tuning of the individual. Reality is experienced as an orderly matrix of separate phenomena (1H 2Q, 3H 2Q), and detailed analysis is used to understand how component parts can best be assimilated into an efficient and smooth-running system (4H 3T). Virgo's placement in the 1H 2T underlines the importance of engaging with that which is other.

The strong focus on establishing and maintaining boundaries (1H 2Q, 3H 2Q) gives rise to a sense that true internal and external assimilation can only be achieved by knowing (and remaining true to) oneself. However, Virgo is endowed with common sense (1H 2Q, 3H 2Q), openness to new knowledge (4H 3T), and a willingness to engage with others (1H 2T), and consequently has the humility to seek guidance from those with more experience – perhaps by serving as a disciple or apprentice. Due to the devotional, transcendent nature of mutability, mundane tasks may be experienced as meaningful rituals, and sensuality may be experienced as a bridge to something beyond the everyday world.

Egoic consciousness tries to alleviate anxiety by, for example: striving to ensure that certain processes always run perfectly smoothly; trying to control outcomes when it would be better to step back and let things take their course; rigidly adhering to routines and procedures; striving to be useful to others, including trying to convince others to take practical advice; and engaging in excessive self-scrutiny, self-censorship and self-possession. A sense that things could fall into chaos at any moment may result in attachment to whichever systems of organisation seem to have worked best so far. This prevents objective assessment of the systems and stifles the kind of playfulness and flexibility that can lead to fruitful changes to the way the individual's world is organised. In Virgo, the radar-like sweep associated with mutability may find expression through the compulsive repetition of practical routines involving, for example, cleaning, tidying or exercising.

Libra

In Libra, a sense of the importance of cooperative, communal living and alignment with higher principles (1H 3Q) combines with a natural ability to see the underlying principles that unite phenomena (air) and an impulsive, self-motivated and goal-oriented approach to effecting tangible change (cardinal).

With the third quarter unfolding in both the 1H and 3H, the drive and initiative of cardinality is applied to the discovery of universal principles, the development of mutual understanding and the building of community. Libra's placement in the 1H 2T adds to the idealism of the 3Q emphasis, and there is a propensity to try to bring people, objects, colours, sounds, etc. into ideal states of alignment in which the value of each thing (including the individual) is optimised. Libra is appreciative of beauty and harmony in all its forms, and may be drawn to the elegant and balanced picture of reality generated by theorems and equations.

Egoic consciousness tries to alleviate anxiety by, for example: avoiding or dismissing that which seems to diminish beauty or harmony; rigidly adhering to a notion of what is reasonable (i.e. logical and/or ethical); affecting the pretence of mutual understanding; accepting a consensus viewpoint too readily; and/or insisting on 'sitting on the fence' rather than committing to a course of action. There may be a sense that discord is the enemy of harmony rather than an inevitable part of life that, when approached creatively, offers a path to a more profound and truthful harmony. Fearful of having nothing of worth to contribute to the group, egoic consciousness tends to socialise in a compulsive, opportunistic and competitive manner.

Rudhyar[*] notes that just as in Aries, the Day Force must assert its new and seemingly precarious dominance, so in Libra, the Night Force must do likewise.

---

[*] *The Pulse of Life* (1970) p. 74; Khaldea.com/rudhyar/ Pt 2, Libra, p. 1. (1st ed. 1943)

Scorpio

In Scorpio, a sense of the importance of cooperative, communal living and alignment with higher principles (1H 3Q) combines with a natural ability to orient oneself and others towards more fulfilling experiences of connectedness (water) and a determined, organisational and idealistic approach to effecting tangible change (fixed).

Scorpio has much capacity to develop and spread consciousness (1H 3Q, 3H 4Q), and is keen to ensure that this consciousness has true value (1H 2T, 4H 2T). The 2T emphasis, combined with an emphasis on unity in the 1H and 3H, results in heightened awareness of the socio-cultural and metaphysical structures that bind individuals together. Structures that impede the watery process of assimilation – both internal structures of consciousness and external socio-cultural structures (i.e. structures of collective consciousness) – must be challenged. Thus, Scorpio has a propensity to break personal and social taboos and to generate radical solutions to personal and social problems. The assimilation that Scorpio seeks enhances the free and creative movement of resources within and between wholes, reducing the potential for the misappropriation or stagnation of those resources.

As limiting structures of consciousness dissolve (water), a clearer understanding of the logic inherent in the phenomenal realm emerges (1H 2T, 4H 2T, 1H 3Q), and this paves the way for the more transcendent viewpoint that will arise during the 1H 3T. Scorpio probes beneath the surface of its current reality in order to get closer to the truth; and its fascination with death may arise largely from a sense that there are things that can never be experienced from within the structures inherent in 'my reality'. The sign also has a propensity to help others undergo transformative experiences that take them beyond their current reality. (Scorpio's position in the 1H 3Q makes it less empathic than the other water signs and therefore less prone to complicity with the limiting fears of those being helped.) The Scorpio individual may appear enigmatic and seductive – or perhaps threatening and repulsive – to others, who sense that the individual can unlock their hidden resources or expose their 'demons'.

Egoic consciousness tries to alleviate anxiety by, for example: pursuing or clinging to relationships or roles that feel empowering; using or withholding knowledge or insight in a manipulative manner; using powers of seduction to control others; compulsively breaking taboos; hiding 'taboo' parts of oneself from oneself and/or others; and/or habitually giving away power or resources. Fear of being shamed, disempowered or violated in some way can trigger withdrawal and/or pre-emptive strikes, and so the fear may become a self-fulfilling prophecy. Scorpio egoic consciousness can be controlling and possessive, and may try to justify vengeful behaviour with distorted notions of social or natural justice. There may be a sense of dependence on – and entitlement to – the resources held by others, but also a sense that declaring one's needs will result in humiliation and alienation; and this may lead to covert, parasitic behaviour. Yet alongside the impulse to maintain control, there can be a longing to surrender to something that has the power to strip away the limiting defences and facades erected by egoic consciousness. Thus, intimacy tends to bring up intense and ambivalent feelings.

Sagittarius

In Sagittarius, a sense of the importance of cooperative, communal living and alignment with higher principles (1H 3Q) combines with a natural ability to act as an agent for creative change and imbue life with meaning (fire) and a holistic, adaptable and insightful approach to effecting tangible change (mutable).

Fire's optimism and need for meaning combine with a focus on underlying archetypal principles (1H 3Q) and a need to understand one's relationship to existence-as-a-whole (1H 3T, 4H 3T). This gives rise to a philosophical outlook and often to a sense of having a part to play in the unfoldment of a purposeful and all-encompassing plan. There may be a tendency to view life as a treasure hunt for clues as to the nature of this plan.

With the idealism of the 1H 3Q, and fire's focus on celebrating one's uniqueness, there may be an inclination to try to become one's 'best self'* – perhaps by aligning one's sense of identity and self-expression with some benevolent deity or archetypal principle. There is a tendency to adhere to a religion or some other school of thought that reinforces one's sense that the development of consciousness and the building of community are meaningful endeavours.

The intuition and initiative of fire may be played out in the social arena (1H 3Q, 3T emphasis), and the individual is primed to act out newly emerging socio-cultural trends. Since fire also endows the individual with optimism and a sense of an abundance of possibilities, there may be a strong

---

* Jupiter is the traditional and modern ruler of Sagittarius, and in *Water and Fire*, Darby Costello suggests that "you imagine yourself in your best light through your Jupiter placement,...as unfolding towards some potential image of completeness". (Kindle book, 63%).

entrepreneurial spirit. The individual may have a natural ability to inspire others with their vision, whether this vision concerns business, religion, spirituality, community or even science. The need for new experiences and broader understanding may be expressed through the exploration of other cultures.

Egoic consciousness tries to alleviate anxiety by, for example: seeking affirmation of one's beliefs – and one's significance as an ambassador for those beliefs – by striving to inspire others to embrace them; trying to be trendy as a substitute for truly meaningful collective involvement; clinging to a sense that one is a 'child of the gods' by testing one's luck and taking the easy route; compulsively using some form of divination (learned or invented) when making decisions; compulsively interpreting experience through the lens of a broad philosophical framework rather than trusting one's own intuition; and/or grasping at new understanding – perhaps to the extent of being gullible. Sagittarius egoic consciousness may be driven relentlessly by wanderlust; as in Gemini, the combination of mutability and the 1Q and 3Q makes it difficult to settle into the here-and-now.

Capricorn

In Capricorn, a sense of the importance of expressing the potential inherent in encompassing wholes by following the guidance from source that arises from within (1H 4Q) combines with a natural ability to work with and enjoy the physical world (earth) and an impulsive, self-motivated and goal-oriented approach to effecting tangible change (cardinal).

Earth's love of order combines with a propensity to take on the needs of encompassing wholes (1H 4Q), resulting in a sense that certain hierarchical structures must be respected and certain rules and traditions honoured. By learning to embody those rules, the individual may become an authority within a particular area and perhaps change the way those laws are implemented, which fulfils the cardinal need for autonomy. The powers of seduction and persuasion inherent in the 1H 4Q combine with the reassuring pragmatism of earth and the inspiring optimism of cardinality to make the Capricorn individual a natural choice of politician/leader.

In order to experience increasing fulfilment, and avoid the onset of a sense of futility or disillusionment, the individual may need to periodically relinquish outmoded values and allegiances (1H 4Q). Since the individual is predisposed to adhere to rules, they may need to withdraw from the influence of others in order to see which values and allegiances have become sources of frustration and dissatisfaction. Such relinquishment brings about external assimilation because it allows the individual to engage with an increasingly diverse range of people in a confident and tolerant manner. It brings about internal assimilation because it allows the individual to accept more of their unique character, freeing the individual to express the licentious side of this the most transcendent of the earth signs more consciously and creatively.

Egoic consciousness tries to alleviate anxiety by, for example: compulsively adhering to traditions, rules, laws or doctrines, and criticising or scapegoating those who fail to do likewise; and/or striving to acquire and retain symbols of status such as positions, social connections, achievements and material possessions. In Cancer, identification with limiting instinctive/feeling responses hinders integration into the larger life; and in Capricorn, over-identification with a limiting collective ego hinders the cultivation of personal authenticity. The combination of cardinality and earth brings issues of individual strength and prowess to the fore, and because this is accompanied by a fear of alienation from the group (1H 4Q), there is an acute sensitivity to humiliation. Fear of humiliation may cause the individual to 'keep their head down' or to get into a 'vicious cycle' wherein overcompensating for this fear increases exposure to possible humiliation, which leads to more intense overcompensation, and so on. The 1H 4Q propensity for martyrdom, combined with the supportiveness of earth, can give rise to a tendency to take responsibility for things too readily. However, the seductiveness of this sign may give rise to an ability to delegate responsibility.

It is interesting to note that the earth signs – Taurus, Virgo and Capricorn – are often associated with the Buddha, Confucius and Jesus, respectively. Taurus occurs in the 1H 1Q, and the Buddha encouraged his disciples to 'be a lamp unto yourself'. Virgo occurs in the 1H 2Q and also the 1H 2T, and Confucius advised people to adhere to particular rules when engaging with family and society. Capricorn occurs in the 1H 4Q, and the biblical narrative of Jesus' life begins with a visitation from a transcendent realm, for which he is said to be an ambassador.

Aquarius

In Aquarius, a sense of the importance of expressing the potential inherent in encompassing wholes by following the guidance from source that arises from within (1H 4Q) combines with a natural ability to see the underlying principles that unite phenomena (air), and a determined, organisational and idealistic approach to effecting tangible change (fixed).

As in Scorpio, there is tension between the 3Q theme of building community and conceptual frameworks and the 4Q theme of dissolving structures that have begun to confine consciousness. Aquarius can potentially work creatively with this tension in order to develop and spread consciousness that has real value. In order to contribute to the continuing blossoming of a collective, the individual must be willing to stand apart from convention and experience some degree of social isolation. Thus, the 4Q themes of sacrifice, scapegoating and martyrdom may be prominent, and Aquarius is often associated with the mythological Prometheus.

Aquarius' need to connect with others in an authentic manner leads to involvement with those who are like-minded. These others may be individuals who have a similar vision of how to improve society, or simply individuals who share the same interests and/or interact according to the same cultural values. While the former involves the pursuit of a society in which all citizens can more easily find fulfilment, the latter involves enjoying the immediate sense of fulfilment that arises with authentic group participation.

Egoic consciousness tries to alleviate anxiety by, for example: embracing alternative behaviours, values or ideas simply for the sake of non-conformity; clinging to a particular way of understanding something and perhaps claiming to know the ultimate truth; and/or being overly idealistic about what can be expected of people and situations. If the questioning of existing social values is compulsive, the same compulsion will make it difficult for the individual to cooperate with others as a part of a progressive movement.

Pisces

In Pisces, a sense of the importance of expressing the potential inherent in encompassing wholes by following the guidance from source that arises from within (1H 4Q) combines with a natural ability to orient oneself and others towards more fulfilling experiences of connectedness (water) and a holistic, adaptable and insightful approach to effecting tangible change (mutable).

In this, the last sign before all of the harmonics are synchronised at the first point of Aries, there is a strong focus on dissolving structures of consciousness and relaxing into a direct experience of source in preparation for some kind of rebirth. The propensity for self-sacrifice is great, because the individual's personal viewpoint is so porous to others' hunger for peace and fulfilment. Sensitivity to the unfulfilled needs of a collective may lead to acts of martyrdom.

Egoic consciousness tries to alleviate anxiety by, for example: clinging to a person or collective onto which the power of redemption has been projected; escaping through drugs and/or fantasy; and/or trying to be 'all things to all people' in order to generate a sense of at-one-ness with others. Where Cancer clings to that which appears to support integration into the corporeal realm, and Scorpio clings to that which seems to offer a way to transcend a limiting and isolating experience of reality, Pisces clings to that which promises to bring redemption by washing away all that has gone before. Desperate to surrender to an intimate experience of source, and yet afraid to fully let go, Pisces egoic consciousness seeks redemption in the phenomenal realm, leading to a cycle of enchantment and disillusionment, and leaving the individual vulnerable to manipulation by others. On the other hand, vulnerability may be used to control others by instilling in them feelings of guilt.

Using the Model to Understand Sign Ingresses

As noted in Chapter 2, mundane astrologers routinely interpret transiting patterns for the moments at which factors move from one zodiacal sign to another. According to the proposed model, the significance of such patterns may be that at these moments, the zodiacal cycle of the factor begins anew at certain harmonic frequencies.

As a factor passes the first point of Aries, its zodiacal cycle begins anew in all harmonics. At the level of one-ness, the transiting pattern at this moment remains relevant until the factor returns to this point. At the level of two-ness, the pattern remains relevant until the factor reaches the first point of Libra, at which point the 2H of the factor's zodiacal cycle begins anew; and the transiting pattern at this moment is significant at the level of two-ness until the factor reaches the first point of Aries. Similarly, the 3H is born anew at the beginning of each fire sign, the 4H is born anew at the beginning of each cardinal sign, the 6H is born anew at the beginning of each positive sign, and the 12H is born anew at the beginning of each sign. In theory, the same principle could be applied to any type of division.

The Thirty-Six-fold Division

Dividing the zodiac into thirty-six 10° stages has a long tradition in many parts of the world. The *decans, decanates* or *dekkans* are usually interpreted in one of three ways. One of these – *rulership by triplicity* – was described in Chapter 4 (page 131). Another is referred to as the system of *Chaldean rulership*, in which the luminaries and visible planets are associated with the decans in the following order: Mars, the Sun, Venus, Mercury, the Moon, Saturn and Jupiter. Thus, the first decan (exactly 0° Aries to exactly 10° Aries) is ruled by Mars, the next by the Sun, and so on. The pattern repeats five times around the zodiac, with the remaining decan given to Mars. Clearly, this approach cannot be accounted for using a harmonic model.

If we wish to adopt a harmonic approach to interpreting the decans, one way to do this is to refer to the 1H and 3H twelve-sign zodiacs simultaneously. In this approach, the first 10° of Aries has the meaning of Aries at the levels of one-ness and three-ness, the second 10° of Aries has the meaning of Aries at the level of one-ness and Taurus at the level of three-ness, and so on. This approach is based on the 1H, 2H, 3H, 4H, 6H, 9H, 12H and 18H (because the 1H twelve-sign zodiac is based on the 1H, 2H, 3H, 4Hand 6H, and the 3H twelve-sign zodiac is based on the 3H, 6H, 9H, 12H and 18H).

An alternative harmonic approach is simply to consider the thirds of the 12H alongside those harmonics that form the basis of the twelve-fold division. In other words, the 1T, 2T and 3T, respectively, of each sign are overlaid with the themes of the 1T, 2T and 3T of the cycle of being.

The One Hundred and Forty-Four-fold Division

When each sign is divided into twelve stages, each spanning 2½° of celestial longitude, each stage is referred to as a *dwad, duad* or *duodenary, dwadasama* or *dwadachamsha*. The original (Vedic) approach to interpreting the one hundred and forty-four-fold division (discussed in Chapter 4 on page 131) is the only system in common use.

The proposed model suggests that the stages of this division can be interpreted by taking the twelve stages within a given sign to form a 12H twelve-sign zodiac that runs from Aries to Pisces. In this case, the harmonics relevant to the one hundred and forty-four-fold division are the 1H, 2H, 3H, 4H, 6H, 12H, 24H, 36H, 48H and 72H. Although alternative harmonic approaches to interpreting this division could be adopted, it seems likely that this would be the most useful and effective.

Jones and Rudhyar on Dividing the Zodiac

The *Sabian symbols* are a collection of 360 images – one for each zodiacal degree – that arose in the mind of medium Elsie Wheeler during an experiment coordinated by astrologer Marc Edmund Jones on one day in 1925. Jones later wrote *The Sabian Symbols in Astrology*, in which he attempts to delineate the meaning of each zodiacal degree by interpreting its Sabian symbol and considering the stage it occupies in each of a number of sub-cycles. In *An Astrological Mandala*, Rudhyar* sets out to improve upon Jones' delineations, offering his own interpretations of the Sabian symbols and referring to an almost identical set of sub-cycles.

Rudhyar divides the zodiac into equal segments in the following ways (with the first stage beginning at the first point of Aries in each case): two stages of 180° each, four stages of 90° each, five stages of 72° each, six stages of 60° each, twelve stages of 30° each, twenty four stages of 15° each, seventy two stages of 5° each, and three hundred and sixty stages of 1° each. It is suggested that the smaller stages within a given stage all carry the meaning of that stage. For example, the unique meaning of a given 5° stage is evident in each of the five 1° stages which it contains; the unique meaning of a given 15° stage is evident in each of the three 5° stages (and thus each of the fifteen 1° stages) which it contains, and so on. Furthermore, the 1° stages that begin their respective 5° stages are suggested to have a particular theme in common, as are the 1° stages that come second in their respective 5° stages, and so on. Thus, the same five-fold pattern of change is said to unfold during each 5° stage, the same three-fold pattern (and the same fifteen-fold pattern) is said to unfold during each 15° stage, and so on.

The Hemicycles of the 12th Harmonic

As noted in Chapter 4, Rudhyar divides each sign into two stages of 15° each and attributes a theme to each stage. Rudhyar does not describe these divisions as arising from a recurring two-fold pattern of change, but given his general approach to sub-dividing cycles, it is plausible that the notion of such a pattern informed his thinking. Regardless of whether or not this was Rudhyar's conscious intention, it could be argued that the terms he uses point to an emphasis on multiplicity during the first half of each sign and an emphasis on unity during the second half. In other words, it could be argued that Rudhyar's interpretation of the 15° stages brings the 1Hem and 2Hem of the 12H into focus. In Aries, for example, a *desire* arises in the consciousness of the individual (1Hem), who uses *potency* to express or fulfil that desire

* *An Astrological Mandala* (1974). (1st ed. 1973)

within the collective sphere (2Hem). In Taurus, something that is *substantiated* in the consciousness of the individual (1Hem) may be *confirmed* through sharing with others (2Hem), and so on.

The Thirds of the 24th Harmonic

Rudhyar suggests that the theme that runs through a given 15° stage manifests at the *actional level* during the 1T of that stage, at the *emotional-cultural level* during the 2T, and at the *individual-mental level* during the 3T. During the 24H 1T, the individual is inclined simply to act out the impulses arising within. During the 24H 2T, the individual engages with that which is other, which requires the navigation of the emotional landscape within and the cultural landscape without. During the 24H 3T, the individual is detached from these emotional and cultural landscapes, allowing clearer mental perception. (Rudhyar often speaks of individuality as something that only blossoms through engagement with one's socio-cultural environment. Here, the term *individual-mental* seems intended to describe a standpoint that transcends the emotional and cultural landscapes.) Jones labels these thirds using the terms *physical/habit, social/emotional* and *spiritual/mental.*

The Fifths of the 72nd Harmonic

Jones and Rudhyar both place great emphasis on the five-fold pattern that is said to unfold during each 5° stage (i.e. each unfoldment of the 72H). Figure 5.5 shows one unfoldment of the 72H divided into five single-degree increments. Most of the pivotal points of the 72H do not coincide with the stage boundaries of the three hundred and sixty-fold division. However, the state of the 72H during the first degree of each 5° stage does reflect the theme that Jones[*] and Rudhyar[†] suggest is common (and unique) to these degrees, with the same applying to the second degree of each 5° stage, and so on.

During the first degree of a 5° stage, the principle of multiplicity is dominant and becoming stronger. New potentiality is released, revealing the purpose and essential nature of the theme to be developed during the 5° stage. Jones uses the term *experimental,* capturing the opportunity to build original and novel form/consciousness while the principle of multiplicity is relatively uncompromised by the principle of unity.

During the second degree of a 5° stage, the polar tide turns, though the

---

[*] *The Sabian Symbols in Astrology* (1993) pp. 146 and 147. (1st ed. 1953)

[†] *An Astrological Mandala* (1973, 1st ed.) pp. 324 to 327

principle of multiplicity remains dominant. Rudhyar suggests that in this degree, the outward expression of the theme is more pronounced, which may be attributable to the turning of the polar tide and thus the need to engage with the orderly matrix. Jones uses the term *sensitive,* capturing the increased capacity to sense the needs and requirements of the environment in which the form/consciousness-building activity is occurring.

During the third degree, emphasis on unity increases. Thus, there is a need to relate "what has been started to its environment or to some larger frame of reference", and there is "some sort of interaction between the new development and what can support it in the greater whole of which it has become a part" (Rudhyar). Jones uses the term *receptive,* capturing the capacity to attune to organising principles and the willingness to become more reliant on external energy sources.

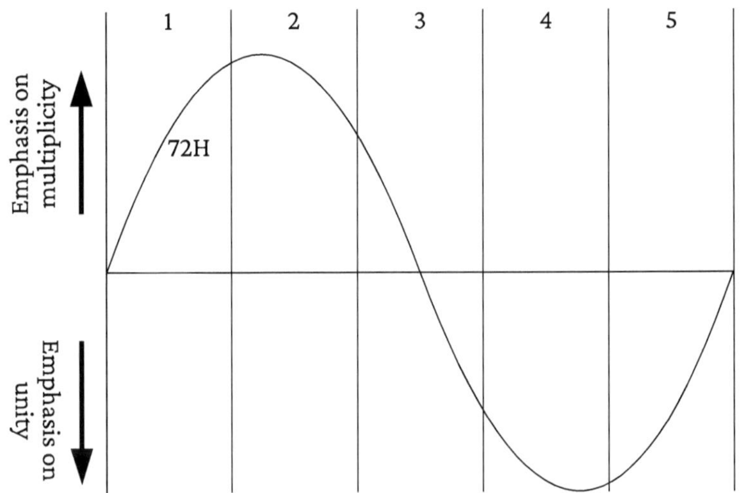

Figure 5.5 An unfoldment of the 72H divided into five single-degree increments

During the fourth degree, the principle of unity remains dominant, but the polar tide turns in favour of the principle of multiplicity. Rudhyar suggests that this degree calls for willingness to surrender to some form of mystical union in order to create the conditions required for the "integration" and "interpenetration" of "polarized life energies". Rudhyar also suggests that "a certain type of method, procedure or technique" becomes apparent that "can be used to make the process work effectively" and that the "principle of effective self-expression" is at work during this stage; and he adds that *self* may refer to the egoic or universal self. With emphasis on unity at its greatest, the notion of a mystical union resulting in the interpenetration of opposites is very apt, as is the expression of the universal self. The ability to see ways to improve the effectiveness of the process could be attributed to abstract thinking (emphasis on unity), and/or a propensity towards re-evaluating (turning of the polar tide). Jones uses the term *responsible,* capturing the importance of playing one's part in the proper functioning of the socio-cultural whole.

During the fifth degree, the principle of unity is dominant, but the strength of the principle of multiplicity is increasing. Rudhyar suggests that here, the events that have occurred during the previous four stages can be understood from a broader perspective and seen to be part of a broader process; and it becomes apparent that something new must now emerge to carry the process forward into another cycle. In other words, during this stage, the personal viewpoint of the individual is porous to the wisdom and agenda of source, and the individual recognises the need to let go of the past in preparation for the future. Jones uses the term *inspired.*

The 90th Harmonic

Given that the stage boundaries of the three hundred and sixty-fold division coincide with the pivotal points of the 90H, we would expect this harmonic to be relevant to the meanings of the 1° stages. When the zodiac is divided into quarters, signs or half-signs as a precursor to interpreting the degree increments, the relevance of the 90H is obscured, because it does not unfold a whole number of times within any of these partitions. However, it may be possible to discern the presence of a 90H influence by considering its relationship with the 72H.

According to the proposed model, the principle of multiplicity becomes dominant in the 72H and 90H at the first point of Aries. Thereafter, the principle of multiplicity becomes dominant in the 72H at intervals of 5° of celestial longitude, in the 90H at intervals of 4° of celestial longitude, and thus in both the 72H and 90H simultaneously at intervals of 20° of celestial longitude. Consequently, with regard to the unfoldment of the 72H and 90H, the same twenty-fold pattern unfolds throughout each 20° stage.

During (and only during) the first degree of each 20° stage, the principle of multiplicity is dominant and becoming stronger in both the 72H and 90H. Thus, if the proposed model is valid, we would expect these degrees to share a theme that expresses the meaning of the first quarter of the cycle of being at the (relatively subtle) levels of seventy-two-ness and ninety-ness. Indeed,

Rudhyar's interpretations for these degrees in *An Astrological Mandala* speak of the release of potentiality and the revelation of the potential for change. In cases where the principle of multiplicity is dominant (and especially when it is becoming stronger) in other harmonics that are relevant to the three hundred and sixty-fold division, these themes are partly attributable to those other (more fundamental) harmonics. However, even Pisces 11 – during which the 72H and 90H may be the only relevant harmonics in which the principle of multiplicity is dominant and becoming stronger – this theme is evident. Rudhyar's* interpretation for Pisces 11 is:

> The capacity inherent in every individual to seek at whatever cost entrance to a transcendent realm of reality.

The Lunar Mansions

The stages of the twenty-seven and twenty-eight-fold divisions of the zodiac are referred to as *lunar mansions*. These divisions would have originally been chosen because, on average, the Moon travels between one twenty-eighth and one twenty-seventh of its orbital path during each rotation of Earth. Just as the significance of the twelve-fold division is synchronous with the ratio of the synodic month to the solar year, so the significances of the twenty-seven and twenty-eight-fold divisions are synchronous with the ratio of the solar day to the sidereal month.

Before exploring these divisions, it is worth considering the relationship between the lunar mansions and the signs, as these two divisions are often discussed alongside one another in modern astrology texts. If a sign is divided into six 5° stages, the meaning that is evident throughout each of those 5° stages incorporates the meaning that is evident throughout the sign. Thus, the interpretation of a factor's placement within a particular 5° stage simply adds further detail to the interpretation of its placement within a particular sign. In terms of the proposed model, we could say that this is because each harmonic that is relevant to the twelve-fold division is also relevant to the seventy-two-fold division. However, the meaning of a lunar mansion is largely independent of the meaning of the sign(s) with which it coincides. Thus, the interpretation of a factor's placement within a particular lunar mansion and the interpretation of its placement within a particular sign give two distinct perspectives. In terms of the proposed model, we could say that this is because some of the harmonics that are relevant to the twelve-fold division are not relevant to, or are divided

* *An Astrological Mandala* (1974) p. 274. (1st ed. 1973)

differently by, the twenty-seven-fold division, and the same may be said of the twenty-eight-fold division.

The harmonic basis of the twenty-eight-fold division* seems to be more complex than that of the twenty-seven-fold division, and while much has been written on the psychological characteristics associated with the twenty-seven lunar mansions, the same does not seem to be true of the twenty-eight lunar mansions. Thus, the remainder of this chapter focuses on the twenty seven fold division.

The Twenty-Seven-fold Division

As discussed below, it seems likely that the twenty-seven-fold division is based on the 1H, 3H and 9H. Given the affinity between Hindu culture and the qualities of three-ness and nine-ness, it is not surprising that this division – rather than the twenty-eight-fold division – was adopted by Vedic astrologers. In Vedic astrology, the twenty-seven lunar mansions are referred to as the *nakshatras*.

The Nakshatras and the Gunas

Guna may be translated as, for example, *thread, energy, tendency, attribute, virtue, quality* or *mode*. According to Vedic philosophy, there are three gunas, which are referred to as *Rajas, Tamas* and *Sattwa*. Each of the twenty-seven nakshatras is said to express one of these gunas at a *primary level*, one at a *secondary level* and one at a *tertiary level* (see Figure 5.6). At the primary level, Rajas finds expression in the first nine nakshatras, Tamas finds expression in the next nine, and Sattwa finds expression in the last nine, with the guna cycle unfolding once around the zodiac. At the secondary level, Rajas finds expression in the first three nakshatras, Tamas in the next three, Sattwa in the next three, Rajas in the next three, and so on, with the guna cycle unfolding three times around the zodiac. At the tertiary level, Rajas finds expression in the first nakshatra, Tamas in the second, Sattwa in the third, Rajas in the fourth, and so on, with the guna cycle unfolding nine times around the zodiac. From the brief account of the gunas given below, we can see that each guna correlates with a different third of the cycle of being, and that the unfoldment of the guna cycle at the primary, secondary and tertiary

---

* It seems likely that the 4H and 7H are relevant to the twenty-eight-fold division, and it is interesting that the twenty-eight lunar mansions are used primarily to time the creation and use of magic talismans in an attempt to materialise (4) an envisioned outcome (7).

levels can be seen as the unfoldment of the cycle of being at the 1H, 3H and 9H frequencies, respectively.

Nakshatra	Gunas		
	Primary (1H)	Secondary (3H)	Tertiary (9H)
1 Ashwini	Rajas	Rajas	Rajas
2 Bharani	Rajas	Rajas	Tamas
3 Krittika	Rajas	Rajas	Sattwa
4 Rohini	Rajas	Tamas	Rajas
5 Mrigashira	Rajas	Tamas	Tamas
6 Ardra	Rajas	Tamas	Sattwa
7 Punarvasu	Rajas	Sattwa	Rajas
8 Pushya	Rajas	Sattwa	Tamas
9 Ashlesha	Rajas	Sattwa	Sattwa
10 Magha	Tamas	Rajas	Rajas
11 Purva Phalguni	Tamas	Rajas	Tamas
12 Uttara Phalguni	Tamas	Rajas	Sattwa
13 Hasta	Tamas	Tamas	Rajas
14 Chitra	Tamas	Tamas	Tamas
15 Swati	Tamas	Tamas	Sattwa
16 Vishakha	Tamas	Sattwa	Rajas
17 Anuradha	Tamas	Sattwa	Tamas
18 Jyeshtha	Tamas	Sattwa	Sattwa
19 Mula	Sattwa	Rajas	Rajas
20 Purva Ashadha	Sattwa	Rajas	Tamas
21 Uttara Ashadha	Sattwa	Rajas	Sattwa
22 Shravana	Sattwa	Tamas	Rajas
23 Dhanishtha	Sattwa	Tamas	Tamas
24 Shatabhisha	Sattwa	Tamas	Sattwa
25 Purva Bhadrapada	Sattwa	Sattwa	Rajas
26 Uttara Bhadrapada	Sattwa	Sattwa	Tamas
27 Revati	Sattwa	Sattwa	Sattwa

Figure 5.6 The guna operative at each level (harmonic frequency) in each of the twenty-seven nakshatras

An account of an archetypal theme is always subject to the biases inherent in the culture in which it is conceived and developed; and in the accounts of the gunas typically found in books and articles on Vedic philosophy this bias is quite stark. Sattwa and Tamas are generally described, respectively, as the highest and lowest gunas, with Rajas described as less positive than Sattwa but less negative than Tamas.

Rajas is described as active and energetic, giving rise to dynamism, passion, initiative, desire, egotism and impatience. This guna is said to be useful for getting things done, but to hinder spiritual attainment by continuously agitating consciousness. Thus, Rajas is an expression of the 1T of the cycle of being.

Tamas is described as sluggish and oppressive, giving rise to lust, greed, indolence, shame and depression. This guna is said to muddy consciousness by drawing it into identification with the material world. Thus, the traditional Vedic view of Tamas focuses on what can go wrong during the 2T of the cycle of being, when the individual tends to engage more intensely with that which is other and to view their own existence through the eyes of others.*

Sattwa is described as calm and harmonious, giving rise to clarity, openness, friendliness, joy, inspiration, balance and lightness. This guna is said to guide consciousness toward its natural, liberated state. This view of Sattwa captures what can be achieved during the 3T of the cycle of being, when the individual is more open to a direct experience of source.

In *The Zodiac and the Soul*, Carter† has this to say about the modes:

> A very common comparison is made to the three Hindu gunas..., but astrologers, as such, do not commonly regard the mutable signs as having the perfection, relative to the others, which Gita ascribes to *Sattva*. However, it is true that the common [i.e. mutable] signs have in them a certain possibility of completeness that is denied to the others.

---

* Having been somewhat vilified in Hindu culture, the Tamas archetype would have been prone to unconscious and destructive expression. This may partly explain why the Hindu caste system, which brought oppression and shame to millions, endured long after the invaders who established it had left India, and perhaps even why the invaders decided that it would be an effective way to control the population.

† *The Zodiac and the Soul* (1968) p.6 (1st ed. 1928)

Fortunately, accounts of the twenty-seven nakshatras found in contemporary Vedic astrological texts tend to describe the positive and negative expressions of each of the nakshatras.

Many Vedic astrologers try to assess the overall strength of each guna in a chart by counting how many times each guna is activated by a significant factor. For example, Rajas is given three counts for each factor in Ashwini; Rajas is given two counts and Tamas is given one count for each factor in Bharani, and so on (see Figure 5.6). However, despite this recognition of the significance of the gunas in the nakshatra cycle, I have been unable to find a single written work or talk in which the meaning of each nakshatra is derived from the meanings of the gunas operative within it. According to the proposed model, this is what determines the essential meaning of each nakshatra; and if the model is valid, anything that has a genuine affinity with a nakshatra – any node, celestial body or deity, or any behaviour or character trait – must express this essential meaning in one way or another. Modern accounts of the nakshatras take the opposite approach, building a description of each nakshatra from the meanings attributed to the deities and celestial bodies, etc. that are traditionally associated with the nakshatra.

The 9th Harmonic

The emphasis on the number nine in Vedic astrology is seen in the extensive use of the 9H twelve-sign zodiac. Each 9H zodiacal sign (referred to in Vedic astrology as a *navamsa*) and each quarter of a nakshatra (referred to as a *pada*) spans 3°20' of celestial longitude. Thus, the first, second, third and fourth pada of each nakshatra coincides, respectively, with a fire, earth, air and water navamsa. Consequently, the four padas of a nakshatra are often viewed simply as the fire, earth, air and water expressions of that nakshatra. According to the proposed model, viewing a 3°20' stage as a 9H zodiacal sign focuses on the 9H, 18H, 27H, 36H and 54H (divided in the same manner that the 1H, 2H, 3H, 4H and 6H, respectively, are divided in the twelve-fold division). Meanwhile, viewing a 3°20' stage as the fire, earth, air or water expression of a particular nakshatra focuses on the 1H, 3H, 9H (each divided into thirds) and the 27H (divided into quarters). Note that the 9H element cycle (the 27H divided into quarters) is relevant to both approaches.

As noted above, at the level of three-ness, the tension inherent in dualism is transcended, giving rise to the capacity for enjoyment and insight. At the level of nine-ness (3 x 3) this is taken to another level, giving rise to the capacity for profound fulfilment and lucidity. Thus, the 9H of a zodiacal cycle is a cycle of change in the way of being that best facilitates an increase in fulfilment and lucidity.

Since all of the higher harmonics that are relevant to the twenty-seven-fold division are powers of three, the twenty-seven-fold division of a zodiacal cycle charts changes in the most natural and effective way for the individual to achieve joy, clarity and a sense of equilibrium.

An astrologer using the twelve-fold division may note that a chart has, for example, a fire emphasis or a fixed emphasis. Similarly, when using the twenty-seven-fold division, it may be useful to note any guna emphasis in a particular harmonic, such as an emphasis on Tamas in the 3H or an emphasis on Tamas and Sattwa (i.e. a lack of Rajas) in the 9H. Figure 5.7 attempts to show how each guna (third of the zodiacal cycle of being) manifests at each level (harmonic frequency).

	1st Harmonic	3rd Harmonic	9th Harmonic
First third	Identifies self as an autonomous individual. Motivated by opportunities to simply be oneself. Acts on instincts.	Enjoys following own impulses. Insight into opportunities to give form to emerging potentiality.	Deep fulfilment and clarity arise through taking the initiative and acting spontaneously.
Second third	Identifies self as a social being and defines self according to effect on others. Strong desire nature. Guided by values and morals.	Enjoys social integration. Insight into value systems, social networks and mechanisms of exchange. Emotional intelligence.	Deep fulfilment and clarity arise through engaging fruitfully and creatively with that which is other, and through healing emotional disquiet.
Final third	Identifies self as a 'child of the universe'. Motivated by opportunities to transcend current sense of reality. Guided by the heart.	Enjoys surrendering to a higher power. Insight into opportunities to expand consciousness.	Deep fulfilment and clarity arise through openness to inspiration and looking beyond what is known.

Figure 5.7 The thirds of the 1H, 3H and 9H

The Nakshatras

The oldest known account of the meanings of the nakshatras is found in the *nakshatra sutras.*[*] Although the sutras are comprised of just six or seven words each, and open to varied interpretations, they serve as a useful complement to modern accounts of the nakshatras. In *Nakshatra – The Authentic Heart of Vedic Astrology*, Vic DiCara[†] gives a detailed and carefully considered translation of each nakshatra sutra. DiCara notes that each sutra speaks of *something above* and *something below*, which he interprets as showing what we must draw upon from above in order to fulfil the potential inherent in the nakshatra, and what fruit will fall to us as this potential is realised. In the account of the nakshatras that follows, all references to the nakshatra sutras are based on DiCara's translations.

The first sutra is on Krittika, probably because when the sutras were written, the segment of the celestial sphere then defined as Krittika contained the vernal point. The nakshatra wheel was later moved in order to align the first point of Ashwini with the first point of Babylonian Aries, and sidereal astrologers continue to align the nakshatras and signs in this way. Thus – as do many modern texts on the nakshatras – we will begin with Ashwini. (Note that just as the empirically observed meanings of the signs only make sense when it is assumed that the principle of multiplicity becomes dominant in all relevant harmonics simultaneously at the first point of Aries, so the empirically observed meanings of the nakshatras only make sense when the same is assumed of the first point of Ashwini.)

In the following account, the three numbers next to the title for each nakshatra show which third of the cycle of being (which guna) is unfolding in each harmonic (at each level). The first, second and third digits refer, respectively, to the 1H, 3H and 9H (the primary, secondary and tertiary levels), and the numbers 1, 2 and 3 refer, respectively, to the 1T, 2T and 3T of the cycle of being (Rajas, Tamas and Sattwa). For example, next to *Ardra* are the numbers *1 2 3*, because Ardra is made up of the 1H 1T, 3H 2T, 9H 3T (Rajas at the primary level, Tamas at the secondary level, and Sattwa at the tertiary level).

1 Ashwini 111

Ashwini is described in modern texts as impulsive, impatient, adventurous, bold, assertive, pioneering and open to new experiences, with the capacity

---

[*] *Taittiriya Brahmana*, Book 1, Ch. 5

[†] *Nakshatra – The Authentic Heart of Vedic Astrology* (2019, 1st ed.)

to accrue power, wealth and fame. Here we see the theme of the 1T operating at all levels, in what might be thought of as the nakshatra equivalent of the sign Aries. Like Aries, Ashwini is traditionally associated with surgeons.

The Sutra for Ashwini speaks of twin horsemen who ride from city to city in order to raise an army. At this stage of the nakshatra cycle, the individual can draw upon the raw potentiality released at the beginning of the cycle by taking the initiative. The raw potentiality is symbolised by the horses and the inhabitants of the cities. The results of taking the initiative to give form to this potentiality are symbolised by the army and the manifest changes that will be brought about by the army's military campaigns (including an increase in the power, wealth and fame of the horsemen).

2 Bharani 112

Much of the impulsiveness and pioneering spirit of Ashwini are present in Bharani (1H 1T, 3H 1T), but this is now overlaid with a sense that true fulfilment can only be found by engaging with that which is other (9H 2T). The individual may become stuck in sensual/sexual overindulgence, jealousy, vanity and rigid moralism, but has a propensity to undergo transformative experiences that unlock the creative power inherent in this nakshatra. The individual is then able to use this power to fight for truth and justice, to regenerate that which has become depleted or stagnant, to engage in artistic creativity, and to achieve emotional tranquillity through practices such as yoga.

The sutra for Bharani does not provide an image, but the above and below aspects, and the meaning of the word *bharani*, encourage restraint. This may refer to the self-restraint needed to endure the discomfort that arises when the passion inherent in this nakshatra is endured and transformed rather than acted out. It may also refer to the need of a society to restrain those who do not adhere to its rules of conduct. The sutra suggests that the potential inherent in Bharani is realised by understanding that restraint yields positive results when used appropriately.

3 Krittika 113

Krittika is often described as a spiritual warrior, cutting through (1T) untruths that blinker consciousness and hinder social progress (3T). This nakshatra is also associated with a passion (1T) for cooking and eating, and protecting one's kin (3T emphasis on assimilation). Other characteristics include passive-aggressive behaviour (1T assertiveness combined with 3T appreciation of harmony) and infidelity (1T passion combined with 3T need to explore/escape). Thus, it is important for the individual to ensure that the passion inherent in Krittika is expressed in ways that open the individual and others to the energy of source, rather than through escapist behaviour that is likely to cause depletion for all concerned.

The sutra for Krittika speaks of the need to draw fuel from above and use it to light up the world. The word *Krittika* means *cutting* or *breaking apart*, and *initiating, activating* or *achieving*; so this name is suggestive of the need to release the energy trapped within, or inhibited by, old structures (3T) in order to pave the way for something new to come into being (1T).

4 Rohini 1 2 1

Rohini is associated with charm, sexual magnetism, passion for life, abundance, prosperity and business acumen, but also materialism, overindulgence and possessiveness. Here we see the 1T emphasis combined with a natural ability to understand and seek pleasure in the phenomenal realm (3T 2T).

The sutra for Rohini seems to liken a plant's need for regular watering to an individual's need to be replenished by their interactions with others and their surroundings. Thus, the sutra encourages interactions that promote the health and growth of all concerned, rather than interactions that result in us becoming emotionally dehydrated or waterlogged.

5 Mrigashira 1 2 2

In Mrigashira, the 1H 1T combines with a 2T emphasis, giving rise to good communication skills, inquisitiveness about one's surroundings, the need for a wide range of experiences, the capacity to relate to a wide range of people and bring about a state of integration between them, and an ability to enjoy life – perhaps to the extent of licentiousness.

The sutra for Mrigashira speaks of a gentle nature and seems to liken the weaving together of individual threads into fabric to the integration of individuals to form a society. This combines a drive to create something new (1T) with a sense of the importance of integration (2T).

6 Ardra 1 2 3

Ardra is said to be complex and emotionally turbulent in its expression; it operates from an individualistic standpoint (1H 1T), wants to enjoy the social and material environment (3H 2T), and yet carries a sense that fulfilment lies beyond all of this (9H 3T). This nakshatra is associated with attempts to improve life through hard work, but also with a propensity to hide from the harsh realities of life through addiction. It is also associated with destruction or sacrifice that leads to revelation.

The sutra for Ardra seems to point to the need to draw upon the power of aggression and predation in order to eliminate destructive forces that cannot be defeated by peaceful means. This combines fighting spirit and courage (1H 1T) with an ability to engage with that which is other (3H 2T) and a sense that true fulfilment lies in acting on behalf of source (9H 3T).

7 Punarvasu 1 3 1

Punarvasu is associated with a sense of boundless expansion and renewal, and a sense that contentment is not dependent upon material possessions (note the absence of the 2T). This nakshatra is also associated with a wise and forgiving nature in which there is little scope for resentment to take hold; however, the capacity for long-term commitment (to people or projects) may be lacking (again, note the absence of the 2T).

The sutra for Punarvasu speaks of the ongoing cycle of renewal that characterises existence. The sutra begins by declaring that this is the nakshatra of *Aditi*, the goddess of indivisible space, which, DiCara notes, is both the womb and the tomb of all phenomena. Here, awareness of the dynamic nature of existence (1T) combines with awareness that all manifest phenomena are but ephemeral expressions of source (3T emphasis). DiCara points out that there may be a tendency to become excessively impatient or perfectionist at this stage of the nakshatra cycle, in which case the creative potential of Punarvasu is diminished.

8 Pushya 1 3 2

Pushya is associated with the ability to understand and teach philosophical and spiritual truths – the individual now inspired to seek fulfilment through engagement with others (9H 2T). This nakshatra is also associated with sensitivity to criticism – which may be masked by condescension and arrogance – and a tendency to adopt conventional ideas. Here, the individualism of the 1H 1T combines with a knowledge-based approach to adapting to life (3H 3T), and a tendency to seek fulfilment by comparing favourably with others (9H 2T) – either by belittling their ideas or by adopting the consensus viewpoint.

The sutra for Pushya speaks of the need to receive guidance from those with knowledge and experience in order to see how best to behave in an efficient and prosperous manner. The need to do something (1T) is accompanied by an awareness of the restrictions and requirements of the phenomenal realm (2T) and an awareness of the importance of breadth of knowledge and perspective (3T).

9 Ashlesha 1 3 3

Ashlesha is associated with the ability to use 'kundalini energy', the tendency to experience sudden leaps of wisdom, and the ability to impose one's will through the use of hypnotic, seductive power. There is also a propensity to be excessively idealistic, and reluctant to accept of what *is*. In all of these traits can be seen the 3T emphasis combined with the passion and dynamism of the 1T.

The sutra for Ashlesha refers to two entwined snakes, suggesting the possibility of reaching a transcendent or mystical state (3T) through passionate, instinctual activity (1T). With the 2T absent, engagement with that which is other is not viewed as an end in itself, but rather as a steppingstone to a direct experience of kundalini energy or source. DiCara associates Ashlesha with the need "to be seductive without being an evil serpent".

10 Magha 2 1 1

In Magha, the individual has a strong sense of being part of a culture and clan (1H 2T) and finds joy and fulfilment through acting on instinct and taking the initiative (3H 1T, 9H 1T). This can manifest as enthusiasm for community-strengthening rituals and ceremonies, loyalty to the clan, and a tendency to make magnanimous gestures. It can also manifest as a defensive and competitive approach to engaging with other clans. In each case, interactions with others (2T) are used as an arena in which to show individual strength (1T).

The sutra for Magha speaks of the importance of condemning those cultural values that threaten one's clan – whether these values are expressed by other clans or members of one's own clan. The sutra advises that adherence to authority dispensed from above helps to maintain stability within the clan below. For the good of the clan, the wilfulness of clan members (1T) must be aligned with the directives of those responsible for maintaining integration (2T). DiCara suggests that this sutra reminds us that at this stage of the nakshatra cycle, we can gain respect or validation by showing that our ideas or actions are in accord with a higher authority or power (i.e. an encompassing organising principle).

11 Purva Phalguni 2 1 2

Purva Phalguni is associated with romance, productivity, creativity, and an ability to enjoy life and materialise desires; but it is also associated with the possibility of vanity and excessive self-indulgence. Here, we see the 2T emphasis combined with a natural ability to make things happen and a love of taking the initiative (1T).

The sutra for Purva Phalguni uses the image of a man approaching a woman whom he hopes will bear his progeny. The image reminds us that a creative impulse can only come to fruition within a 'field' or 'womb' (using these terms in their widest sense) that is suited to the purpose and that has been cared for in the appropriate manner. Here, insight into creative potential (3H 1T) combines with the ability to engage fruitfully with the phenomenal realm (2T emphasis).

12 Uttara Phalguni 2 1 3

In Uttara Phalguni, identification with the group (1H 2T) is overlaid with a natural ability to take the initiative (3H 1T) and a sense that fulfilment comes through opening to the larger life (9H 3T). Thus, this nakshatra is associated with acts of kindness and compassion and the desire to form meaningful connections with one's kin. It is also associated with a tendency to feel bereft when this connection is lacking, and to try to control others through generosity or other means.

The sutra for Uttara Phalguni refers to a woman who is enabled by the strength of a man, and seems to follow from the image given in the previous sutra. This sutra reminds us that it is necessary to give sufficient support to creative processes in order to maximise the benefit and pleasure derived from them. This requires a sense of relatedness to that which is other (1H 2T), a natural ability to make things happen (3H 1T) and an attunement to the true source of all creativity (9H 3T).

13 Hasta 2 2 1

Hasta is associated with the capacity to take the initiative (1T) in 2T areas such as manifestation, business and self-transformation, and to assert one's own viewpoint (1T) when engaging with others (2T). This nakshatra is also associated with craftsmanship and self-control.

The sutra for Hasta speaks of the need to draw upon the life force in order to realise goals and objectives. The image given by this sutra is a hand, which we use to work with the world around us. DiCara notes that at this stage of the nakshatra cycle, we can open to a steady stream of inspiration by paying "more attention to the small details in the everyday things all around". There is a need for some kind of motivating input from a 'higher plane' (9H 1T), but this must come through contact with the phenomenal realm, because this is where the individual's consciousness is focused (1H 2T, 3H 2T).

14 Chitra 2 2 2

In Chitra, the 2T is unfolding in all three harmonics, giving rise to a propensity to create and appreciate beauty in all its forms, and perhaps a propensity to manipulate the phenomenal realm in a deceptive manner and become obsessed with worldly things. This nakshatra is also associated with regenerative power and the potential to develop a 'strong ego' (in response to the emotional and cultural pressures associated with the 2T). The issue of laying karma to rest is said to be especially pertinent during this stage of the nakshatra cycle.

The sutra for Chitra is translated by DiCara as: "Brilliant sensual creativity needs genuinity for true beauty". This sutra speaks very clearly of the creative potential inherent in the phenomenal realm, but reminds us that genuineness is crucial in fully realising this potential. Egoic consciousness carries a distorted sense of genuinity, and creates a false or shallow kind of beauty that pacifies, indulges and glorifies the egoic sense of self. The sense of genuinity carried by unconditioned consciousness gives rise to that which is truly beautiful.

15 Swati 2 2 3

The emphasis on the 2T is now overlaid with a sense that in order to find fulfilment, it is necessary to adopt a transcendent viewpoint. Thus, while Swati shows much of Chitra's business acumen and potential for material indulgence, it is also associated with restlessness, eagerness to learn, a charitable nature and a tendency to evaluate the rightness of one's actions from a broader perspective. It is said that the individual may be inclined to follow a spiritual path, but perhaps only after a certain degree of material success has been achieved.

The sutra for Swati speaks of the need to expand in one's own direction – getting beyond the flaws inherent in one's culture and society – rather than being limited by excessive conformity. Here, awareness of being immersed in a particular socio-cultural matrix (2T) combines with a need to connect directly with source (3T), and there is potential to play a progressive role in society.

16 Vishakha 2 3 1

Vishakha is associated with an ambitious and determined nature that can achieve much, but also with a tendency to try to achieve too many goals simultaneously. This nakshatra is also associated with the potential for social adeptness and intelligence, but with a propensity to be quarrelsome and pushy and to become alienated from others. Here we see the difficulty that can arise during a stage where all three thirds are unfolding.

The sutra for Vishakha encourages teamwork with the right individual(s) and the securing of necessary resources in order to achieve a goal. The sutra also speaks of the importance of honouring the uniqueness of each individual and phenomenon by allowing each to play the role which best suits its inherent nature. Here we see how the combination of all three thirds can be expressed positively in the social arena (2T unfolding in the most fundamental harmonic)

17 Anuradha 2 3 2

Anuradha is associated with a willingness to honour the needs of others and an ability to maintain mutually satisfying relationships of all kinds. Here we see the 2T emphasis combined with an enjoyment of, and capacity for, inclusiveness and compassion (3H 3T). There is also said to be a propensity to achieve business success (2T) after moving away from one's homeland (3T).

The sutra for Anuradha speaks of the potential for the love expressed between people to reach a point of climax following sufficient arousal. This may refer to the potential for any experience of relatedness (2T) to become so heightened during a period of sustained attention that it takes on a transcendent quality (3T).

18 Jyeshtha 2 3 3

Jyeshtha is associated with the potential to acquire great power, skill and wisdom, and to be seen by others as a guide or elder. This nakshatra combines an awareness of one's connection to collectives and the phenomenal realm in general (2T) with the insight conferred by the 3T emphasis.

DiCara summarises his translation of the sutra for Jyeshtha with the following:

> Those who wield power achieve their ambitions by provoking enemies to attack, which exposes their weaknesses and intentions, justifying and legitimizing counter-attack.

Thus, DiCara notes, we are warned against reacting to the taunts of those who try to manipulate us into attacking them (2T), and encouraged instead to maintain a healthy detachment and clear perspective (3T), which gives them the space to expose themselves.

19 Mula 3 1 1

Mula begins the final third of the nakshatra cycle and is associated with the need to take action (1T) to uphold the Truth (3T) and challenge anything seen to be false or illusory. Mula is also associated with difficult – possibly self-destructive – experiences that may prompt the individual to move from a state of restless agitation to a more focused pursuit of wisdom and understanding.

The sutra for Mula reminds us that delusions and falsehoods naturally contradict and thus destroy one another. Here, identification with knowledge and understanding (1H 3T) combines with bold self-assertion (1T emphasis); thus, untruths are quickly exposed as they clash with one another and with truth.

20 Purva Ashadha 3 1 2

The shift from the 1T to the 2T in the 9H gives rise to good debating skills and an interest in matters relating to law and morality, and perhaps a tendency to be pushy and argumentative when communicating with others. The need to arrive at a consensus viewpoint (2T) is also said to be greater than in the previous nakshatra.

The sutra for Purva Ashadha advises that success is assured when people cooperate enthusiastically, integrating their diverse talents. Thus, the message of this sutra is similar to that of the sutra for Vishakha (2 3 1).

21 Uttara Ashadha 3 1 3

With an emphasis on the 3T, Uttara Ashadha is associated with a friendly, humanitarian nature, a strong sense of ethics, and an ability to relate to others, but there is also an ability to take the initiative where necessary (3H 1T). Oratory skills and a propensity for self-righteousness are also possible, though this nakshatra is said to be less combative than the previous one. There is a tendency to approach tasks with great enthusiasm (1T) if inspired to do so, but to become apathetic and directionless when uninspired (3T emphasis), and staying power may be lacking (absence of 2T). Uttara Ashadha is said to be conducive to success in goals that benefit others (goal-oriented 1T combined with 3T connection to source).

The sutra for Uttara Ashadha speaks of the natural tendency to regard one's own understanding as superior and thus to attempt to influence the lives of others. This sutra encourages each of us to achieve the broadest understanding possible before undertaking such action, including awareness that we are not separate entities. As DiCara notes:

> Ultimately, when we realise the unity of all things, we can effortlessly achieve victory, not by conquering others, but by harmonizing with everyone.

22 Shravana 3 2 1

Shravana is associated with the propensity to engage with others in order to learn and share one's own understanding. With all of the thirds represented, this is a complex nakshatra, requiring periods of engagement with others and periods of seclusion, and seeking new understanding while respecting tradition. Interest in others may manifest more negatively as a propensity to gossip, and the individual may be disagreeable and touchy when feeling insecure.

The sutra for Shravana points to the importance of continually taking stock of our direction in life, regardless of how experienced and worldly wise we may feel ourselves to be. To get the best from this stage of the nakshatra cycle, we must use our worldly experience wisely (3H 2T), remaining open to change (1T and 3T). With the 1T unfolding in the 9H, it feels fulfilling simply to be taking the next step, but with the 3T unfolding in the 1H, there is a need for a broad vision of a 'direction in life'.

23 Dhanishtha 3 2 2

In Dhanishtha, a propensity to find joy and fulfilment by engaging with the phenomenal realm (3H 2T, 9H 2T) is underpinned by a need to be connected to, and guided by, something otherworldly. Thus, this nakshatra is associated with ability in music and dance, and more broadly with an uncanny ability to dance effortlessly through the phenomenal realm, prospering by being in the right place at the right time. The combination of the 2T and 3T can give rise to a charitable nature, but also a deep yearning (3T) for material things (2T). Engaging with others is important (2T emphasis); with the 3T unfolding in the 1H, this is approached in an inclusive, attentive, perceptive and charitable manner, with a tendency to try to bring people together under a shared ideal. However, a tendency to be overly idealistic may cause problems. This nakshatra is often said to bestow marital discord and to bring marital karma to the fore. (The 2T is concerned with relationships and confronting 'karma', while the idealism of the 3T can give rise to dissatisfaction with what *is*.)

The sutra for Dhanishtha speaks of the creation of objects that are universally admired and appreciated. DiCara suggests that the lesson of this sutra is that beauty generates beauty, wealth generates wealth, etc., and that recognising and honouring our particular assets leads to the creation of things that have value to others and ourselves. In other words, when we value what source has endowed us with, source flows creatively through us. Compared to Chitra (2 2 2), Dhanishtha is more concerned with the creation of beauty that transcends the values of any particular culture (3T).

24 Shatabhisha 3 2 3

In Shatabhisha, a 3T emphasis combines with a natural ability to work with the phenomenal realm (3H 2T); thus, this nakshatra is associated with the ability to harness the life force and use it to thrive and heal, and to defeat enemies. The strong idealism of the 3T emphasis combines with the 2T attunement to the phenomenal realm, making it difficult for the individual to relax and enjoy life. There may be a tendency to take responsibility for upholding the 'law' (whatever that may mean to the individual), to view life as a burden, to be aloof and secretive, and to need solitude. The individual may try to understand their life – and the human condition in general – in order to try to make sense of periods of loneliness and depression. With the 1T absent, the individual may sink into apathy at times, perhaps feeling victimised and overwhelmed. Shatabhisha is also said to be prone to health problems if the right action is not taken.

The sutra for Shatabhisha reminds us that the phenomenal is the abstract made manifest. If abstract ideas and ideals are adhered to rigidly, it is difficult to be satisfied with anything that is produced in the phenomenal realm; and if one's sense of what is required to function in the phenomenal realm becomes too rigid, one's sense of the bigger picture is lost. When both realms are approached in a spirit of openness and flexibility, the tangible makes the abstract more vivid, while the abstract gives meaning to the tangible.

25 Purva Bhadrapada 3 3 1

Purva Bhadrapada begins the final ninth of the nakshatra cycle; thus, both the 1H and 3H are now in the 3T, and the 9H is beginning its final unfoldment before all three harmonics are synchronised at the first point of Ashwini. Purva Bhadrapada is associated with a drive to become liberated from destructive emotions and attitudes through a process of inner purification. It is also associated with a drive to break away from cultural norms and to seek ever-broader understanding through the exercise of independent thinking. Oratory skills and generosity are also indicated. This nakshatra is said to be very active and – unless inner purification has been achieved – prone to impulsiveness and outbursts of anger. In all of these characteristics, we see the 3T emphasis combined with the passion and initiative of the 1T.

The sutra for Purva Bhadrapada seems to refer to the process of inner purification mentioned in the previous paragraph. DiCara summarises his interpretation of this sutra as follows:

> Material things should be piled before the altar of sacrifice. 'Burning' these things by deep and thorough perception will allow us to comprehend the true meaning and purpose of life and become disinterested in the differentiated, tangential material world.

The animal associated with Purva Bhadrapada is the male lion. Interestingly, alchemical texts use the image of a lion trapped in a heated alembic with its paws cut off to depict a process of psychological transformation referred to as *calcinatio,** in which the individual must endure frustration without acting it out in order to burn away destructive emotions.

26 Uttara Bhadrapada 3 3 2

Uttara Bhadrapada is similar to Purva Bhadrapada in many respects, but with the 2T now unfolding in the 9H, Uttara Bhadrapada is said to be milder in temperament and better able to contain anger and pain in order to burn away 'karma'. Increased connectedness to others brings strong psychic ability and feelings of protectiveness towards kin. There is a tendency to become increasingly indifferent to material concerns as spiritual growth

* See, for example, *The Dynamics of the Unconscious,* in which Greene discusses four 'alchemical processes', correlating one with each element.

proceeds, but in the absence of such growth, there is said to be a propensity for manipulative behaviour, laziness and perhaps addiction.

Like the sutra for Shatabhisha (3 2 3) the sutra for Uttara Bhadrapada seems to remind us that the tangible and the intangible realms are not distinct. The sutra for Uttara Bhadrapada refers to a sacrificial altar, but while the sutra for Purva Bhadrapada refers to the burning away of karma/delusion (1T), the sutra for Uttara Bhadrapada refers to the sanctification of one's experience of the phenomenal realm through intimate experience of it (2T). Thus, while Purva Bhadrapada uses the image of fire, Uttara Bhadrapada uses the image of water.

27 Revati 3 3 3

In what might be thought of as the nakshatra equivalent of Pisces (interestingly, one of the symbols used to denote Revati is a pair of fish), the 3T unfolds in all three harmonics. Revati is associated with intuition and psychic ability, a devotional and spiritual nature, talent for the arts, the ability to heal and nourish, and empathy, compassion and forgiveness. There is great sensitivity to the feelings of others and an openness to visions of what might be. A sense of low self-esteem may lead the individual to give too much in an attempt to make the world a better place. Revati is associated with transitions from one world to another, and the individual may not feel settled on the material plane.

DiCara refers to Revati as the nakshatra of the *nourished nourisher*. Such an individual is open to sustainment and guidance from source, and is able to channel this sustainment to others. The individual who takes on the role of nourisher without being open to nourishment from source – the 'wounded healer' – meets with various disappointments and complications. We may not have learned in childhood to be open to the compassion and nourishment of source, but it is always possible to relinquish the structures of consciousness that prevent such openness. To the extent that we do this, we are better able to help others to do likewise.

CHAPTER SIX

INTERPRETING DIURNAL POSITION

The first part of this chapter gives a brief summary of the explanation of the diurnal cycle given in Chapter 1* and discusses the meaning of this cycle in psychological astrology. The remainder of the chapter shows how the proposed model can help to make clear the core meaning of each stage of the two, three, four and twelve-fold divisions of this cycle.

The Diurnal Cycle

In order to interpret the significance of celestial events for particular locations on Earth's surface, astrologers use frames of reference that take location into account (see Figure 1.28 and Figure 1.29 on pages 44 and 45).

The vertical line that passes through Earth's centre and a location on Earth's surface meets the celestial sphere at the location's *zenith* (above) and the location's *nadir* (below). The plane that is perpendicular to the zenith-nadir axis and that passes through Earth's centre is the *horizon plane*, which meets the celestial sphere at the *rational horizon* (a great circle). The rational horizon divides the celestial sphere into an upper half and a lower half, and approximately coincides with the boundary between earth and sky. The arc-length between the rational horizon and a point on the celestial sphere (measured perpendicular to the rational horizon) is referred to as the *altitude* or *elevation* of the point.

The *meridian plane* of a location passes through the location, Earth's rotation axis, the location's zenith and nadir, all points on the location's line of terrestrial longitude, and all points on the opposite line of terrestrial longitude. Thus, all locations on a given line of terrestrial longitude and the

---

* This is mostly for the reader who skipped the relevant parts of Chapter 1; however, for others it may serve as useful revision of the main points. Those who skipped all of Chapter 1 are advised to read pages 1 to 6 before continuing.

opposite line of terrestrial longitude share the same meridian plane. The meridian plane meets the celestial sphere at the *celestial meridian* – a great circle that is perpendicular to the rational horizon and that passes through the zenith and nadir and the north and south points on the rational horizon. If you face directly north or south, the celestial meridian divides the celestial sphere into the half to the right of you and the half to the left.

Earth's rotation axis meets Earth's surface at the *geographic poles* and meets the celestial sphere at the *celestial poles*. The *equatorial plane* passes through Earth's centre and is perpendicular to Earth's rotation axis, meeting Earth's surface at the *terrestrial equator* and meeting the celestial sphere at the *celestial equator*, which is a great circle (see Figure 1.1 on page 2). The celestial equator passes through the east and west points on the rational horizon and reaches its highest and lowest altitudes as it crosses the celestial meridian. The *declination* of a point on the celestial sphere is the arc-length between the celestial equator and the point, measured perpendicular to the celestial equator.

As Earth rotates, a given location on Earth's surface moves eastwards around Earth's rotation axis; and consequently, to an observer at the location, each point on the celestial sphere appears to move westwards parallel with the equatorial plane, completing one *diurnal cycle* during each rotation of Earth. Because the equatorial plane is not parallel with the horizon plane (unless the location is a geographic pole), each point on the celestial sphere undergoes a cycle of changing altitude during each unfoldment of its diurnal cycle. A point on the celestial sphere reaches its highest and lowest altitudes as it crosses the celestial meridian.

Whether a given point on the celestial sphere actually rises and sets across a location's rational horizon during each rotation of Earth depends on the declination of the point and the terrestrial latitude of the location. The closer the location to the equator, the greater the northerly and southerly declinations of the north and south points on the rational horizon, and so the wider the band of the celestial sphere that can cross the rational horizon. At a location on the equator, the north and south points on the rational horizon are the celestial poles, and all points on the celestial sphere (apart from the celestial poles themselves) rise and set during each rotation of Earth. At a geographic pole, the rational horizon coincides with the celestial equator, and so no points on the celestial sphere rise or set. At locations with terrestrial latitude between 0° and 66.6° north or south, all points on the ecliptic rise and set.

Charting the Diurnal Cycle

The *horizon axis* is the nodal axis (line of intersection) of the ecliptic plane and the horizon plane. Thus, the nodes of the horizon axis (the points at which it meets the celestial sphere) are the points of intersection of the ecliptic and the rational horizon. The node at which points on the ecliptic move upwards across the rational horizon is referred to as the *ascendant* (ASC), and the node at which points on the ecliptic move downwards across the rational horizon is referred to as the *descendant* (DES). Because the ecliptic and rational horizon are great circles, the horizon axis passes through Earth's centre, and the ascendant and descendant are diametrically opposed. The horizon axis may be represented on an astrological chart by a straight line between the ascendant and descendant.

The *meridian axis* is the nodal axis of the ecliptic plane and the meridian plane. Thus, the nodes of the meridian axis are the points of intersection of the ecliptic and the celestial meridian. The node above the rational horizon is referred to as the *midheaven* or *medium coeli* (MC), and the node below the rational horizon is referred to as the *lower heaven* or *imum coeli* (IC). Because the ecliptic and celestial meridian are great circles, the meridian axis passes through Earth's centre, and the midheaven and lower heaven are diametrically opposed. The meridian axis may be represented on an astrological chart by a straight line between the midheaven and lower heaven. The ascendant, descendant, midheaven and lower heaven are referred to as the *angles* of the chart.

A frame of reference that divides the celestial sphere into segments for the purpose of charting diurnal position is called a *diurnal wheel*. Where a diurnal wheel divides the celestial sphere into twelve segments, each segment is referred to as a *house*, each boundary-line between two segments is referred to as a *house cusp*, and the method used to construct the wheel is referred to as a *house system*.

The houses are numbered from 1 to 12 anticlockwise around the chart wheel. The semicircle on the celestial sphere that separates the twelfth and first houses is referred to as the *cusp of the first house*; the semicircle that separates the first and second houses is referred to as the *cusp of the second house*, and so on. In almost all houses systems (the most commonly used exception being the Koch system), the cusps of the first and seventh houses are always two halves of the same great circle, as are the cusps of the second and eighth houses, the third and ninth, and so on; and the six great circles used to divide the celestial sphere mutually intersect at two diametrically opposed points. In all houses systems, the points at which the first and seventh house cusps cross the ecliptic are always diametrically opposed, as are the points at which the cusps of the second and eighth houses cross the ecliptic, and so on.

Whichever house system is used, the half of an astrological chart that is comprised of houses 1 through 6 is referred to as the *lower hemisphere*, and the half that is comprised of houses 7 through 12 is referred to as the *upper hemisphere* (see Figure 1.39 on page 72). The half of the chart that is comprised of houses 1 through 3 and 10 through 12 is referred to as the *left hemisphere,* and the half that is comprised of houses 4 through 9 is referred to as the *right hemisphere.* (For a location outside the Arctic and Antarctic circles, the ascendant is always the more easterly node of the horizon axis, and so the left and right hemispheres are often referred to, respectively, as the *eastern* and *western hemispheres.*) Thus, the chart divides naturally into four quadrants: houses 1 through 3 make up the *lower left quadrant*; houses 4 through 6 make up the *lower right quadrant*; houses 7 through 9 make up the *upper right quadrant*; and houses 10 through 12 make up the *upper left quadrant.*

Where a *quadrant house system* is used, the cusps of the first, fourth, seventh and tenth houses always intersect the ecliptic at the ascendant, lower heaven, descendant and midheaven, respectively. Thus, where a chart is drawn using a quadrant house system, the upper and lower hemispheres are separated by the horizon axis, and the left and right hemispheres are separated by the meridian axis. Where the house system used is not a quadrant system, it is common practise to add the ascendant and/or midheaven to the chart.

On an astrological chart, each house cusp is represented by the point at which it crosses the ecliptic. Because each point on a chart wheel represents all points on a particular line of celestial longitude, if a house system is used in which the house cusps are not lines of celestial longitude, then the house placement of any factor that is not on or near the ecliptic may not be accurately represented on the chart. When an astrologer uses such a house system and assumes that the house placements suggested by the astrological chart are correct, they are (knowingly or unknowingly) using a modified version of that house system – one in which the original house cusps are usurped by the lines of celestial longitude that intersect the house cusps at the ecliptic.

The actual position of a celestial body relative to the rational horizon and celestial meridian can be found using astro-mapping, and a more accurate way of representing house position on an astrological chart is shown in

Figure 1.37 on page 67. It should be noted that the type of discrepancy discussed above also has implications for charting the movement of transiting factors through the houses of a whole's natal chart, and for locating the positions of one whole's natal factors in the houses of another whole's natal chart.

As a location revolves eastwards around Earth's rotation axis, the diurnal wheel of that location revolves eastwards around the celestial sphere, and each point or factor on the celestial sphere appears to move westwards, passing through the houses in reverse numerical order. However, the eastward motion of a transiting, progressed or directed factor – when superimposed onto a chart drawn for a particular time and location – is seen to proceed through the houses in numerical order.

As noted at the end of Chapter 1, no one can say for sure whether there is a particular house system that always gives the best results, or whether the best system to use varies according to culture, geographical region, the astrological techniques used and/or the approach and goal of the astrologer. Amongst the issues that prevent clarity in this area are: 1) inaccuracy in the timing of events (especially births); 2) the misrepresentation of diurnal positions on the astrological chart when certain house systems are used; 3) confirmation bias on the part of the astrologer; 4) the widespread belief that – unlike zodiacal signs – houses blur into one another over several degrees; 5) the apparent limitations of statistical research as a tool for studying the meanings of discrete stages of celestial cycles. (Note that the second, third and fourth of these issues tend to exacerbate one another.)

The Meaning of the Diurnal Cycle

As noted in the previous chapter, just as Earth is the standpoint from which we observe the celestial sphere, so the Earth-function in the individual human psyche gives rise to a focal point from which values and drives (corresponding to zodiacal stages and celestial bodies, respectively) are experienced as 'my' values and drives. From the standpoint of the individual, each point on the celestial sphere lies in a particular direction relative to Earth-as-a-whole, and thus corresponds to a particular perspective from which a value or drive can be experienced as 'my' value or drive.

For the purposes of interpretation, each distinct segment of a diurnal wheel is assumed to correspond to a distinct type of perspective and the type circumstance – or area of life – that naturally invokes that type of perspective. The placement of a factor in a particular diurnal segment signifies that the individual is predisposed to associate the corresponding value or drive with the corresponding type of perspective/circumstance. Thus, there is a tendency to express, notice and encounter the value or drive whenever the type of circumstance is met, and there is a tendency for the individual to experience their circumstances as being more akin to those associated with the house whenever the value or drive is expressed or encountered.

That the diurnal cycle corresponds to a cycle of changing self-consciousness makes sense when we consider that the consciousness arising in the individual alternates between sleep and wakefulness in step with the diurnal cycle of the Sun. (Similarly, that the zodiacal cycle corresponds to a cycle of changing values and motivation makes sense when we consider that the priorities of the individual have historically changed in step with the tropical zodiacal cycle of the Sun.)

The Diurnal Cycle as a Cycle of Being

The large waveform at the top of Figure 6.1 shows the 1H of the diurnal cycle unfolding anticlockwise around the chart wheel (eastwards around the celestial sphere for all locations). Displacement of the waveform above the line corresponds to emphasis on multiplicity, and displacement of the waveform below the line corresponds to emphasis on unity. We can see that at the 1H frequency: the pivotal points are the first, fourth, seventh and tenth house cusps; the principle of multiplicity is dominant throughout the lower hemisphere (houses 1 through 6); the principle of unity is dominant throughout the upper hemisphere (houses 7 through 12); emphasis on multiplicity is increasing throughout the left hemisphere (houses 10 through 12 and 1 through 3); and emphasis on unity is increasing throughout the right hemisphere (houses 4 through 9).

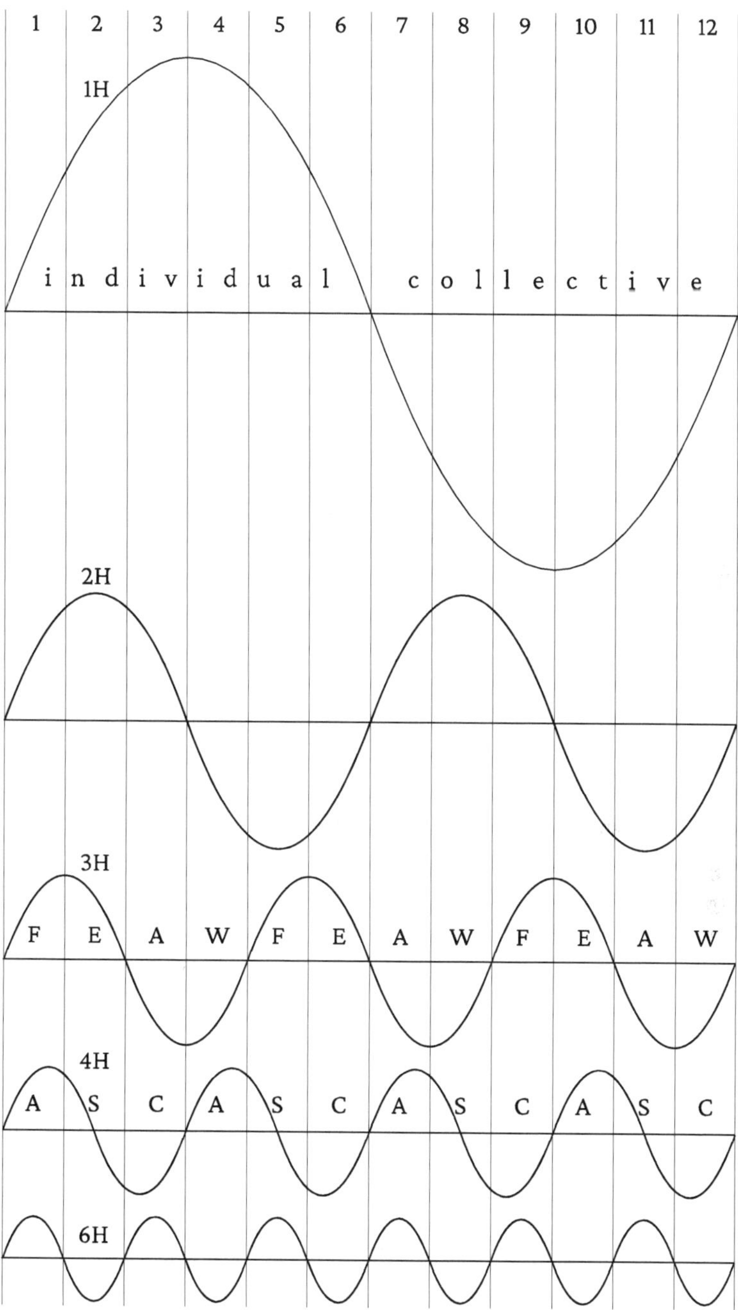

Figure 6.1 The harmonic basis of the division of the diurnal cycle into the twelve houses, with waves shown separately

Dividing the Diurnal Cycle

The two, three, four and twelve-fold divisions seem to be the only divisions used by contemporary astrologers to interpret diurnal position. In Ancient Egypt, the diurnal cycle was initially divided into eight *watches*, but at some point, Egyptian astrologers switched to the twelve-fold division. The harmonic basis of the division of the diurnal cycle into the twelve houses is shown with the waves separated in Figure 6.1 and on a single graph in Figure 4.4 (page 127). As discussed in Chapters 4 and 5, the two and three-fold divisions are based solely on the 1H, and the four-fold division is based on the 1H and 2H. All that is said about these harmonics and divisions in Chapter 5 may be applied to the diurnal cycle; thus, to avoid unnecessary repetition, most sections of the following discussion are relatively brief.

Given the complexities and uncertainties surrounding the division of the diurnal cycle, and the potential difficulty in defining a larger number of distinct types of circumstances, it makes sense to limit the number of diurnal stages to twelve. In theory, however, a diurnal cycle could be divided in as many ways as a zodiacal cycle, and where the Equal House, Whole Sign or Porphyry system is used, this could be done very easily without the use of a computer. Where the zodiac around the chart wheel is divided into the twenty seven nakshatras, for example, a case could be made for a *Whole Nakshatra* system (in which each diurnal stage coincides with a nakshatra, beginning with the rising nakshatra), or an *Equal Mansion* system (in which the first of twenty-seven equal diurnal divisions begins at the ascendant). With regard to the use of such divisions, it is interesting to note that while the importance of the twelve-fold division is synchronous with the relationship between Earth's orbital period and the Moon's orbital period, the importance of the twenty seven-fold division (and the twenty eight-fold division) is synchronous with the relationship between the Moon's orbital period and Earth's rotational period.

The 1st Harmonic

As noted in Chapter 5, the quality of one-ness is that of wholeness itself. Thus, the 1H of the diurnal cycle corresponds to a shift of emphasis back and forth between a sense of being someone who is first and foremost an individual whole and a sense of being someone who is first and foremost a constituent part of encompassing wholes.

The Angles

In Chapter 1, we saw that whichever house system is used, one or both pairs of angles play a part in defining the pivotal points of the diurnal cycle (i.e. the cusps of houses 1, 4, 7 and 10). In fact, the ascendant, and the first house cusp of any valid diurnal wheel, each express, in a unique way, the meaning of the point of the cycle of being at which the principle of multiplicity becomes dominant. Similarly, the lower heaven and any fourth house cusp express the meaning of the point at which emphasis on multiplicity peaks, and so on. However, the significance of the angles is observed to extend beyond their role in the construction of diurnal wheels. This section explores how an understanding of the cycle of being can help to make clear the core meanings of the angles.

The Ascendant and Descendant

The ascendant correlates with the point at which the principle of multiplicity becomes dominant. This is the most subjective point of the cycle of being, where potentiality first emerges into consciousness as an impulse to act, and where there is little or no objective understanding of the nature of the potentiality. Thus, the ascendant corresponds to the experience of moving forwards through life from one moment to the next in response to impulses (potentiality) arising from within; it represents the experience of simply being in one's own skin – of being oneself as opposed to being *conscious of* oneself. By acting out the impulse/potentiality arising in each moment, the individual not only creates something new, but also becomes something new. Thus, the ascendant is often referred to as the point of self-discovery.

The ascendant in the birth chart shows the qualities – i.e. drives/functions (celestial bodies) and values (zodiacal stages) – that come to the fore when the individual is not aware of being in any particular type of circumstance. However, these qualities set the tone for the entire diurnal cycle, colouring the individual's experience of all types of circumstances to some extent. These qualities are experienced as being an important and unavoidable part of life in general, and the individual instinctively meets life accordingly. The individual may not be aware of how subjective and personal their way of perceiving and meeting the world is. However, these qualities tend to stand out to others, and the individual may notice that others tend to respond to them in a particular way. These qualities also come to the fore as the individual enters into – or anticipates entering into – a new situation or venture. The more relaxed the individual is in expressing these qualities, the more spontaneous and growthful are their responses to impulses arising from within and opportunities arriving from without.

The descendant correlates with the point at which the principle of unity becomes dominant. At this point of the cycle of being, the individual becomes more aware that they are just another participant in the sphere of collective wholeness. Thus, the descendant corresponds to the experience of being someone who exists in relationship with others, and who can potentially interact with others in a fruitful manner and thus be of value to collectives and to other members of those collectives. While the ascendant is the point of awareness of oneself as a subject of experience, the descendant is the point of awareness of oneself as an object of the experience of others.

The descendant is often referred to as the point of the 'significant other'. Essentially, the significant thing is our experience of being in relationship with the other, for this is how we assess how much value we have for encompassing wholes. Any interaction, with any person, is significant to some extent, and it is interesting to observe how the significance of interactions tends to vary according to the age, respectability, gender, familiarity, like-mindedness, attractiveness, class/caste, etc. of the other. It is also interesting to observe one's under or oversensitivity to the viewpoints of others, in order to see how what kinds of defences are being deployed at the descendant.

The descendant in the birth chart shows the qualities that the individual experiences as being an important and unavoidable feature of all relating, but that come to the fore to the extent that the individual tries to use the interaction to self-evaluate through the eyes of the other. There is often a tendency to retreat into the ascendant way of being and depend on others to bring the qualities associated with the descendant to interactions. To the extent that the individual is reliant on others to do this, there is a tendency become disorientated and frustrated when the other does not oblige. To the extent that the individual can 'own' their descendant qualities and express them in a relaxed manner, they will tend to be more creative in their interactions and relationships with others, and more tolerant of others' natural ways of relating.

Rudhyar* refers to the horizon axis as the *axis of consciousness*, and to the ascendant and descendant, respectively, as the subjective and objective poles of this axis. He notes that in the experience of the observer, the rational horizon approximately coincides with the earth-surface, which is the arena of human consciousness and interaction.

---

* *The Astrological Houses* (1986) pp. 40 and 41. (1st ed. 1972)

The Lower Heaven and Midheaven

The lower heaven correlates with the point at which the principle of multiplicity peaks in strength. At this point of the cycle of being, the individual realises that they coexist with other phenomena as part of an orderly matrix, and sees the potential to harness and focus the power inherent in the matrix (both within and without) more effectively. Thus, the lower heaven corresponds to the experience of being someone who has inner resources and depths (including a racial and cultural heritage) and who can cultivate a sustaining and fruitful relationship with the phenomenal/corporeal realm.

The lower heaven in the birth chart shows the qualities that the individual experiences as being important and unavoidable when trying to become more centred and grounded as a person, and more integrated into a supportive environment. The more relaxed the individual is in expressing these qualities, the more at home they feel within their own being and in the world, and the more creatively they can navigate the restrictions, and exploit the opportunities, inherent in the orderly matrix.

The midheaven correlates with the point at which the principle of unity peaks in strength. At this point of the cycle of being, the unique viewpoint of the individual acquires renewed significance, and they are better able to see how cultural values are obscuring their own and others' connection to source. Thus, the midheaven corresponds to the experience of being someone who can connect with, and act as an ambassador for, some greater power, and who can tap into the unrealised potential inherent in a collective.

The midheaven in the birth chart shows the qualities that the individual experiences as being important and unavoidable when pursuing a vocation or calling – qualities that colour the individual's experience of authority figures and their sense of what will earn the respect of others. As the expression of these qualities becomes more relaxed, and the individual becomes less anxious about the image that they present to the world at large, their participation in the cultural, political and spiritual life of collectives becomes more fruitful and fulfilling.

Rudhyar* refers to the meridian axis as the *axis of power*. He associates the lower heaven with the power generated by virtue of internal integration, and the midheaven with the power generated by virtue of collective

* *The Astrological Houses* (1986), pp. 40 and 41. (1st ed. 1972)

integration. It is interesting to note that the plants that sustain us draw energy from the earth below and the sunshine above, and goddesses and gods are generally depicted as dwelling in the earth or sky.

The meridian axis is often referred to as the *parental axis*. Parental figures provide a stable foundation (lower heaven) and social guidance (midheaven), ideally helping the child to achieve, internal, familial and social integration by modelling integrity and the appropriate use of power. Traditionally, the midheaven has been associated with the father and the lower heaven with the mother. This makes sense when we consider that the traditional role of the father is that of the authority figure, who goes out into the world to make a living and perhaps a name for himself; and the traditional role of the mother – after acting as a vessel for the incarnation of the child – is that of homemaker and carer. However, Greene[*] argues that the midheaven is generally more indicative of the mother, while the lower heaven is more indicative of the father. Greene notes that the child is socialised during its time at home with the mother, and that an individual's sense of what it means to be a productive member of society may be strongly influenced by their mother's unlived ambitions. Greene also notes that the role of the father in the child's incarnation and upbringing is traditionally more hidden and mysterious.

Since the individual's parents were probably attracted to one another largely because each found the other to be a suitable projection screen for relatively unconscious traits, it is likely that each parent will embody both poles of the individual's meridian axis to some extent. Furthermore, parental roles are becoming less gender-specific over time. By approaching each natal chart with an open mind, and by dialoguing with the individual about their experiences of being parented, the astrologer can interpret the meridian axis in a way that is relevant to the individual.

The poles of the 1H coincide with the points at which the principle of unity becomes dominant in the 2H. Thus, it is interesting to note that the people associated with the individual's lower heaven and midheaven are 'significant others' in that they help the individual to adjust to the turning of the 1H polar tide. At the lower heaven, the significance of others is measured by their effect on the individual's ability to find stability and sustainment; and at the midheaven, the significance of others is measured by their effect

---

[*] See, for example, *The Development of the Personality* (chapter entitled *The Parental Marriage in the Horoscope*) and *Relating – An Astrological Guide to Living with Others* (chapter entitled *Honour Thy Father and Mother – with Reservations*).

on the individual's ability to define and pursue a vocation or calling.

****

The point of intersection of the horizon and meridian axes at the centre of the birth chart represents the centre of the individual's reality. For egoic consciousness, it is from this centre that the individual strives to make the best of the experiences that life throws at them. For relaxed consciousness, all experience flows outwards from this centre.

The Two, Three and Four-fold Divisions

The Hemicycles of the 1st Harmonic

The 1H 1Hem is represented on an astrological chart by the lower hemisphere, which consists of houses 1 through 6 – traditionally referred to as the *personal* or *individual houses* (see Figure 6.1). This hemicycle corresponds to the experience of being first and foremost an individual, and thus circumstances that prompt the development of individual identity, test the individual's capacity for self-sufficiency and autonomy, and call for the generation of form/consciousness.

The 1H 2Hem is represented on an astrological chart by the upper hemisphere, which consists of houses 7 through 12 – traditionally referred to as the *social* or *collective houses*. This hemicycle corresponds to the experience of being first and foremost a constituent part of various collectives or other encompassing wholes, and thus circumstances that prompt the cultivation of a sense of relatedness, test the individual's capacity for cooperation and mutual understanding, and call for the development and spreading of consciousness.

The hemicycle during which emphasis on multiplicity is increasing in the 1H is represented by the left hemisphere, which consists of houses 10 through 12 and houses 1 through 3. This hemicycle corresponds to the experience of being someone with a unique viewpoint, and thus circumstances that test the individual's capacity to respond to impulses arising from within.

The hemicycle during which emphasis on unity is increasing in the 1H is represented by the right hemisphere, which consists of houses 4 through 9. This hemicycle corresponds to the experience of being someone who is an integral part of a consensus reality, and thus circumstances that test the individual's capacity to respond to opportunities for enhanced integration.

The Quarters of the 1st Harmonic

The 1H 1Q is represented by the lower left quadrant (houses 1 through 3). This quarter corresponds to the experience of being an individual whose identity is defined from within, and circumstances that provide space for self-discovery through spontaneous self-expression.

The 1H 2Q is represented by the lower right quadrant (houses 4 through 6). This quarter corresponds to the experience of being an individual who is subject to an internal and external order, and circumstances that call for internal and external integration.

The 1H 3Q is represented by the upper right quadrant (houses 7 through 9). This quarter corresponds to the experience of being a collective participant who can grasp underlying principles and achieve mutual understanding with others, and circumstances that call for cooperation, the acquisition and sharing of knowledge, and the building of community.

The 1H 4Q is represented by the upper left quadrant (houses 10 through 12). This quarter corresponds to the experience of being a collective participant who can express the potential inherent in encompassing wholes by following the guidance from source that arises from within, and circumstances that call upon the individual to act as a catalyst for socio-cultural transformation. On another level, this quarter corresponds to the experience of being someone who can find immediate fulfilment through relating to others in an authentic manner, and circumstances that provide opportunities for this.

The Thirds of the 1st Harmonic

While the hemispheres and quadrants of the astrological chart have been discussed a great many times in astrological literature, I know of only one source that discusses the thirds of the diurnal cycle. In *The Twelve Houses*, Howard Sasportas* refers to houses 1 through 4 as constituting the *personal phase* of the diurnal cycle, during which the individual "becomes conscious of their own existence" and a sense of *me-in-here* is established. Houses 5 through 8 are said to constitute the *social phase*, during which the individual tries "to express and share the autonomous self with others", thus establishing a sense of *me-in-here meets you-out-there*. Houses 9 through 12 are said to constitute the *universal phase*, which involves "integration...with society-at-large and the greater whole of which we are a part" and the

* *The Twelve Houses* (1985, 1st ed.) p. 111

development of a sense of *us-in-here*.

The 3rd Harmonic

In Figure 6.1, the letters F, E, A and W refer to the *fire, earth, air* and *water houses*, respectively. Each fire house (1, 5 and 9) corresponds to an experience of being someone who can adapt to and enjoy life by acting on intuitive impulses and imbuing life with meaning, and circumstances that encourage self-discovery and self-expression. Each earth house (2, 6 and 10) corresponds to an experience of being someone who can adapt to and enjoy life by working with the order inherent in one's own nature and the world in general, and circumstances that involve dealing with concrete reality. The earth houses are often jointly associated with the individual's work-life, sense of self-worth, and (along with the ascendant and the first and fourth houses) body-awareness. Each air house (3, 7 and 11) corresponds to an experience of being someone who can adapt to and enjoy life through clear thinking and adherence to principles, and circumstances that involve learning and communicating. The air houses are often jointly associated with the individual's social life and conceptual thinking. Each water house (4, 8 and 12) corresponds to an experience of being someone who can adapt to and enjoy life through the process of internal and external assimilation, and circumstances in which people can connect intimately with one another and with source. The water houses are often jointly associated with the individual's sensitivity to feelings circulating in their environment, and in particular to unresolved issues within the family, community, society, etc.

The 4th Harmonic

In Figure 6.1, the letters A, S and C refer to the *angular, succedent* and *cadent houses*, respectively. Like the cardinal, fixed and mutable signs, the angular, succedent and mutable houses coincide with the 1T, 2T and 3T, respectively, of the 4H.

Each angular house corresponds to an experience of being an agent of change, and circumstances in which there is ongoing opportunity to initiate change. Each succedent house corresponds to an experience of being attuned to organising principles, and circumstances in which there is ongoing opportunity to create value by engaging with that which is other in accordance with those principles. Each cadent house corresponds to an experience of being someone who can sense and reveal the harmony and synthesis at the heart of life, and circumstances in which there is ongoing opportunity to develop a broader and more holistic viewpoint.

In *The Astrological Houses*, Rudhyar* summarises the meanings of the angular, succedent and cadent houses, respectively, using the key words: *to be*, *to use*, and *to understand* or *transform*.

The Twelve-fold Division

The First House

The meanings attributed to the ascendant and first house are generally interchangeable. Thus, when interpreting the ascendant in a birth chart, the astrologer may include any celestial bodies or zodiacal stages in the first house that are not conjunct or on the ascendant. This affinity between the ascendant and the first house is to be expected given that the ascendant and first house cusp both correlate with the point at which the principle of multiplicity becomes dominant in the 1H, 2H, 3H, 4H and 6H, and each of these harmonics continues that theme, in one way or another, throughout the first house.

The Second House

The second house corresponds to the experience of being a unique and autonomous individual who can be self-sufficient and potent, and who can express this unique individuality in tangible ways by utilising available resources. This house corresponds to circumstances in which capacities and other resources are acquired, developed, maintained and utilised, and circumstances in which a personal value-system is used to make decisions. Thus, the second house is associated with, for example: talents and inherent traits; the body as the instrument of the personality and the will; income, finances and wealth; self-worth; security; and values. In the birth chart, the second house shows the qualities that the individual experiences as important and unavoidable when focusing on such things. (The previous sentence is, of course, applicable to each of the houses; it is not repeated in the remaining sections.)

The Third House

The third house corresponds to the experience of being a unique and autonomous individual who can become familiar with objects, ideas, tasks, people and locations in order to ensure freedom of movement, to facilitate further learning and exploration, and to communicate their viewpoint to others. It corresponds to circumstances in which the individual navigates

* *The Astrological Houses* (1986) p. 43. (1st ed. 1972)

their environment 'on automatic pilot' and which tend to be seen as having little significance in the wider scheme of things, and circumstances in which the mind is discovering and learning. Thus, the third house is associated with, for example: interactions with familiar people such as neighbours, relatives and peers; communication and information exchange; local travel; school; categorising, labelling, analysing and problem solving; and the mind as the instrument of the personality and the will.

The Fourth House

The fourth house corresponds to the experience of being someone who is an inseparable part of an orderly matrix, and who must maintain a state of internal and external assimilation in order to ensure the well-being of oneself and one's progeny (using this term in its widest sense). It corresponds to circumstances that involve withdrawing into oneself or some compartment of the world in order to gestate and nurture new life, consciousness, art, etc., and in order to experience a sense of safety and belonging. Thus, the fourth house is associated with, for example: self-nurture and the nurture of others; emotional security; self-acceptance; the childhood environment; the current home and home-life; the homeland; art that gives form to feelings and the imagination; the private self – who we are deep down; and ancestral origins.

The meaning of the lower heaven is very similar to that of the 1H 2Q. However, where the diurnal wheel is divided into twelve houses, the same degree of affinity does not exist between the lower heaven and the fourth house. This is because the fourth house is not just an expression of 2Q themes, but also the themes of water and cardinality. The same discrepancy is found between the midheaven and the tenth house. Despite these discrepancies, the lower heaven and midheaven, and the fourth and tenth houses, are all associated with the experience of being parented. (Note that the earthiness of the tenth house does mirror the 2Q theme of the IC, while the wateriness of the fourth house mirrors the 4Q theme of the MC.)

The Fifth House

The fifth house corresponds to the experience of being someone who is an inseparable part of an orderly matrix, and who can use the resources inherent in this matrix to radiate one's unique character and vision out into the world. It corresponds to circumstances in which the individual can engage with the world creatively and spontaneously, and see their vitality and specialness reflected back to them by the results. Thus, the fifth house is associated with; for example: recreational activity, including spontaneous play, hobbies and the fun aspect of sport; creativity, including the procreation of offspring; the inner child; romantic relationships; entrepreneurial activity; and gambling.

The Sixth House

The sixth house corresponds to the experience of being someone who is a compartment of an orderly matrix, and who can acquire the skills and understanding necessary to achieve a state of internal and external integration. It corresponds to circumstances in which constituent parts must operate as a smooth-running system as a matter of practical necessity, and circumstances in which the individual is trying to become a more effective facilitator of this. Thus, the sixth house is associated with, for example: mundane tasks; interactions with co-workers, employers and employees; training, apprenticeship and discipleship; the healing and maintenance of the body-mind; the body as intermediary between the personality and the greater whole; and self-purification.

The sixth house is also associated with animals, but involvement with animals does not fit neatly into one type of circumstance, and it should always be remembered that the houses correspond to types of circumstances rather than types of phenomena. Keeping an animal is a sixth-house experience in that the individual maintains the conditions necessary for the continuing well-being of the animal, and in so far as the animal serves a useful function such as mountain rescue, detecting drugs and explosives, herding sheep, deterring intruders, or compensating for one or more sensory impairments. However, using an animal to compensate for one or more sensory impairments also involves the first four houses; embracing the animal as a family member is largely a fourth-house experience; showing the animal in competition is largely a fifth-house experience; using the animal as a source of income (for example, through breeding) is largely a second-house experience; expressing feelings of disempowerment and resentment through abusive behaviour towards an animal is largely an eighth-house experience; and rescuing an animal that has been neglected by others is largely a twelfth-house experience.

The Seventh House

The meaning of the seventh house is similar to that of the descendant. The discrepancy is more than between the ascendant and first house, but less than between the lower heaven and fourth house, or the midheaven and tenth house. This is because in the seventh house, the same quarter is unfolding in the 1H and 3H.

Both the sixth and seventh houses correspond to circumstances in which a high degree of cooperation is called for; but while sixth house cooperation is pragmatic and involves the synthesis of the form/consciousness-building activity of the participants, seventh house cooperation is idealistic and involves the alignment of the communal aspirations of the participants. In the sixth house, a hierarchal structure may be deemed useful or acceptable if some participants are more skilled or equipped.* In the seventh house, we are equals embarking on a new adventure in the collective sphere of wholeness. While the third house is associated with the mind as the instrument of the personality and will, the seventh house is associated with the mind as intermediary between the personality and the greater whole.

The Eighth House

The eighth house corresponds to the experience of being someone who is sustained by shared resources, and who can work more creatively within this state of symbiosis by transcending one's current reality and by understanding and achieving the right balance between control and surrender. It corresponds to circumstances in which the individual has the opportunity to achieve this transcendence/balance, either voluntarily or because their identity/reality/understanding breaks down to some extent. Thus, the eighth house is associated with, for example: shared resources, banking, investment and 'big business'; inheritance; ecology; emotional/sexual intimacy; shared emotional experiences in general; sensitivity to emotional undercurrents; traumatic or transformative experiences; deaths; investigation and research; that which is buried or hidden; psychoanalysis, psychotherapy, etc.; the astral plane; the study of metaphysics and the occult; taboos; and power struggles.

The Ninth House

The ninth house represents the experience of being a protagonist in the unfolding of a story of some significance – someone who has a meaningful connection with a greater power or plan and is sustained and vitalised by this. It corresponds to circumstances in which the individual is trying to formulate a broader understanding of life or align their identity and will with something universal and archetypal. Thus, the ninth house is associated with, for example: the god-image; divination; assumptions about what lies over the horizon; travel to other cultures; philosophy and religion; teaching and publishing; advertising and propaganda; collective trends and

* As when the employer possesses the 'means of production'.

aspirations; and communication through symbols.

The Tenth House

The tenth house corresponds to the experience of being someone who can play a productive role in the advancement of a collective by maintaining a sense of personal integrity. It corresponds to circumstances that involve working to make practical improvements to a collective by following the lead of a higher authority and/or by exercising authority. Thus, the tenth house is associated with, for example: career, vocation and calling; authority figures; the government; prestige and influence; public image; and the body as an instrument of source or spirit.

The Eleventh House

The eleventh house corresponds to the experience of being someone who can relate to others in a way that draws maximum pleasure from, and/or promotes the further advancement, of a culture. It corresponds to circumstances that involve joining with others of like mind, especially where there is a strong sense of group-identity. Thus, the eleventh house is associated with, for example: friends; clubs and societies; hopes and wishes; progressive ideas and movements; group identity and group consciousness; and the mind as an instrument of source or spirit.

The Twelfth House

The twelfth house corresponds to the experience of being someone who is ultimately at-one with source, and who is bereft when alienated from source and deeply fulfilled when connected with source. It corresponds to circumstances in which the individual aligns their personal will with the needs of others and the greater whole, and circumstances in which the personal will is undermined by unconscious forces within the psyche, by other individuals, or by forces operating within some greater whole. Thus, the twelfth house is associated with, for example: spirituality and redemption; meditation, prayer and retreat; enemies working behind the scenes; the dissolving of structures of consciousness; confusion and enchantment; sacrifice and martyrdom; sensitivity to the unresolved issues of collectives; hospitals and prisons; museums as storehouses of the past successes and failures of collectives; and inspiration from a higher realm.

(A collective may deem it necessary to confine an individual within some kind of institution as a means of cleansing society. Ideally, this is done in an attempt to heal the individual so that they can be integrated back into society, and is accompanied by collective soul-searching about what could be done to improve society so that in future such individuals are better supported right from birth. Historically, there has been a tendency to try to deal with social dysfunction by 'sweeping it under the carpet', though attitudes seem to be gradually improving in many parts of the world.)

The House Axes

In *The Astrological Houses*, after summarising the meanings of the angular, succedent and cadent houses using the keywords cited above, Rudhyar[*] defines six "basic operations". Rudhyar suggests that the same six operations bring about the development of "subjective consciousness of self" in houses 1 through 6, and "the kind of consciousness which results from relationship, cooperation and finding one's place in society" in houses 7 through 12. These operations are referred to as: *being* (houses 1 and 7), *having* (2 and 8), *informing* (3 and 9), *maintaining* (4 and 10), *expressing* (5 and 11) and *transforming* (6 and 12). Greene[†] also comments on the theme shared by each pair of opposite houses, associating houses 1 and 7 with *interaction with others*, 2 and 8 with *substance*, 3 and 9 with *knowledge*, 4 and 10 with *family background and parental inheritance*, 5 and 11 with *identity*, and 6 and 12 with *synthesis*. Rudhyar's and Greene's terms are also useful in understanding the zodiacal sign axes.

According to the proposed model, a six-fold pattern of change that unfolds once during each 1H hemicycle is founded upon two or all of the following: the 2H (divided into its 1Hem and 2Hem), the 4H (divided into thirds) and the 6H (divided into its 1Hem and 2Hem).[‡] The terms listed in the previous paragraph seem to embrace all three of these.

The contributions of the 2H, 4H and 6H combine in the most straightforward manner in the 1/7 axis and the 6/12 axis.

In the 1/7 axis, the 1Hem is unfolding in the 2H and 6H, highlighting (at the level of three-ness) the importance of freedom and expansion (dominant principle becoming stronger in the 1H and 3H); and this is reiterated by the 4H 1T theme of autonomy. Thus, in this axis, the individual is free just to *be* and to engage with others as opportunities arise.

---

[*] *The Astrological Houses* (1986) p. 43. (1st ed. 1972)

[†] *The Art of Stealing Fire: Uranus in the Horoscope* (1996, 1st ed.)

[‡] All even-numbered harmonics repeat the same pattern of change in each 1H hemicycle, while no odd-numbered harmonics do.

In the 6/12 axis, the 2Hem is unfolding in the 2H and 6H, highlighting (at the levels of one-ness and three-ness) the importance of the relationship between constituent part and encompassing whole (dominant principle becoming weaker in the 1H and 3H); and this is reiterated by the 4H 3T theme of synthesis. Thus, in this axis, the individual is able to bring about, or undertake, some kind of transformation through the synthesis of the right ingredients.

In the remaining house axes, the 2H, 4H and 6H combine in a less straightforward manner.

In the 2/8 axis, the 2H 1Hem signifies a strong focus on one sphere of wholeness at the level of one-ness; but the 6H 1Hem shows that at the level of three-ness, there is a need to integrate the principles of multiplicity and unity. As noted in Chapter 5, the juxtaposition of the principles of multiplicity and unity gives rise to the sense of containment within space-time; in other words, it gives rise to the substantiality of reality. In the 2/8 axis, this combines with the heaviness and need for integration associated with the 4H 2T; thus, attention is focused on working with substance and dealing with the issue of who possesses this or that piece of this substance.

In the 5/11 axis, the 2H 2Hem signifies a need to integrate the spheres of wholeness at the level of one-ness, and the 6H 1Hem shows that at the level of three-ness, the individual adapts to life by discovering and expressing new ways of being. What is discovered and expressed is a sense of identity, by virtue of which the individual can identify as a unique example (multiplicity) of a group of others (unity). Awareness of the juxtaposition of individuality and collectivity is also a feature of the 2T (4H 2T).

In the 3/9 axis, the 2H 1Hem and 6H 1Hem signify a strong emphasis on building new consciousness at the levels of one-ness and three-ness, and the 4H 3T signifies a focus on synthesis and knowledge.

In the 4/10 axis, the 2H 2Hem and the 6H 2Hem signify an emphasis on sustaining the relationship between constituent part and encompassing whole, and the 4H 1T brings dynamism and initiative. Thus, this axis is concerned with taking action to maintain the relationship between constituent part and encompassing whole in order to try to ensure that the interaction between them remains fruitful.

CHAPTER SEVEN

INTERPRETING SYNODIC POSITION PART I

This chapter discusses the meaning in psychological astrology of the synodic cycle viewed through a frame of reference comprised of equally spaced lines of celestial longitude. It also shows how the proposed model can help to make clear the core meanings of the stages of the two, four, eight and twelve-fold divisions of this cycle, and considers the question of which of its pivotal points are the points of equilibrium and which are the poles.

The Synodic Cycle

A *synodic cycle* is a cycle of change in the relative positions of three or more celestial bodies, usually measured between two successive occurrences of a particular state of alignment. In geocentric astrology, a synodic cycle is a cycle of change in the relative positions of two celestial bodies – as 'seen' from Earth's centre – measured between successive perfect conjunctions of those bodies.

When a synodic cycle is divided into stages for the purposes of observation or interpretation, each stage is referred to as a *phase*. Synodic cycles other than the Sun-Mercury, Sun-Venus and Mercury-Venus cycles can be interpreted by dividing the entire celestial sphere into equal segments using equally spaced lines of celestial longitude. One of these lines always passes through the slower-moving body, and as this body moves, the segments move in tandem with it. Between successive perfect conjunctions, the faster-moving body moves through each segment in turn.

Any synodic cycle of the Sun and a body that orbits the Sun may also be divided into phases using an alternative approach, which distinguishes between the direct and retrograde motion of the orbiting body. This approach is discussed in Chapter 8.

The Meaning of the Synodic Cycle

As noted in Chapter 2, each astrologically significant celestial body corresponds to a function operating within terrestrial wholes; and as noted in Chapter 5, a cycle of changing celestial longitude corresponds to a cycle of change in the way terrestrial wholes are predisposed or motivated to utilise the energy available to them. Thus, the synodic cycle of two celestial bodies corresponds to a cycle of change in the way terrestrial wholes are predisposed to use the corresponding functions together to utilise available energy. Psychological astrology is concerned with how the corresponding psychological functions work together within the psyche of the individual.

The Synodic Cycle as a Cycle of Being

As noted in Chapter 2, there are two schools of thought regarding which pivotal points of the synodic cycle are the points of equilibrium and which are the poles, and thus two approaches to correlating the synodic cycle with other types of celestial cycle, with the cycle of being in general, and with the seasonal cycle. It is also noted that since the perfect conjunction is always taken to be the beginning of the synodic cycle, each approach to defining the pivotal points of the synodic cycle implies a different notion of where other types of celestial cycle, the cycle of being in general, and the seasonal cycle begin anew.

Figure 2.6 (page 90) represents the approach that takes the perfect conjunction and opposition to be the points of equilibrium of the synodic cycle, and the perfect squares to be the poles. According to this approach, the points of equilibrium are the points of alignment, and the poles are the points of maximum misalignment. Thus, the polar-opposite trends that operate within the cycle consist of the motion of the faster-moving body back and forth across the plane that is perpendicular to the ecliptic and passes through the centres of Earth and the slower-moving body. This is shown in Figure 7.1, in which the larger dot represents the zodiacal position of the slower-moving body at any given time, and the smaller dot represents the faster-moving body, with the arrow showing its motion relative to the slower-moving body.

Figure 2.7 (page 91) represents the approach that takes the perfect conjunction and opposition to be the poles, and the perfect squares to be the points of equilibrium. According this approach, the poles are the points at which the difference between the bodies' celestial longitudes reaches its minimum and maximum values of 0° and 180°, and the points of equilibrium are the points at which this difference is 90°. Thus, the polar-opposite trends that operate within the cycle are the movement of the faster-moving body towards and away from the slower-moving body. This is shown in Figure 7.2.

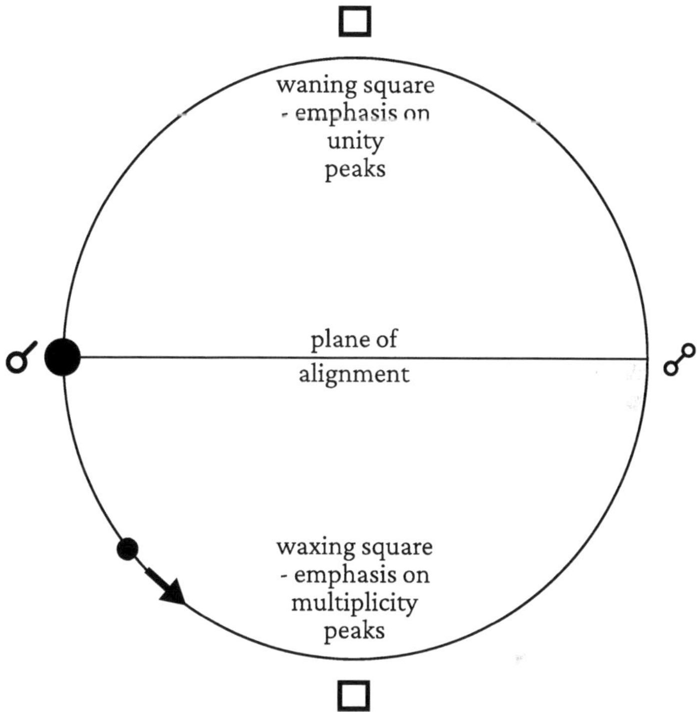

Figure 7.1 Taking the perfect conjunction and opposition to be the points of equilibrium of the synodic cycle

Michael Erlewine and Steven Forrest are amongst those who have adopted the latter approach. They each note that, from the geocentric viewpoint, the Moon is invisible at the Sun-Moon conjunction and fully illumined at the opposition, with half of the Moon visible at each square.

Erlewine* divides the synodic cycle into twelve phases, correlating the phase that begins at the perfect conjunction and ends at the perfect semi-sextile with Capricorn, the phase that begins at the perfect semi-sextile and ends at the perfect sextile with Aquarius, and so on.

* *Full Phase Aspects* (1998, 1st ed.)

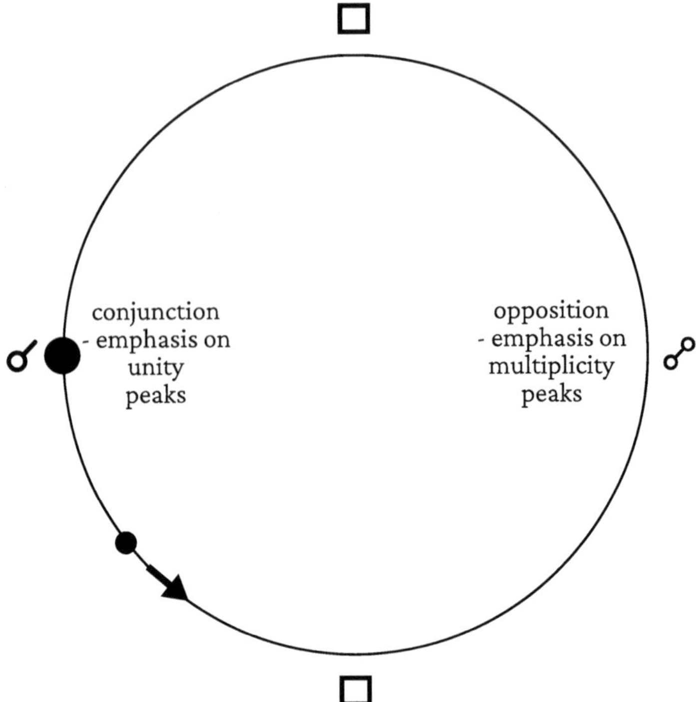

Figure 7.2 Taking the perfect squares to be the points of equilibrium of the synodic cycle

Forrest* divides the lunation cycle into eight phases rather than twelve. He broadly agrees with Rudhyar's† interpretations of these phases, except that where Rudhyar correlates the new and full moons, respectively, with the spring and autumn equinoxes, Forrest correlates them with the winter and summer solstices. Forrest also correlates the first, second, third and fourth quarters of the lunation cycle, respectively, with the elements fire, earth, air and water, which (in my view) is a valid correlation that Rudhyar missed. However, because of the way Forrest correlates the lunation and seasonal cycles, he effectively correlates spring, summer, autumn and winter, respectively, with the elements earth, air, water and fire.

As noted in Chapter 2, I agree with Rudhyar and others‡ that the perfect

---

* *The Book of the Moon* (2010, 1st ed.)

† *The Lunation Cycle* (1982). (First published under the title *The Moon – The Cycles and Fortunes of Life* in 1976)

‡ For example, Michael R Meyer (see *A Handbook for the Humanistic Astrologer*).

conjunction is the point of the synodic cycle at which the principle of multiplicity becomes dominant, and thus correlates with the ascendant, the first point of Aries and the spring equinox. From this standpoint, the conjunction of the Sun and the (then invisible) Moon symbolises the subjectivity and blind instinct associated with the ascendant and the first point of Aries; and the opposition of the Sun and the (then fully illumined) Moon symbolises the objectivity and capacity for evaluation and reflection associated with the descendant and the first point of Libra.

It is my view that only when the cycles are correlated in this way are they seen to unfold in parallel with one another, expressing the same core themes at each pivotal point and stage. (The question of which pivotal points of the synodic cycle are the points of equilibrium and which are the poles is touched on again in Chapter 9.)

Dividing the Synodic Cycle into Equal Segments

Very little has been written about dividing the celestial sphere into equal segments for the purposes of interpreting phase position. For the most part, this is probably because the technique of interpreting aspects (and nowadays midpoint structures, also) is seen to reveal the most significant features of the way functions work together within a whole. The interpretation of certain synodic cycles as the alternation of direct and retrograde motion has attracted considerably more attention (see Chapter 8).

For any given division of the synodic cycle (whether using the approach discussed in this chapter or that discussed in Chapter 8), the astrologer can note any emphasis on one or more phases within the chart, by noting the phase relationship between each pair of celestial bodies.* (Some astrological software can perform this operation.) This way of looking for themes in a chart is connected with the interpretation of *chart shaping* (the distribution of celestial bodies around the chart wheel). In the chart shown on pages 265 and 266, for example, the chart is a reasonably close to a *bucket shape*, because all of the bodies (excluding Chiron†) form a bowl shape apart from Saturn – the bucket handle. In this chart, one-half of the phase relationships

---

* Thank you to Antony Milner for bringing this type consideration to my attention and for computing a table showing the phase count for my natal chart.

† Consideration of chart shaping is generally limited to the luminaries, planets and Pluto. The more bodies that are included, the less distinct is the shaping. To include Chiron while excluding other similar bodies seems arbitrary.

are between 0° and 90°, so there is a clear emphasis on the first phase of the four-fold division (the 1H 1Q). This is related to the fact that most of the celestial bodies form a bowl, and amongst these, the faster-moving bodies tend to be to the east of the slower-moving bodies.

Interpreting the phase relationship(s) of one or more pairs of slower-moving celestial bodies during a given period can help the astrologer to discern the characteristics shared by individuals (or other types of wholes) born during that period, and can help the mundane astrologer to discern the general characteristics of a given period.

In the discussion that follows, where a phase is said to begin at one aspect and end at another, this refers to the perfection of those aspects. To avoid unnecessary repetition, the following account is kept brief. All that is said in previous chapters about the harmonic basis of the two, four and twelve-fold divisions may be applied to the context of the synodic cycle.

The Two and Four-fold Divisions

As noted in previous chapters, the two-fold division is based solely on the 1H, while the four-fold division is based on the 1H and 2H (see Figure 7.3).

During the 1H 1Hem (the waxing hemicycle), the individual uses the functions jointly in an autonomous and self-sufficient manner to give form to the potentiality released at the conjunction, and to express their unique nature. During the 1H 2Hem (the waning hemicycle), the individual uses the functions jointly in a cooperative and idealistic manner to develop and spread the consciousness that has arisen during the first hemicycle, and to form mutually satisfying relationships with others.

During the 1H 1Q (conjunction to waxing square), the individual uses the functions jointly in an enthusiastic, impulsive and relatively subjective manner to give distinctive form to the emerging potentiality and to express their potency and capacity for innovation. During the 1H 2Q (waxing square to opposition), the individual uses the functions jointly in a productive and pragmatic manner to manifest the potentiality in useful forms and to bring about internal and external integration. During the 1H 3Q quarter (opposition to waning square), the individual uses the functions jointly in an objective and civilised manner to build community and develop new understanding. During the 1H 4Q (waning square to conjunction), the individual uses the functions jointly in a progressive manner to remove outmoded social institutions and reverse the effects of social conditioning, thus helping to bring about the evolution of collectives, and helping individuals to find true fulfilment.

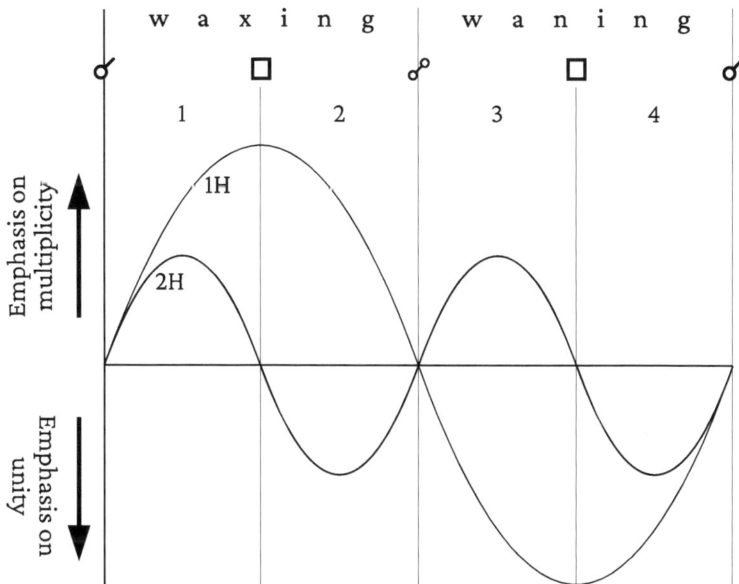

Figure 7.3 The harmonic basis of the four-fold division of the synodic cycle

As emphasis on unity increases (waxing square to waning square), the individual uses the functions jointly in line with consensus reality, prioritising integration and organisation. As emphasis on multiplicity increases (waning square to waxing square), the individual uses the functions jointly to express impulses arising from within, prioritising diversification and personal authenticity.

The Eight-fold Division

In contrast to the twelve-fold division, the eight-fold division is based solely on harmonics that are powers of two (see Figure 7.4). Thus, the eight-fold division focuses on how the individual applies effort to achieve tangible results.

In theory, the eight-fold division could be applied to any type of celestial cycle, but is generally applied only to the synodic cycle. It could be that this has come about because the synodic cycle has a greater affinity with two-ness than do other types of celestial cycle. If this is the case, it may be due to a fundamental difference between cycles involving the motion of one celestial body relative to another (synodic) and cycles involving the motion of a celestial body relative to a node (zodiacal or diurnal).

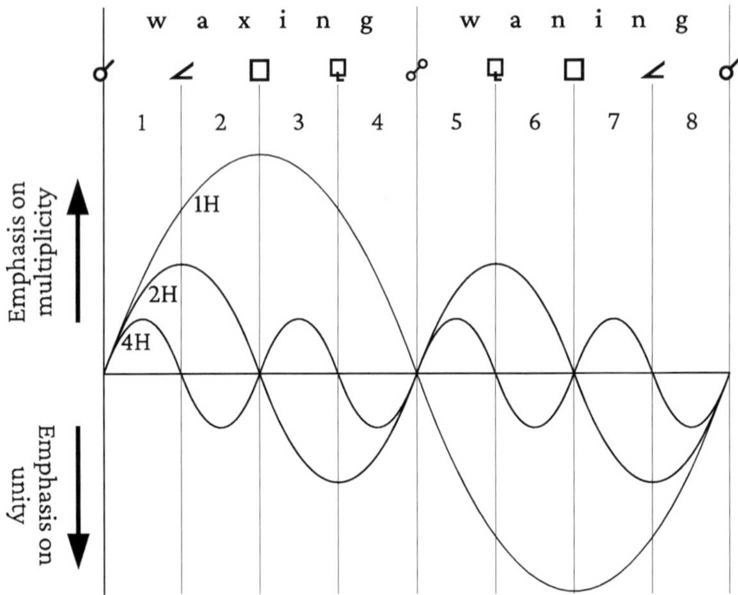

Figure 7.4 The harmonic basis of the eight-fold division of the synodic cycle

The Hemicycles of the 4H

The stage boundaries of the eight-fold division divide the 4H into its 1Hem and 2Hem. As noted in Chapter 5, the 4H of the cycle of being is a cycle of changing emphasis between multiplicity and unity in the way power is used to effect tangible change. Thus, during the 4H 1Hem, power is used in a relatively autonomous manner to give tangible form to something new; and during the 4H 2Hem, power is used with greater awareness of the wider sphere within which the individual is functioning, resulting – hopefully – in tangible shifts of values and understanding for the individual and others.

As far as I am aware, the only modern astrological texts that give meanings for the stages of the eight-fold division refer specifically to the synodic cycle of the Sun and Moon, with the interpretations given in Rudhyar's* *The*

---

* *The Lunation Cycle* (1982). (First published under the title *The Moon – The Cycles and Fortunes of Life* in 1976)

Lunation Cycle serving as the basis for works by other authors. The discussion that follows is relevant to the eight-fold division of any synodic cycle; and in theory, these meanings could be applied to other contexts such as the zodiacal and diurnal cycles.

In the following account, we will focus on the significance of the 1H and 4H during each phase. As noted in Chapter 5, the meanings of the 2H 1Hem and 2H 2Hem are largely implicit in the meanings of the 1H quarters with which they coincide; and the meanings of the 4H 1Hem and 4H 2Hem quarters reiterate the meanings of the 2H quarters with which they coincide. Thus, for the purposes of this discussion, we can simply consider each phase as a combination of a 1H quarter and a 4H hemicycle.

Phase 1

During the first phase (conjunction to waxing semi-square), the principle of multiplicity is dominant and becoming stronger in the 1H and is dominant in the 4H. The functions work together dynamically and impulsively, acting out the potentiality released at the conjunction with little objective awareness of its nature or the wider implications of the activity. Consequently, the individual can experiment freely when using the functions jointly to effect tangible change, and the potentiality can acquire vivid and distinctive form.

Phase 2

During the second phase (waxing semi-square to waxing square), the principle of multiplicity is still dominant and becoming stronger in the 1H, but the principle of unity is now dominant in the 4H. Thus, although the form/consciousness-building continues to be rather compulsive and subjective (1H 1Q), there is now a greater tendency to relate the activity to its surroundings. On the one hand, this means that inner or outer obstacles to the activity may become apparent, challenging the individual to try to overcome them. On the other hand, it means that the individual understands better how to navigate and manipulate the surroundings when effecting tangible change.

Phase 3

During the third phase (waxing square to waxing sesquiquadrate), the principle of multiplicity is dominant but becoming weaker in the 1H, and is dominant in the 4H. Awareness of the orderly matrix now arises at a more fundamental level (1H 2Q), but the functions are used jointly in a dynamic and headstrong manner to effect tangible change (4H 1Hem). Thus, this is very industrious phase, during which much building can occur, along with the demolition of anything that stands in the way of this.

Phase 4

During the fourth phase (waxing sesquiquadrate to opposition), the principle of multiplicity is still dominant but becoming weaker in the 1H, but the principle of unity is now dominant in the 4H. There is now greater understanding of the nature of the orderly matrix, and the headstrong industriousness of the previous phase gives way to a more reflective approach to working with it. Thus, during the fourth phase, the individual tries to achieve clarity of purpose and the refinement of the form/consciousness-building process (including the builder).

Phase 5

During the fifth phase (opposition to waning sesquiquadrate), the principle of unity is dominant and becoming stronger in the 1H, and the principle of multiplicity is dominant in the 4H. As in any division in which the number of stages is a power of two, opposite stages are identical except that they mirror one another in the 1H. Thus, the first and fifth stages of the eight-fold division are identical except that the principles of multiplicity and unity, respectively, are newly dominant in the 1H. During the fifth phase, the individual uses the functions jointly in an impulsive and enthusiastic manner in the collective sphere, resulting in the prolific building of concepts, symbols and community, with perhaps an influx of new values.

Phase 6

During the sixth phase (waning sesquiquadrate to waning square), the principle of unity is still dominant and becoming stronger in the 1H, and is also now dominant in the 4H. As in the previous phase, the individual uses the functions jointly in an enthusiastic and impulsive manner to build concepts, symbols and community, but now there is a deeper understanding of the socio-cultural context in which it is occurring, and a greater tendency to reflect upon what is being achieved. On the one hand, this means that the joint use of the functions is more easily influenced by waves of collective emotion. On the other hand, the functions can be used jointly to generate propaganda with which to effect tangible changes in the behaviour of others.

Phase 7

During the seventh phase (waning square to waning semi-square), the principle of unity is dominant but becoming weaker in the 1H, and the principle of multiplicity is dominant in the 4H. The 1H 4Q calls for the relinquishing of those values and allegiances that prevent the functions from working together under the guidance of source; yet during the first half of this quarter, the functions must engage in some kind of form/consciousness-building (4H 1Hem). To the extent that outmoded values and allegiances are relinquished, the functions can work together to give form to a progressive ideal, resulting in a sense of fulfilment. To the extent that the relinquishing falters, the functions must work together within the confines of the outmoded values and allegiances, generally leading to a sense of futility.

Phase 8

During the eighth phase (waning semi-square to conjunction), the principle of unity is dominant but becoming weaker in the 1H, and is also now dominant in the 4H. The propensity to take the initiative and embody progressive ideas during the seventh phase is now replaced by a more complete surrender to source. The way in which the functions work together becomes very receptive to inspiration from source and the unfulfilled needs circulating in collectives. Attempts to control the way the functions work together tend to be unsuccessful, while surrendering control leads to deep fulfilment.

The Twelve-fold Division

Figure 7.5 shows the 1H, 2H, 3H, 4H and 6H against the twelve-fold division of the synodic cycle. These harmonics are shown on a single graph in Figure 4.4 (page 127). In the account that follows, the title given for each phase is taken from *Astrological Aspects – A Process Oriented Approach*, by Leyla Rael and Dane Rudhyar.*

---

* *Astrological Aspects – A Process Oriented Approach* (1980, 1st ed.)

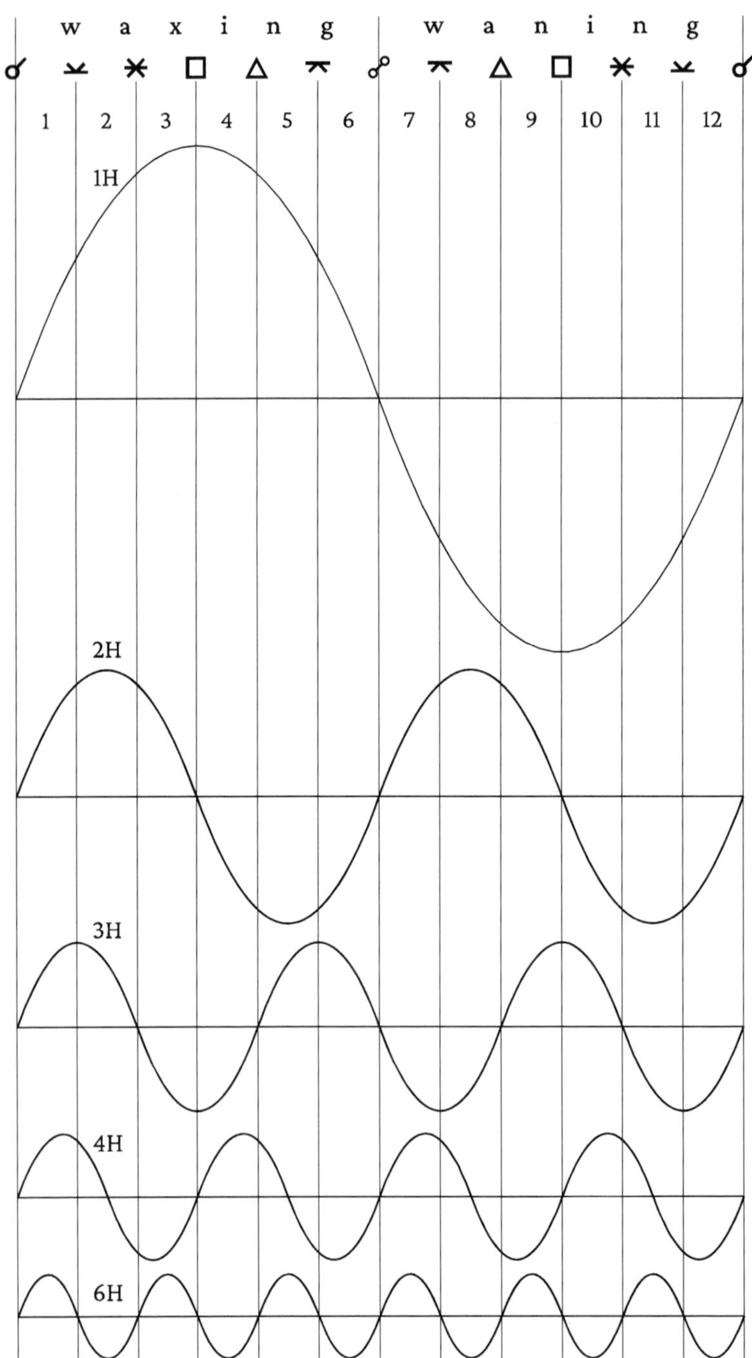

Figure 7.5 The harmonic basis of the twelve-fold division of the synodic cycle

Phase 1 – Subjective Being

During the first phase (conjunction to waxing semi-sextile), the functions are used jointly to act out emerging potentiality in a dynamic and impulsive manner. When using the functions together, the individual may feel challenged to prove their uniqueness and potency.

Phase 2 – Focusing

During the second phase (waxing semi-sextile to waxing sextile), the functions are used jointly in a more grounded manner with a view to producing something of enduring worth. The individual tends to insist on doing this on their own terms, perhaps resulting in stubbornness or bullishness. The individual may view the ability to use the functions jointly as an asset in itself – a talent worth developing.

Phase 3 – Organising

During the third phase (waxing sextile to waxing square), the individual uses the functions jointly to explore, navigate and interact with their immediate environment. The individual may try to rationalise their essentially subjective approach to using the functions together, and there may be an element of eccentricity or mischief.

Phase 4 – Deciding

During the fourth phase (waxing square to waxing trine), the functions are used jointly to nurture emerging potentiality, and the form/consciousness-building that takes place during this phase, while typically dynamic, may be somewhat sheltered from exposure to the outer world. There is an ongoing need to decide what truly supports this process and what impedes it, with increasingly fruitful judgments arising with the expansion of the subjective sense of self.

Phase 5 – Expressing

During the fifth phase (waxing trine to waxing quincunx), the functions are used jointly to make a strong impression on the environment. In this phase, the individual can shine by using available resources to create something that will be valued by others; but this is best achieved by finding a balance between self-belief and humility.

Phase 6 – Improving

During the sixth phase (waxing quincunx to opposition), the functions are used jointly to achieve and maintain internal and external integration, perhaps to the extent of becoming overly fastidious due to a fear of chaos and disintegration. Using the functions together may be seen as a useful skill to develop.

Phase 7 – Realising

During the seventh phase (opposition to waning quincunx), the individual is able to understand the working relationship between the functions at a more abstract level and to express this understanding through the building of concepts, symbols and community. Excessive idealism and/or the need to be valued by others may affect the joint expression of the functions.

Phase 8 – Sharing

During the eighth phase (waning quincunx to waning trine), the functions are used jointly to navigate intimate relationships and the use of shared resources. The working relationship between the functions may need to undergo a series of transformations as part of the development of a deeper understanding of how to share resources in a truly fruitful and fulfilling manner.

Phase 9 – Understanding

During the ninth phase (waning trine to waning square), the functions are used jointly to achieve a broader understanding of life, and perhaps to try to bring others together under a shared vision. The joint use of the functions may be a channel for the release of new potentiality into a collective. Fanaticism, unrealistic expectations and/or a reluctance to deal with practicalities may lead to the functions being used together in a destructive manner.

Phase 10 – Revaluing

During the tenth phase (waning square to waning sextile), the functions are used jointly to make a tangible contribution to the building of a better world. Fulfilment comes through ensuring that the contribution is not only productive and useful, but also an authentic expression of the individual's unique viewpoint and sense of purpose.

Phase 11 – Reorganising

During the eleventh phase (waning sextile to waning semi-sextile), the functions are used jointly with an understanding of how to capitalise on the resources inherent within a collective. This may involve enjoying the company of like-minded others and/or trying to advance the principles according to which a collective is organised. The creative potential of the functions' combined operation may be hindered by rigid adherence to an ideology and/or blinkered group identification.

Phase 12 – Releasing

During the twelfth phase (waning semi-sextile to conjunction), the functions are used jointly to reveal to the individual and to others the possibility of a direct experience of source, unaffected by limiting structures of consciousness (both individual and collective). The combined use of the functions is responsive to needs circulating in collectives; thus, the individual may use the functions jointly to try to bring about some sort of healing or redemption. The ability to consciously direct the joint use of the functions may be limited, and deep fulfilment follows from relinquishing control.

Phases and Aspects

When a synodic cycle is divided into stages using equally spaced lines of celestial longitude, there is a strong correlation between the meaning of a given stage and the meaning of the most fundamental aspect that is perfected at the beginning of that stage. In the two-fold division, for example, the 1H 1Hem is characterised by the subjectivity of the conjunction, while the 1H 2Hem is characterised by the sense of relatedness of the opposition. In the four-fold division, the 1H 1Q is strongly characterised by the subjectivity of the conjunction, while in the 1H 2Q, this is subjectivity is overlaid by the type adjustment associated with the waxing square. Also in the four-fold division, the 1H 3Q is strongly characterised by the sense of relatedness of the opposition, while in the 1H 4Q, this sense of relatedness is overlaid by the type of adjustment associated with the waning square.

It is by virtue of these correlations that the 12H aspects can be incorporated into the *astrological alphabet*, in which each one of twelve 'letters' is represented by one zodiacal sign, one house, one phase, one 12H aspect and one celestial body. For example, the first letter is represented by Aries, Mars, the first house, phase one of twelve, and the conjunction; the second letter is represented by Taurus, Venus, the second house, phase two of twelve, and the waxing semi-sextile. (The astrological alphabet is to be discussed in the next book in this series.)

The aspect perfected at the beginning of a phase comes into orb before the phase begins; thus, two bodies may form a 12H aspect that represents a different 'astrological letter' to that represented by their phase relationship. For example, two bodies begin to form an applying conjunction before the twelfth phase of their synodic cycle ends.* More generally, two bodies form numerous aspects during each phase of their synodic cycle, and the meaning of such an aspect may contradict the meaning of their phase. Thus, it is generally useful to consider any aspect formed between two bodies alongside consideration of the phase reached in their synodic cycle.

In *Astrological Aspects – A Process Oriented Approach*, Rael and Rudhyar interpret the sequential formation of a selection of aspects as the unfoldment of a meaningful pattern of change. My own sense is that when doing this, it is better to select aspects that have a particular harmonic in common, so that the sequence expresses a single, consistent narrative. Without such consistency, the inclusion of certain aspects and not others is somewhat arbitrary, and the filter – or 'harmonic lens' – through which meaning is being attributed suddenly changes a number of times mid-sequence.

The Waxing and Waning Hemicycles

As noted in Chapter 1, part of the meaning of a given aspect is dependent upon whether it occurs in the waxing or waning hemicycle (the 1H 1Hem or 1H 2Hem). It is interesting to note that while an astrologer would never attribute the same meaning to, for example, phases 3 and 7 of an eight-fold division, many astrologers tend to attribute the same meaning to both waxing and waning squares. This practise may have come about because waxing and waning aspects are less distinct from one another than are opposite phases (and opposite stages of celestial cycles in general). However, as Antony Milner has pointed out to me, there may be an entrenched bias towards viewing aspects simply as angles of separation – i.e. with no consideration of whether aspects are waxing or waning – because the concept of the cycle only began to play a significant role in astrological interpretation in the mid-twentieth century.

---

* This may be relevant to the widespread belief that a factor near the end of a house seems connected to the following house; for example, a factor forms a 'diurnal trine' with the ascendant while at the end of the fourth house.

For the purposes of using the proposed model to understand phase position, we must assume that the passage of the faster-moving factor through the harmonic waves of the slower-moving factor has greater significance than vice versa. Otherwise, it would not be possible to distinguish between the waxing and waning hemicycles.

It is suggested in Chapter 4 that a 4H aspect between two factors is essentially an alignment of their 4H waves – an alignment that would, of itself, be the same at the perfection of each 4H aspect. Thus, it seems plausible that the difference between the waxing and waning expression of an aspect is the result of the phase position of the bodies, rather than something that is inherent to the aspect alone.

CHAPTER EIGHT

INTERPRETING SYNODIC POSITION PART II

This chapter discusses the meaning of the direct-retrograde cycle in psychological astrology, and shows how the proposed model can help to make clear the core meaning of each hemicycle and quarter of this cycle.

The Meaning of the Direct-Retrograde Cycle

As noted in Chapter 7, the synodic cycle of the Sun and a body that orbits the Sun may be charted in two ways. The approach discussed in Chapter 7 uses a frame of reference that could be constructed in the same manner if Earth were actually positioned at the centre of the solar system. The approach discussed in this chapter uses a frame of reference in which some of the phase boundaries are determined by changes in the direction of the geocentric motion of the orbiting body – i.e. a frame of reference founded upon the fact that Earth is a satellite of the Sun. Thus, while the former approach focuses on changes in the working relationship between the solar function and the orbiting function, the latter approach focuses on changes in the subjective viewpoint from which the orbiting function operates. Just as the diurnal cycle arises because the observer is not positioned at Earth's centre, so the direct-retrograde cycle arises because Earth is not positioned at the centre of the solar system; and both types of cycle are concerned with changes in the individual's subjective viewpoint.

As discussed in Chapter 1, the pattern according to which the direct-retrograde cycle of an inferior body* unfolds is different to the pattern according to which the direct-retrograde cycle of a superior body† unfolds. The remainder of this chapter discusses each pattern in turn.

---

* An *inferior body* is a body that orbits the Sun inside Earth's orbit.

† A *superior body* is a body that orbits the Sun outside Earth's orbit.

The Direct-Retrograde Cycle of an Inferior Body as a Cycle of Being

The geocentric motion of an inferior body is retrograde as the body passes between Earth and the Sun, with the retrograde speed of the body peaking as it perfects an inferior conjunction with the Sun (as it passes between Earth and the Sun). The body's direct speed peaks as it perfects a superior conjunction with the Sun (as it passes behind the Sun). A detailed explanation of this cycle is given in Chapter 1, with Figure 1.17 (page 31) showing the cycle from the geocentric viewpoint.

Figure 8.1 shows the direct-retrograde cycle of an inferior body as a cycle of being. A 1H point of equilibrium is reached at each perfect conjunction, with the 1H 1Hem beginning at the inferior conjunction and the 1H 2Hem beginning at the superior conjunction. A 1H pole is reached at each station,* with the 1H 2Q beginning at the direct station and the 1H 4Q beginning at the retrograde station. Thus, the principle of multiplicity is dominant while the body is west of the Sun; the principle of unity is dominant while the body is east of the Sun; emphasis on multiplicity increases while the body has westward (retrograde) geocentric motion; and emphasis on unity increases while the body has eastward (direct) geocentric motion.

During the 1H 1Q, the body is west of the Sun with westward geocentric motion (principle of multiplicity dominant and becoming stronger). During the 1H 2Q, the body is west of the Sun with eastward geocentric motion (principle of multiplicity dominant but becoming weaker). During the 1H 3Q, the body is east of the Sun with eastward geocentric motion (principle of unity dominant and becoming stronger). During the 1H 4Q, the body is east of the Sun with westward geocentric motion (principle of unity dominant but becoming weaker).

Figure 1.24 (page 39) shows that the closer a body's orbit is to Earth's orbit, the greater the proportion of time the body has direct geocentric motion. It is also the case that the closer a body's orbit is to Earth's orbit, the more inherently subjective is the corresponding psychological function. Thus, the more subjective – or 'personal' – the function, the greater the proportion of

---

* Some astrologers take the points of maximum easterly and westerly elongation to be the poles of the cycle, in which case consideration of whether the body's geocentric motion is direct or retrograde is replaced by consideration of whether the body's elongation is becoming more easterly or more westerly. (The elongation of a body is the difference between its celestial longitude and that of the Sun.)

time it is focused on engaging with consensus reality.

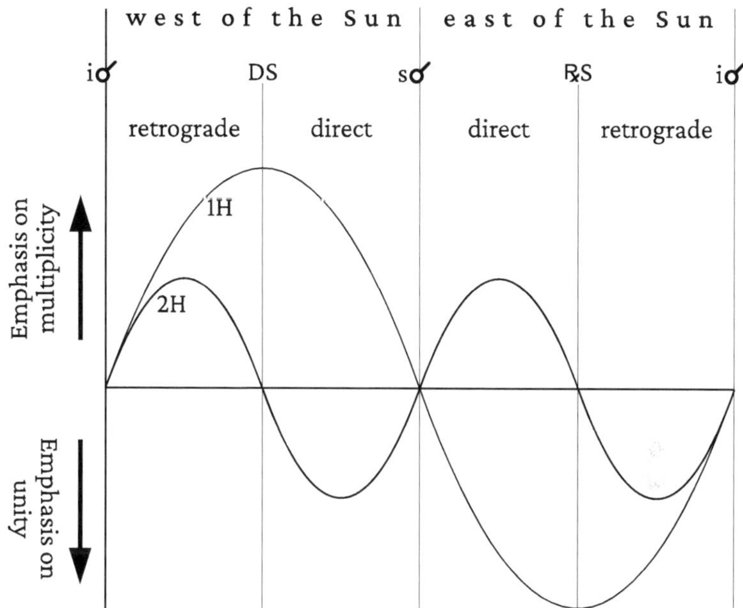

Figure 8.1 The direct-retrograde cycle of an inferior body as a cycle of being

The Hemicycles and Quarters of the Direct-Retrograde Cycle of an Inferior Body

The following discussion includes examples of how each inferior planetary function operates during each hemicycle and quarter.* The meanings of these functions may be summarised very briefly as follows: The Mercury-function acquires skills and understanding, and uses these to rationalise perceptions, exchange information with others, and solve problems. The Venus-function develops aesthetic sensibility and a sense of value, and uses these to enjoy and create beauty, engage in mutually satisfying relations with others, and appreciate one's own worth. (The meanings of the

* Rudhyar discusses the hemicycles in Chapters 8 (Mercury) and 11 (Venus) of *An Astrological Study of Psychological Complexes* Khaldea.com/rudhyar/ (1st ed. 1976). With regard to the quarters, Rudhyar describes only those of Mercury's cycle. The only account of the quarters of Venus's cycle that I have come across is Meyer's essay, *The Four Faces of Venus*, which can be found at Khaldea.com, along with Meyer's *The Four Faces of Mercury*.

planetary functions are to be discussed in the next book in this series.)

To avoid unnecessary repetition, the following account is relatively brief. All that has been said about the 1H hemicycles and quarters (and the 2H 1Hem and 2H 2Hem) in previous chapters may be applied to the context of the direct-retrograde cycle.

The First Hemicycle

During the 1H 1Hem, the function is used in a relatively self-contained and headstrong manner to generate new form/consciousness.

Rudhyar refers to Mercury during this hemicycle as *Mercury-Prometheus.* According to Greek mythology, Prometheus (*pro* means *forward, methes* means *thinking*) saw the potential for humanity to think independently and creatively, and acted to realise this potential by giving fire to humanity, despite this being against the will of the gods. During the Prometheus phase, there is emphasis on putting ideas into practise in order to substantiate them, and a sense of self-reliance colours the individual's approach to learning and problem solving.

While west of the Sun – and therefore seen as the Morning Star when far enough from the Sun – Venus has traditionally been referred to as *Lucifer* (Latin) or *Phosphorus* (Greek), these terms meaning *bringer of light*. During the Lucifer phase, immediate perceptions are used as the basis for making evaluations, and there is a tendency to give tangible expression to values and talents. Self-worth is enhanced by a sense of self-sufficiency, and there is a need for some degree of autonomy in relationships.

The Second Hemicycle

During the 1H 2Hem, the function is used in a relatively cooperative and reflective manner to develop and spread consciousness.

Rudhyar refers to Mercury during this hemicycle as *Mercury-Epimetheus*, a label suggestive of thinking that occurs after the act (*epi* means *subsequent or additional*) and that provides an overview (*epi* also means *above*). Mercury-Epimetheus is concerned with developing and sharing thoughts and ideas in such a way that they become sources of meaning and facilitate a sense of unity and togetherness. The rational mind is more inclined to abstraction than in the Promethean phase, and there is a tendency to rationalise perceptions to the extent of becoming relatively detached from them.

While east of the Sun and seen as the Evening Star, Venus has traditionally been referred to as *Hesperus* (Greek for *evening star*). Venus-Hesperus is concerned with developing and sharing visions of beauty and harmony in such a way that they become sources of meaning and enhance the sense of unity and togetherness. The individual's sense of self-worth is affected by how well they can connect with others, and talents are valued insofar as they facilitate this. The determination of value is approached from a more abstract perspective than during the Lucifer phase, and the natural idealism of the Venus-function tends to be more pronounced.

Note that the inferior and superior conjunctions are distinct from one another in that the former is essentially a point of release of potentiality, while the latter is essentially a point of illumination.

The Direct Hemicycle

During the direct hemicycle, the function is used in an organised and structured manner in accordance with consensus reality.

The direct hemicycle brings out the natural clarity, objectivity and rationality of the Mercury-function. It is often said that disruption to travel, confused and delayed communications, and the forming of contractual agreements that prove to be problematic later, are less likely when transiting Mercury is direct than when it is retrograde.

The direct hemicycle emphasises the Venus-function's capacity for cooperation and integration. There is a tendency to adhere to convention in matters of values and tastes, and to value order and rationality.

The Retrograde Hemicycle

The direct-retrograde cycle differs from the types of celestial cycle discussed in Chapters 5, 6 and 7 in that it is founded upon apparent changes in the direction of travel of the factor concerned. In the direct-retrograde cycle, the orbiting body seems to 'go into reverse' while emphasis on multiplicity is increasing, and this has a bearing on the individual's experience of this hemicycle. It seems that the themes normally associated with increasing emphasis on multiplicity (attunement to a personal viewpoint, heightened intuition and imagination, etc.) are overlaid with a sense of 'swimming against the tide' and going over the past. Rudhyar* refers to the retrograde hemicycle as an opportunity "to repair the damage done by life experiences, when these experiences were frustrated by social shams and prejudices" (i.e. destructive features of a consensus reality).

---

* *An Astrological Guide to Psychological Complexes*, Khaldea.com/rudhyar/ Ch. 12 (1st ed. 1976)

The retrograde hemicycle undermines the natural clarity, objectivity and rationality of the Mercury-function, but lends itself to introspection, intuitive thinking, heartfelt communication, and 'thinking outside the box' to solve problems.

The retrograde hemicycle emphasises the use of the Venus-function to develop truly personal tastes and values. There is a greater propensity to engage in relating and artistry (using these terms in their widest sense) in ways that inspire others to see beyond existing norms.

Note that the direct and retrograde stations are distinct from one another in that the former is essentially a point of crisis in action, while the latter is essentially a point of crisis in consciousness.

The First Quarter

During the 1H 1Q, the function is used to act out impulses (potentiality) arising within, with pioneering spirit, determination to overcome the inertia of habit and convention, and a sense of an abundance of possibilities. However, due to the nature of retrogradation, these qualities may not translate readily into tangible activity.

Mercury in the Prometheus-retrograde phase suggests eagerness to learn, passionate communication, and a tendency to identify strongly with ideas and opinions. Thinking tends to be intuitive and inventive, with a direct and perhaps impatient approach to problem solving. There may be difficulty in taking in information from others, as the mind is carried along – inwardly or outwardly – by the individual's emotional life.

Venus in the Lucifer-retrograde phase suggests a tendency to reject established value systems and to value that which is truly alive and enlivening in any given moment. Subjective identification with some vision of a more beautiful and harmonious world, and a tendency to associate self-worth with potency and uniqueness, may hinder cooperation and mutual understanding, but there is a capacity to relate to others in ways that inspire them to express their own potency and uniqueness.

The Second Quarter

During the 1H 2Q, the function is used in a structured, pragmatic and industrious manner to create form/consciousness that honours and contributes to consensus reality.

Mercury in the Prometheus-direct phase suggests that the mind is oriented towards making sense of, and navigating, the concrete realm. Thinking tends to be organised and pragmatic, and oriented towards the acquisition of understanding and skills that are deemed to have practical benefit. There may be awareness that current understanding has a developmental history, and a wish to contribute to the advancement a body of knowledge.

Venus in the Lucifer-direct phase suggests a tendency to value convention, while at the same valuing cultural change that leads to increasingly harmonious integration. Self-worth is associated with productivity and responsibility, and there is a tendency to relate to others through gestures that have practical benefit. There is a preference for stability in relationship, and for relationships in which the participants enhance one another's productivity and effectiveness.

The Third Quarter

During the 1H 3Q, the function is used in a relatively objective and rational manner to reveal archetypal principles and to build community according to an ideal of social cooperation.

Mercury in the Epimetheus-direct phase suggests a tendency to reflect on past events and experiences in order to develop a clear, broad, and relatively abstract understanding of some facet of life. Communication and problem solving are oriented towards bringing about unification and harmonisation.

Venus in the Hesperus-direct phase suggests an idealistic and principled approach to relating, perhaps resulting in the stifling of emotions that would reveal the individual's self-indulgent side. Values tend to be clearly thought-out, with a tendency to place adherence to principles above the exercising of personal preference. There may be social gregariousness and an ability to relate to a diverse range of people.

The Fourth Quarter

During the 1H 4Q, the function is used to achieve a more intimate experience of source by attuning to impulses arising within; it is sensitive to the unfulfilled needs of collectives, and able to act as a vehicle for voicing these needs.

Mercury in the Epimetheus-retrograde phase suggests an essentially introspective mind that is oriented towards understanding one's role as an ambassador for source. The question of how people can experience true fulfilment is at the forefront of attempts to make sense of life, and making progress towards this may seem the only rational thing to do. There may be a sense that a greater power is communicating through the individual, as ideas of how to create a better world arise. Problem solving and learning may occur at an almost unconscious level, and the mind readily withdraws into the imaginal realm.

Venus in the Hesperus-retrograde phase suggests a tendency to place great value on peace and serenity, and thus to avoid interactions that disrupt this. Self-worth is associated with the capacity to help others to find peace, and the individual may need to connect with source and/or seek out mutually nourishing intimate relationships in order to avoid depletion. There is a tendency towards social idealism, and the individual may question those cultural values that prevent people from achieving a sense of fulfilment. This placement is also associated with capacity for inspired artistic creativity.

The Direct-Retrograde Cycle of a Superior Body as a Cycle of Being

The geocentric motion of a superior body is retrograde as Earth passes between the body and the Sun, with its retrograde speed peaking at the opposition and its direct speed peaking at the conjunction. A detailed explanation of this cycle is given in Chapter 1, with Figure 1.22 (page 37) showing the cycle from the geocentric viewpoint.

Figure 8.2 shows the direct-retrograde cycle of a superior body as a cycle of being. The 1H 1Hem is the waning hemicycle (beginning at the opposition), during which the Sun approaches the body from the west. The 1H 2Hem is the waxing hemicycle (beginning at the conjunction), during which the Sun departs eastwards. Emphasis on multiplicity increases during the retrograde hemicycle and emphasis on unity increases during the direct hemicycle.

During the 1H 1Q, the Sun is to the west of the body (making waning aspects) and the body has retrograde motion. During the 1H 2Q, the Sun is to the west of the body (making waning aspects) and the body has direct motion. During the 1H 3Q, the Sun is to the east of the body (making waxing aspects) and the body has direct motion. During the 1H 4Q, the Sun is to the east of the body (making waxing aspects) and the body has retrograde motion.

We can see from the above that in the direct-retrograde cycle of a superior body, the principle of multiplicity becomes dominant in the 1H at the opposition. However, when a synodic cycle is interpreted using the approach discussed in Chapter 7, the principle of multiplicity becomes dominant in the 1H at the conjunction. We may be able to go some way towards understanding this apparent discrepancy by recalling that the synodic cycle of the Sun and a body that orbits the Sun can only be charted as a direct-retrograde cycle because the Sun is actually the centre of the solar system.

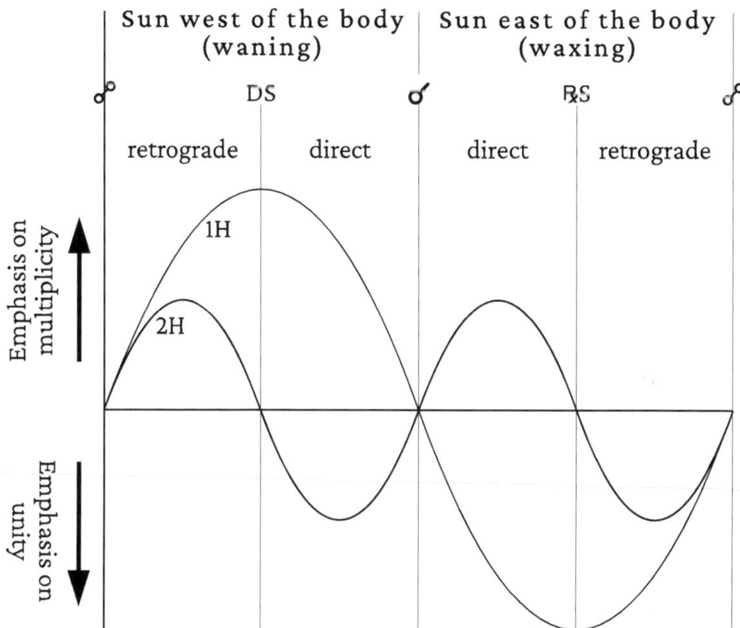

Figure 8.2 The direct-retrograde cycle of a superior body as a cycle of being

If we observe the synodic cycle of the Sun and a superior body from the heliocentric viewpoint, we see that the faster-moving body (Earth) passes and overtakes the slower-moving body at the opposition; and if we observe the cycle from the geocentric viewpoint, the faster-moving body (the Sun) passes and overtakes the slower-moving body at the conjunction. Thus, the cycle of being always begins as the faster-moving body overtakes the slower-moving body, but this applies to the heliocentric viewpoint when the cycle is interpreted as a direct-retrograde cycle.

The Direct and Retrograde Hemicycles of a Superior Body

When the synodic cycle of the Sun and superior body is charted as a direct-retrograde cycle, it is generally only divided into its direct and retrograde hemicycles (i.e. using only the stations as stage boundaries). This would seem to be sensible practise given the issues discussed in the previous two paragraphs. The general themes associated with the direct and retrograde hemicycles are described above.

CHAPTER NINE

PRINCIPLES OF CORRESPONDENCE

This chapter attempts to shed light on the principles that govern which trend within a celestial cycle corresponds to increasing emphasis on multiplicity and which trend corresponds to increasing emphasis on unity. It considers whether these principles are analogous to those behind the Doppler Effect.

The Doppler Effect

If the distance between the source of a continuous wave and a point of detection of that wave remains constant, the peaks of the wave reach the point of detection at the same rate at which they leave the source. In other words, the apparent frequency of the wave – as recorded at the point of detection – is equal to the frequency at which the wave is emitted. While the distance between the source and the point of detection is decreasing, however, the apparent frequency is raised; and while this distance is increasing, the apparent frequency is lowered. This is referred to as the *Doppler Effect* and the difference between the actual frequency and the detected frequency of a wave is referred to as a *Doppler shift*. The greater the rate of change of the distance between source and point of detection, the greater the Doppler shift. (Diagrams and animations illustrating the Doppler Effect can be found online.)

The lower the frequency of an audible sound wave, the lower the pitch of the sound; and the higher the frequency, the higher the pitch. Thus, by virtue of the Doppler Effect, the apparent pitch of an audible sound wave is lower while the distance between source and observer is increasing, and higher while this distance is decreasing. This difference is perceived when the pitch of the sound of a vehicle is heard to drop suddenly as the vehicle passes.

The lower the frequency of a visible light wave, the nearer the colour is to the red extreme of the visible spectrum; and the higher the frequency, the nearer the colour is to the violet extreme. Thus, by virtue of the Doppler Effect, the apparent colour of a visible light wave is closer to the red extreme while the distance between source and observer is increasing, and closer to the violet extreme while this distance is decreasing. Doppler shifts of light are too small to register with the naked eye, because even the fastest-moving objects that we can see with the naked eye are moving too slowly relative to the speed of light.

The Doppler Effect is of interest here because changes in the frequency of light or sound waves affect our attunement to multiplicity or unity – a phenomenon that is utilised when a different colour and pitch is used to attune to each of the seven primary chakras. The primary chakras are the seven primary energy centres within the body, positioned along the spinal axis from the *base chakra* at the coccyx – or tailbone – to the *crown chakra* above the head. Each primary chakra resonates with a different way of being, ranging from instinctive self-preservation at the base chakra (greatest emphasis on multiplicity) to surrender to unity at the crown chakra (greatest emphasis on unity). Each primary chakra has affinity with one of the seven colours of the rainbow, from red at the base chakra to violet at the crown chakra; and when sound is used to energise and attune to the chakras, the lowest pitch is used to focus on the base chakra, building up to the highest pitch at the crown chakra.

The phenomenon described in the previous paragraph is, of course, a more subtle expression of a broader principle that affects our everyday experience. We naturally experience a heightened sense of multiplicity during separation from that which is important to us, and a heightened sense of unity during reunion.

The shifts of emphasis between multiplicity and unity discussed so far in this chapter are a result of increasing and decreasing proximity. The shifts of emphasis studied by astrologers arise in synchrony with more complex motions. This complexity, and the diversity of the types of celestial cycles that may be interpreted as cycles of being, make it difficult to discern the principles that determine which trend within a celestial cycle corresponds to increasing emphasis on multiplicity and which trend corresponds to increasing emphasis on unity.

The following discussion is essentially an attempt to frame each type of celestial cycle in such a way that increasing emphasis on multiplicity and increasing emphasis on unity can each be described in the same terms in each type of celestial cycle. I had hoped for a clearer outcome; I am including the chapter in the hope that others will develop these thoughts further, or, in refuting them, become aware of alternative approaches to solving this puzzle.

The terms used in the following discussion refer to whether the motion being charted is *congruous with*, or *contradictory to*, a slower or broader motion. Congruous motion is suggested to correspond to increasing emphasis on multiplicity, and contradictory motion is suggested to correspond to increasing emphasis on unity. These correlations may seem counterintuitive, but congruous motion can also be thought of as a trend that leads to breaking out in front, while contradictory motion can be thought of as a trend that leads to following behind. In each case, 'ahead' and 'behind' are separated by a *plane of equilibrium*, with multiplicity emphasised while the factor whose motion is being charted is 'ahead' of this plane, and unity emphasised while the factor is 'behind' this plane.

The Tropical Zodiacal Cycle

Since a sidereal zodiac does not have an Aries node – i.e. is not derived from the juxtaposition of two planes – it can only be defined as the alternation of two polar-opposite trends by treating it as a synodic cycle (with a particular star chosen as the slower-moving body). Thus, the only zodiacal cycle discussed in this chapter is the tropical zodiacal cycle.

The tropical zodiac is founded upon the relationship between the planes that are defined by Earth's rotational and orbital motions. Thus, it seems reasonable to assume that Earth's rotation relative to the ecliptic plane causes some kind of localised distortion within the energy field that surrounds Earth. Just as the perception of distant objects is altered by using different spectacle lenses, so the meaning of a celestial factor may be altered as it is 'seen' through different parts of this tropical zodiacal distortion.

In any case, as noted in Chapter 5, the tropical zodiacal cycle of a factor is the cycle of changing declination of the point at which the factor's line of celestial longitude meets the ecliptic; thus, in this case, the plane of equilibrium is the equatorial plane. Emphasis on multiplicity increases while the declination of this point is becoming more northerly (0°♑ to 0°♋), and emphasis on unity increases while the declination of this point is becoming more southerly (0°♋ to 0°♑). Thus, multiplicity and unity are emphasised while the point has northerly and southerly declination, respectively.

The question that arises now is, 'Why this way around?' To find a possible answer to this question, we can refer to a third celestial motion: the motion of the Sun – and thus the entire solar system – through space. Our solar system is currently moving towards the star Vega, a northern hemisphere star that serves as the pole star during part of the cycle of equinoctial precession. Thus, increasing northerly declination (increasing emphasis on multiplicity) is relatively congruous to the motion of the solar system-as-a-whole, while increasing southerly declination (increasing emphasis on unity) is relatively contrary to this motion.

The Diurnal Cycle

The diurnal cycle of a factor may be charted in many ways, with some diurnal wheels being more true to the actual cycle of rising and setting than others. The frame of reference used in the Equal House system, for example, is essentially a zodiacal wheel whose Aries node is derived from the intersection of the ecliptic and rational horizon; and the frame of reference used in the Whole Sign system is essentially a zodiacal wheel that is yet further from the actual cycle of rising and setting, because the first house cusp is placed at the beginning of the ascending zodiacal sign. Furthermore, a diurnal wheel is converted to a 'diurnal zodiac' when the house cusps are converted to lines of celestial longitude (which is what happens when a house cusp is represented by a point on a chart wheel). Nonetheless, all approaches to charting the diurnal cycle are derived, in one way or another, from the actual diurnal cycle, and a 'diurnal zodiac' may be a perfectly valid means of charting and interpreting diurnal position.

As noted in Chapters 1 and 6, the diurnal cycle of a factor is the cycle of change in the factor's position relative to Earth's centre, as 'seen' from a particular location on Earth's surface. When the diurnal cycle is viewed as a cycle of being, the cycle unfolds in an eastward direction (anticlockwise around the chart wheel), which is the typical direction of travel of celestial bodies and points through the fixed diurnal wheel shown on an astrological chart.

The plane of equilibrium of the diurnal cycle is the horizon plane or a plane derived from it. However, the individual does not actually exist in this plane, but rather sits 'on top' of the world, between Earth's centre and the zenith. As Earth rotates eastwards, the zenith (representing the observer on the celestial sphere) moves eastwards around the celestial sphere. When the diurnal wheel is frozen in time as a chart, transiting factors continue to move eastwards through it, crossing the upper half of the celestial meridian and continuing to move towards the lower half through the chart's left hemisphere. We can think of this motion through the chart's left hemisphere (which corresponds to increasing emphasis on multiplicity) as being congruous with the motion of the observer, and motion through the right hemisphere (which corresponds to increasing emphasis on unity) as being contradictory to that of the observer. On this basis, the factor is 'ahead' of the plane of equilibrium while in the lower hemisphere (emphasis on multiplicity) and 'behind' the plane of equilibrium while in the upper hemisphere (emphasis on unity).

The Synodic Cycle

As discussed in Chapters 2 and 7, there are two schools of thought regarding which pivotal points of the synodic cycle are the points of equilibrium and which are the poles. According to the approach adopted in this book, a point of equilibrium is reached at the perfect conjunction or opposition, with emphasis on multiplicity and unity, respectively, peaking at the waxing and waning squares (see Figure 2.6 on page 90). This being the case, the plane of equilibrium is the plane of the slower-moving body's line of celestial longitude – the 'plane of alignment'. This applies to all of the types of synodic cycle discussed in Chapters 7 and 8.

The Synodic Cycle Charted by Dividing the Celestial Sphere into Equal Segments

In this case, the motion of the faster-moving body is congruous with that of the slower-moving body between the perfect waning and waxing squares (increasing emphasis on multiplicity), and contrary to that of the slower-moving body between the perfect waxing and waning squares (increasing emphasis on unity). The faster moving body is 'ahead' of the plane of alignment between the perfect conjunction and opposition (emphasis on multiplicity), and 'behind' the plane of alignment between the perfect opposition and conjunction (emphasis on unity).

The Direct-Retrograde Cycle

As discussed in Chapter 8, direct-retrograde cycles only occur because the solar system is actually heliocentric rather than geocentric; thus, the meaning of each point of the direct-retrograde cycle is related to the arrangement of the bodies at that point, but viewed heliocentrically. Consequently, when both types of synodic cycle are interpreted as cycles of being, a given point of the cycle of being looks the same in each type, if the heliocentric viewpoint is adopted in the case of the direct-retrograde cycle.

In the case of an inferior body, the principle of multiplicity becomes dominant as the body passes between and Earth and the Sun and moves 'ahead' of the plane of alignment.* The principle of unity becomes dominant as Earth and the body are aligned on opposite sides of the Sun and the body falls 'behind' the plane of alignment.†

In the case of a superior body, the principle of multiplicity becomes dominant as the Earth passes between the body and the Sun and moves 'ahead' of the plane of alignment.‡ The principle of unity becomes dominant as Earth and the body are aligned on opposite sides of the Sun, and Earth falls 'behind' the plane of alignment.§

The poles of the direct-retrograde cycle are more difficult to define in these terms. This is largely because we have been viewing the cycle heliocentrically, and yet the poles are only seen to coincide with a reversal in the direction of change if the cycle is viewed geocentrically. This applies whether the poles are defined as the stations or the points of peak elongation. (The poles can only be defined as the points of peak elongation in the case of an inferior body.)

---

* Geocentrically speaking, this is the perfection of the inferior conjunction.

† Geocentrically speaking, this is the perfection of the superior conjunction.

‡ Geocentrically speaking, the body and the Sun perfect an opposition aspect.

§ Geocentrically speaking, the body and the Sun perfect a conjunction aspect.

EPILOGUE

The emergence of single cell organisms on Earth was followed by the emergence of increasingly complex multicellular organisms (i.e. collectives of cells), leading eventually to the emergence of the nervous system and then the brain. In a parallel process, human beings are becoming increasingly integrated into the evolving 'body of humanity'. The nervous system of humanity-as-a-whole has evolved through the development of more effective means of acquiring, processing and communicating information; and with the introduction of the World Wide Web, and the increasing prominence of artificial intelligence, we are currently moving closer to a world in which humanity is coordinated by a single artificial brain.

We would not attribute free will to artificial intelligence any more than we would a single cell organism. Each is seen as simply responding to input according to the nature of its programming. From our subjective viewpoint, it appears that human beings are endowed with a marked degree of free will; however, the results of experiments conducted by psychologists during the last decade or so have challenged this assumption. It may become apparent that free will is illusory, and that the sentience upon which this illusion rests is not the pinnacle of the whole-forming process, but merely a necessary step in the evolution of an artificially intelligent (i.e. non-sentient) whole that is more complex than any sentient organism.*

The belief that human beings have free will and autonomy has become stronger over the millennia, and the paradigms used to explain astrology and guide astrologers have – inevitably and necessarily – changed accordingly. The current consensus is that we are fated to be a particular type of person, and free to choose how we respond to this; and this sense of a dance between fate and free will is something that astrology – with its

---

* Interestingly, Rudhyar suggests that consciousness is generated by the organised activity that arises within any whole – whether an individual human being, a society, a galaxy or an atom. On this basis, what we refer to as consciousness is merely a narrow band within a wider spectrum of consciousness, just as visible light is a narrow band within the wider electromagnetic spectrum. (See *The Essential Rudhyar* (1983) Khaldea.com/rudhyar/ Pt. 2, Section 8.)

ability to predict themes but not concrete events – can obligingly reflect back to us. However, humanity's ability to predict outcomes is constantly improving, and we do not know how predictable life will turn out to be. And if anything *is* truly unpredictable, this may be due to an element of spontaneity in existence itself, rather than any degree of individual free will.*

Fortunately, whoever and whatever we are – and whether or not we understand who and what we are – we can find peace simply by relaxing.

Like any conceptual framework, astrology offers a window on life – a particular vantage point from which to engage with life without fully exposing ourselves to it. Thus, when using astrology, it is important to keep in mind that a window is still part of the wall, and that the real value of astrology lies in its ability to help us to understand why we are reluctant to turn away from the window and step outside.

* If this is so, then this spontaneity may be more pronounced to the extent that the principle of multiplicity is dominant and/or increasing in strength in the context concerned.

CHART & ASPECT GRID OF THE AUTHOR

15:15 (14:15 UT) February 16th 1971
Walsall, UK 52°N35' 001°W58'

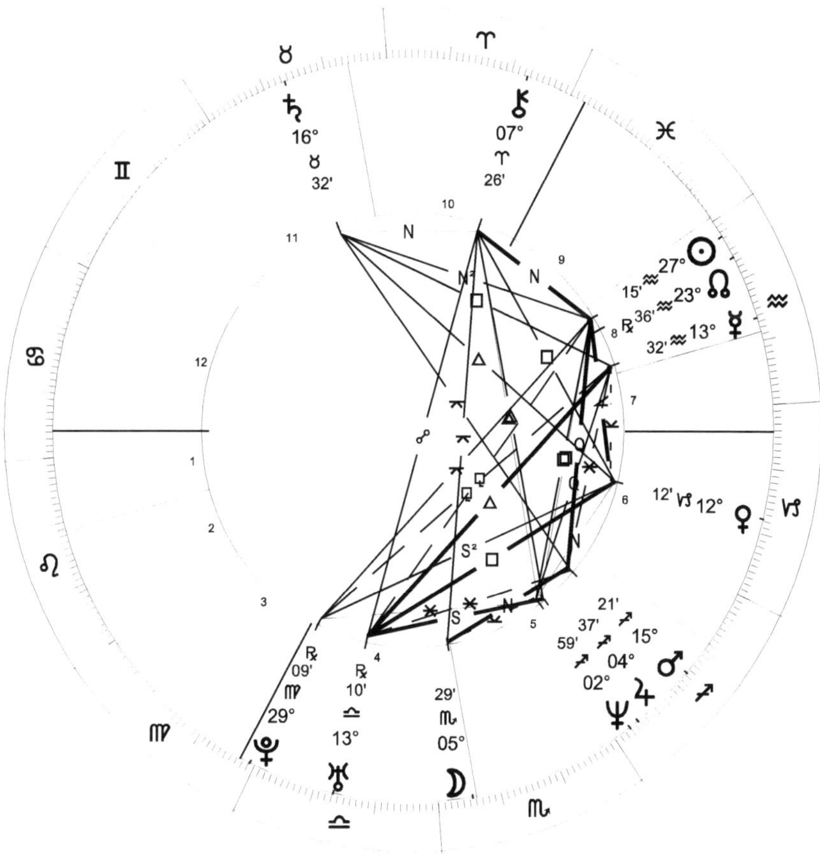

Geocentric
Tropical zodiac
Placidus houses
True lunar nodes
Birth time given to mother by a hospital staff member on the day of birth (unrectified)

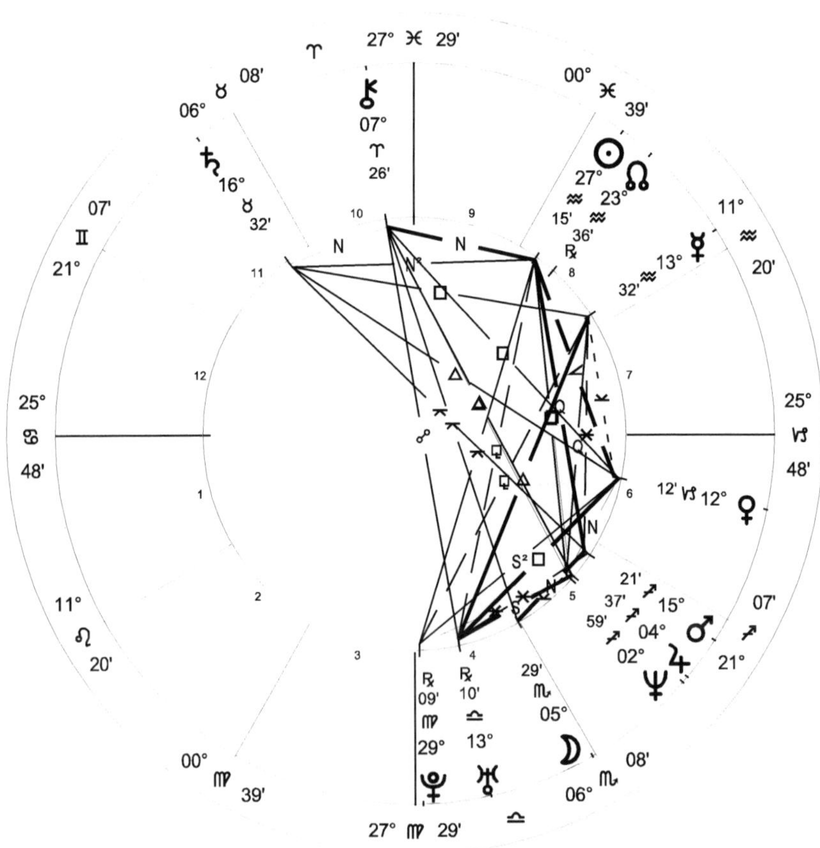
27° ♓ 29'
♈
06° ♉ 08'
⚷ 07° ♈ 26'
♄ 16° ♉ 32'
00° ♓ 39'
☉ 27° ♒ 15'
☊ 23° ♒ 36'
℞
11° ♒ 20'
☿ 13° ♒ 32'
07' ♊ 21°
10
9
11
8
12
7
1
6
2
5
3
4
N
N
N
N
25° ♋ 48'
25° ♑ 48'
♀ 12° ♑ 12'
11° ♌ 20'
♂ 15° ♐ 21'
♃ 04° ♐ 37'
♆ 02° ♐ 59'
07' ♐ 21°
℞ 09' ♍ 29° ♇
℞ 10' ♎ 13° ♅
☽ 05° ♏ 29'
00° ♍ 39'
06° ♏ 08'
♎
27° ♍ 29'

	☽	☉	☿	♀	♂	♃	♄	♅	♆	♇	⚷	☊	As	Mc
☽			// 0A30											
☉														
☿									// 0S31					
♀		∠ 0A02	⚺ 1S19			// 0A35							# 0A14	
♂	N 0S07	Q 0A05	✱ 1A48											
♃	⚺ 0S51	□ 7A21											# 0A50	
♄		N^2 0S43	□ 2A59	△ 4A19	⚻ 1A10					// 0A37				
♅		⚼ 0A55	△ 0S22	□ 0A57	✱ 2S10	S 0S00					# 0S28			
♆		□ 5A43	Q 1A26	N 0A46		☌ 1S37								
♇		⚻ 1A54	⚼ 0A37	S^2 0S11					✱ 3S49					
⚷	⚻ 1A57	N 0A11		□ 4S46		△ 2A49	N 0A54	☍ 5A44	△ 4S27					
☊		☌ 3S39							N^2 0A36	Q^2 0S26	∠ 1A09			
As		⚻ 1A27								✱ 3A21		⚻ 2S12		
Mc	Q^2 1A59	⚺ 0S14	∠ 1A03		S^2 0A43				△ 5A29	☍ 1A40			△ 1S41	

REFERENCES

John Addey

Harmonics in Astrology, Eyebright Books (2009)

A New Study of Astrology, The Urania Trust (1996)

Michael Baigent, Nicholas Campion, Charles Harvey

Mundane Astrology, Thorsons (1995)

Charles Carter

Essays on the Foundations of Astrology, Theosophical Publishing House (1978)

The Zodiac and the Soul, Theosophical Publishing House (1968)

Darby Costello

Water and Fire, Centre for Psychological Astrology Press (1998)

Vic Dicara

Nakshatra – The Authentic Heart of Vedic Astrology, Published Independently (2019)

Michael Erlewine

Full Phase Aspects, Startypes.com (1998)

Stephen Forrest

The Book of the Moon, Seven Paws Press (2010)

Liz Greene

Barriers and Boundaries, Centre for Psychological Astrology Press (2002)

Relating – An Astrological Guide to Living with Others, The Aquarian Press (1986)

Saturn – A New Look at an Old Devil, Samuel Weiser, Inc. (1987)

The Art of Stealing Fire: Uranus in the Horoscope, Centre for Psychological Astrology Press (2004)

Liz Greene, Howard Sasportas

The Development of the Personality, Routledge & Keegan Paul Ltd (1987)

Dynamics of the Unconscious, Samuel Wesiner, Inc. (1988)

The Luminaries, Weiser Books (1992)

Z'ev ben Shimon Halevi

The Tree of Life, Gateway Books (1981)

Robert Hand

Horoscope Symbols, Para Research, Inc. (1981)

Michael Harding, Charles Harvey

Working with Astrology, an Arkana book, Penguin Group (1990)

Ralph William Holden

The Elements of House Division, L. N. Fowler & Co. Ltd. (1977)

Richard Idemon

The Magic Thread, The Wessex Astrologer (2010)

Rok Koritnik

The secret meeting of East and West – Understanding divisional and/or harmonic charts, RokKoritnikAstrologer.com (2019)

Michael R. Meyer

A Handbook for the Humanistic Astrologer, iUniverse.com, Inc. (2000)

Eric Meyers

Elements and Evolution, Astrology Sight Publishing (2010)

Leyla Rael

The Essential Rudhyar (1983)

Leyla Rael, Dane Rudhyar

Astrological Aspets – A Process-oriented Approach, Aurora Press (new edition 1980)

Dane Rudhyar

The Astrological Houses, Doubleday and Company (1972)

An Astrological Mandala, Random House (1973)

An Astrological Study of Psychological Complexes, Shambhala Publications (1976)

Astrological Timing: The Transition to the New Age, Harper Colophon (1972)

The Astrology of Personality, Aurora Press (1991)

Beyond Individualism, a Quest book, Theosophical Publishing House (1979)

The Fullness of Human Experience, a Quest book, Theosophical Publishing House (1976)

How to Interpret the Lunar Nodes (June and July 1966) Horoscope Magazine

The Lunation Cycle, Shambhala Publications (1971). Originally published under the name The Moon – The Cycles and Fortunes of Life (1967)

A New Approach to the Zodiac, Horoscope Magazine (June 1962)

The Pulse of Life, Shambhala Publications (1970)

Howard Sasportas

The Twelve Houses, The Aquarian Press (1985)

Alex von Schlieffen

When Chimpanzees Dream Astrology, Centre for Psychological Astrology Press (2004)

Rudolph Steiner

The Gospel of St. John, Hamburg Cycle, Anthroposophic Press (1962)

Erin Sullivan

The Signs (Talk on You Tube)

Made in the USA
Coppell, TX
20 January 2024

27935236R00160